IMAGES
of America

BEMISTON

On the Cover: Members of the Bemiston Main Office staff enjoy a day at Talladega Creek. They are either playing hooky or cooling off after a hard day at the office. From left to right are Billie Vickers, Imogene Costner, and Lula Maxwell. (Courtesy of J. W. Baker.)

IMAGES
of America

BEMISTON

Bobbye Baker Trammell

ARCADIA
PUBLISHING

ISBN 978-0-7385-6803-4

Published by Arcadia Publishing
Charleston, South Carolina

Printed in the United States of America

Library of Congress Control Number: 2009925164

For all general information contact Arcadia Publishing at:
Telephone 843-853-2070
Fax 843-853-0044
E-mail sales@arcadiapublishing.com
For customer service and orders:
Toll-Free 1-888-313-2665

Visit us on the Internet at www.arcadiapublishing.com

Contents

Acknowledgments

This book was made possible by the many people and friends of Bemiston, Alabama, who so willingly shared so many memories and photographs with me. I want to especially thank my brother, J. W. Baker, who was the last employee of Bemis Brothers Bag Company and had the foresight to save and preserve many items, such as pictures, records, and other items of interest, when the plant was sold. Also, I want to thank Doug Hill and Todd Wilson, who so graciously helped with the photographs. I would be remiss if I didn't thank my son, Gary Trammell, who spent so much time on the computer, and Willene Senn Hughston, who had the intuition to save all the *Parkway News* papers and so willingly shared them.

I especially want to thank the many mentors I had through the years, who encouraged me to want to write this book and preserve all these memories for my children, grandchildren, and other generations. I think it is very important to leave a legacy of not just a cotton mill village in just a time of hard work, but also trying to attain a better standard of living for one's family, as well to develop a more healthy and happy community for future generations.

Clarice Sawyer, the editor of the *Parkway News* and *Bemistory* magazine, was a major source of the material and pictures used in this book; although a photograph was not available, it is most important that she be recognized in gratitude.

I would like to dedicate this book to my parents, John W. Baker and Minnie Giles Baker, who saw a future in Bemiston, Alabama, for their family of six children. In doing so, they were left with many beautiful and lasting memories.

INTRODUCTION

In the early 1920s, a group of business men from St. Louis, Missouri, came to the area to purchase property for the purpose of building a cotton mill and village in south Talladega County, Alabama. However, the city fathers of Talladega were not very receptive to bringing another cotton mill to the area.

At that time, there was already a textile mill in the city, and the fear was that a new mill would draw employees away from Talladega. After they were told the purposed site was not in the city limits of Talladega, city officials agreed on the sale of the property to Bemis Brothers, and finally, the plant and village became Bemiston, Alabama.

The location was a beautiful valley consisting of approximately 3,000 acres bordered on the east by clear-running Talladega Creek and on the west by Alabama Highway 21 and the big imposing mountain range known as the "Sleeping Giant." A railroad ran parallel to Highway 21, making the delivery of supplies and other necessities to the plant convenient. In the years to come, visitors to Bemiston would ride the train, and during World War II, servicemen coming home on leave could walk from the train to their homes, a distance which was never more than three blocks.

Since there were no electric tools nor cranes, mules with scoops were used to move the vast amounts of dirt to build the foundation of the 700,000-square-foot plant. At a time when there were few passable roads in most parts of the state and almost no paved roads, Bemis built a paved, divided four-lane parkway in front of the plant as an entrance. It still remains a beautiful entrance to the village.

The plant began operating in 1929, the year the Great Depression came. When industries all over America were closing, Bemiston continued to operate at one shift all through the Depression. During World War II, the plant made bags for sandbags for the war effort, operating three shifts with seven-day workweeks.

The community of Bemiston was independent. Its residents built their own school, churches, recreation center, general store, garage and filling station, barbershop, beauty parlor, fire department, and even a nurses' office with a registered nurse on duty at all times. Bemiston also owned and maintained a local power plant that supplied power to the cotton mill and to the residents. The company also built and maintained a water and sewer plant.

Although this was a time when automobiles were almost nonexistent in the area, each house had a garage—doubles (duplexes) had a double garage. Every house had a complete bathroom with running hot and cold water. However, it must be mentioned that in the summer, the only hot water available was when a fire was built in the cook stove next to the water heater.

The Raymond L. Young Memorial School Foundation was the first building to be erected during the time the plant was also being built. This continued to be the Raymond L. Young Memorial School Foundation until 1980, when the school was turned over to the City of Talladega. At that time, it became R. L. Young Elementary School.

The school served students from kindergarten through sixth grade. After sixth grade, students were transported to Talladega High School by bus. Two additions have since been built in order to accept students from other parts of the city of Talladega.

The Community Building was built in 1938 for recreational purposes. A full-time recreational director was brought in to work with the children and to develop the baseball and basketball teams. The basement of the building was divided to allow the boys' teams half and the girls' teams half for shower and dressing space. It was also furnished with lockers for every player. When basketball season was over, the gymnasium was used as a skating rink. Skates were available for a small fee of 15¢ for all afternoon. Of course, the floor would have to be refinished when basketball season began.

On the main floor, adjacent to the gymnasium, was a lobby with rooms for playing pool and Ping-Pong and a room especially used for table games such as checkers, cards, and dominos. There were also rooms used for a barbershop, a beauty parlor, and a completely stocked library.

On the second floor, there was an auditorium used for banquets, dances, and other social events. It was complete with a fully stocked kitchen. A ladies lounge was primarily used by the women for bridal showers, baby showers, and other small parties. Adjacent to the ladies lounge, a sewing room, complete with sewing machines, was furnished for use by the citizens. A seamstress was available to instruct, if needed.

A fenced-in, lighted tennis court was available behind the building—large enough for two sets at any time—with an instructor. Because it was such a popular gathering place, Bemiston's Community Building eventually came to be known as the "glory hole" by the young people of the community. The director had a lady assistant to help work with the girls. They both played a big part in directing extracurricular activities. A summer theater was formed for the children who were not a part of the athletic teams.

Boy and Girl Scouts were very active. Edith Moore was the Girl Scout leader, with Anci Huddleston and Howard Chappell as Boy Scout leaders.

To ensure the beauty of the village, a landscaper was hired to plant trees and shrubs, and to sod all the yards around the houses, as well as other buildings.

The landscaping included the two-way drive, which was carefully maintained at all times. Mrs. Z. D. Dugan designed and implemented all of the work, which resulted in a beautiful setting. Vern Scott, a local newspaper columnist and historian, stated in the December 9, 1987, edition of the *Daily Home*, "One manager, R. A. Wells, cooperated with Mrs. Dugan, to build the most beautiful drive this town has every seen." The 1930s were not trouble-free. The labor union came and tried to organize, but they were not successful. This resulted in a short-term strike. After things calmed down, full-time security guards were installed at the gateway of the village, with the position of security guard becoming permanent for the security of the families in the community. The guards continued throughout the life of the community, but later they just patrolled the streets in the village in an auto or Jeep, and during the war, they rode a horse to conserve fuel. So Bemiston was ahead of its time. It probably became the first "gated" community in the South. The two brick pillars at the entrance of the village where the guardhouse stood remain today.

The 1940s in Bemiston were much the same as for the rest of the country. The plant converted to making sandbags. Citizens pulled together, collecting scrap iron and newspapers. Employees started buying war bonds, and the children were buying stamps to fill up their war books to buy a bond. Workers started working long hours. In their spare time, women rolled bandages and volunteered for anything they could do to help the war effort.

Men and women went off to war—some did not come back. When the war was over, Bemiston had the same problems as other parts of the country. The men coming home wanted to go back to work, and the ones who had families needed housing. This became an all-important priority. Baseball and basketball games resumed, and dances were held regularly. Gradually, life became as normal as circumstances would allow.

The churches were built in the early 1950s. Before that, services were held in the auditorium at the school and later in the Community Building or in a company house. The Bemis Brothers Bag Company did not build the churches but donated the land for both a Methodist and Baptist church. Both churches held fund-raisers and accepted donations to help build the churches. Bemis Brothers matched the fund-raising efforts: with each dollar raised, the company would match it. The labor was furnished by members of each church. The Bemiston Baptist Church was dedicated in 1952 and the Bemiston Methodist Church in 1956. Both are located in close vicinity to the school.

The 1950s and 1960s went smoothly as the babies of the 1930s began having babies, mostly staying close by, remaining in the village, and continuing to work in the plant while raising their families.

The 1970s brought foreign imports, and the labor union began to try to organize again. Some were of the opinion that this was a factor in the closing of the plant in 1979, but it was never verified.

Bemiston Village played host to some five generations of children. In 1987, a group of its second generation got together and organized a reunion for anyone who had ever worked, played, or lived in Bemiston over the years. After 50 years, an estimated 1,000 people attended the reunion to relive the memories of times past. Since then, a reunion is held regularly in the Community Building, with everyone invited.

One

The Early Years

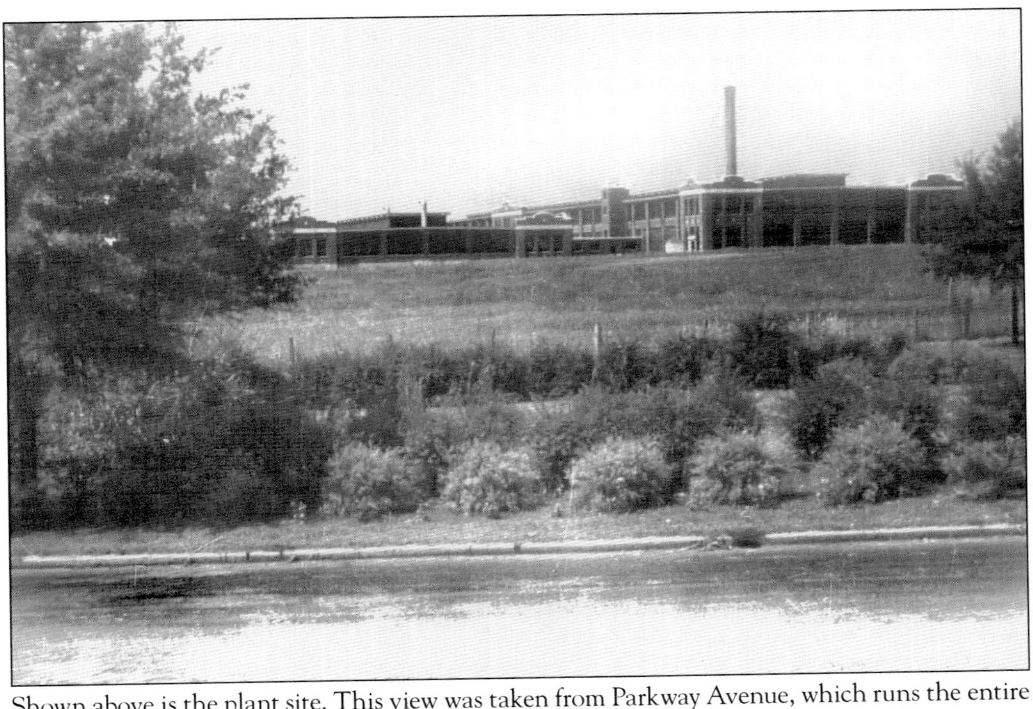

Shown above is the plant site. This view was taken from Parkway Avenue, which runs the entire length of the village. The plant has 700,000 square feet of space and has employed as many as 1,400 at one time. (Courtesy of the Talladega Public Library.)

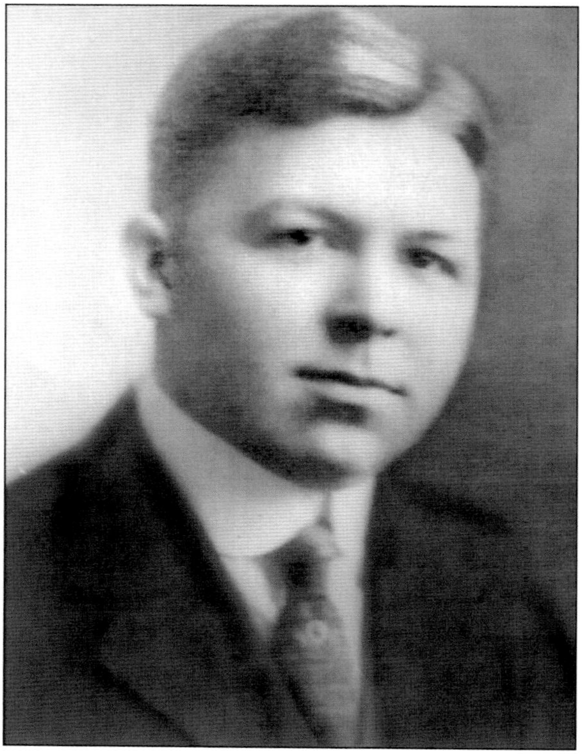

Raymond L. Young was selected to be the general manager of the plant, but he died on the way to Bemiston, and R. A. Wells was named to the office. The R. L. Young Elementary School was named for him, and his portrait still hangs in its hall. (Courtesy of J. W. Baker.)

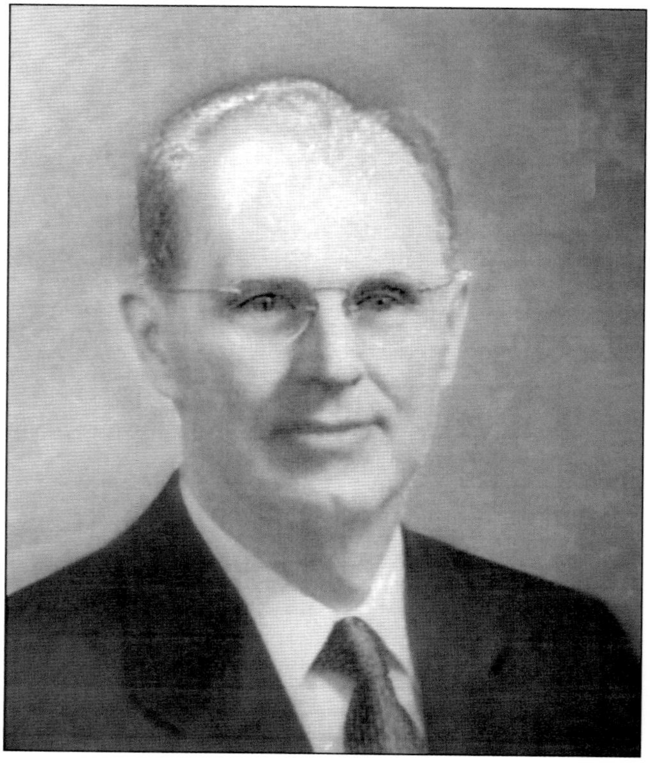

Russell A. Wells succeeded Raymond L. Young as general manager. During his tenure, he was also the construction engineer for the plant, school, and village houses. He remained in this capacity until his retirement in 1958. His portrait also hangs in the R. L. Young Elementary School. (Courtesy of J. W. Baker.)

D. L. Wall was plant supervisor and president of the First Village Council from 1931 to 1932. (Courtesy of Sam and Yvonne Grice.)

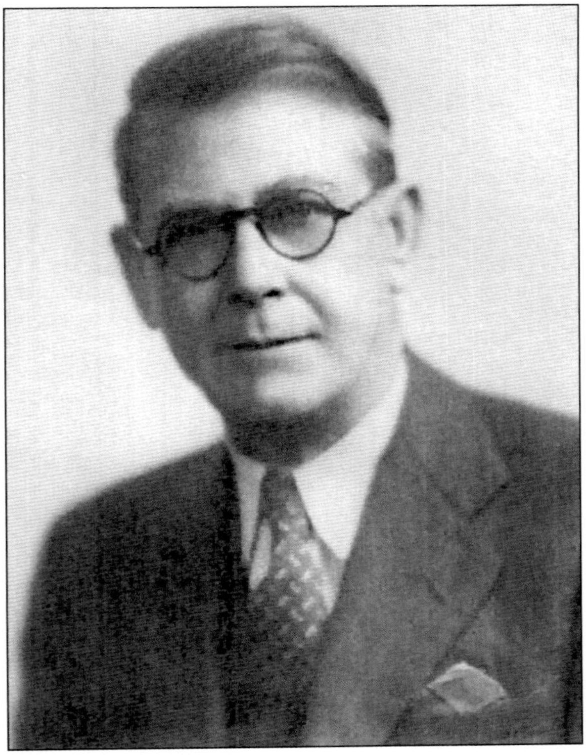

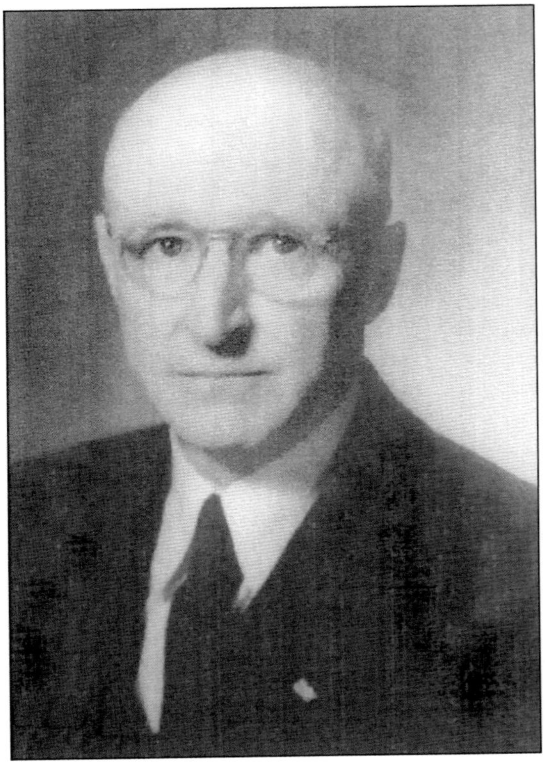

Henry B. Bergfeld was plant superintendent and president of the Village Council from 1933 to 1939. (Courtesy of Sam and Yvonne Grice.)

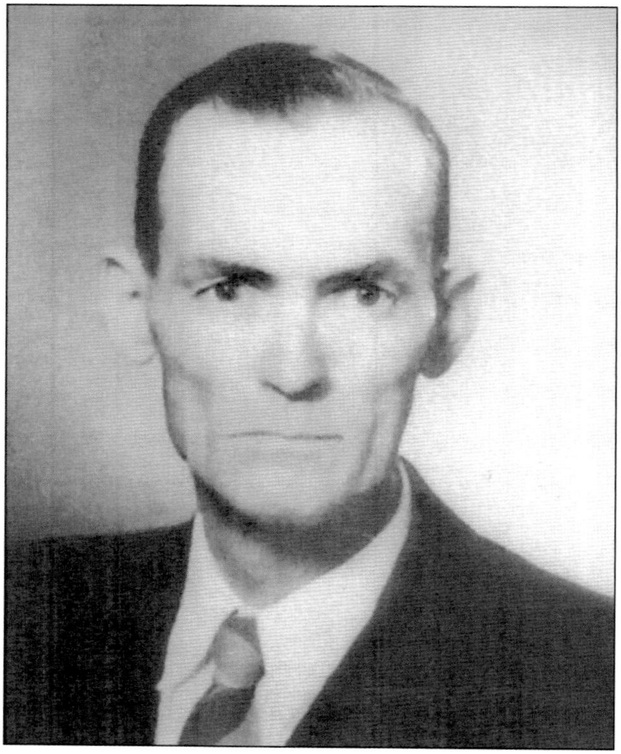

S. W. Grice was the village's maintenance supervisor and president of the Village Council in 1940. (Courtesy of Sam and Yvonne Grice.)

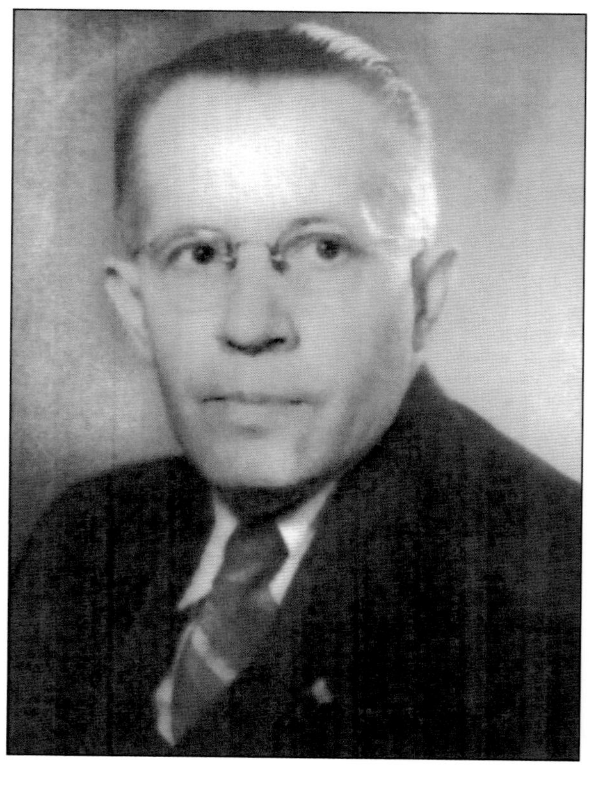

W. Bert Garner was overseer of the Carding Department and served as the Village Council president in 1941. (Courtesy of Sam and Yvonne Grice.)

R. T. Butler was principal of the R. L. Young Elementary School, bandmaster of the Bemiston Marching Band, and president of the Village Council from 1942 to 1943. (Courtesy of Sam and Yvonne Grice.)

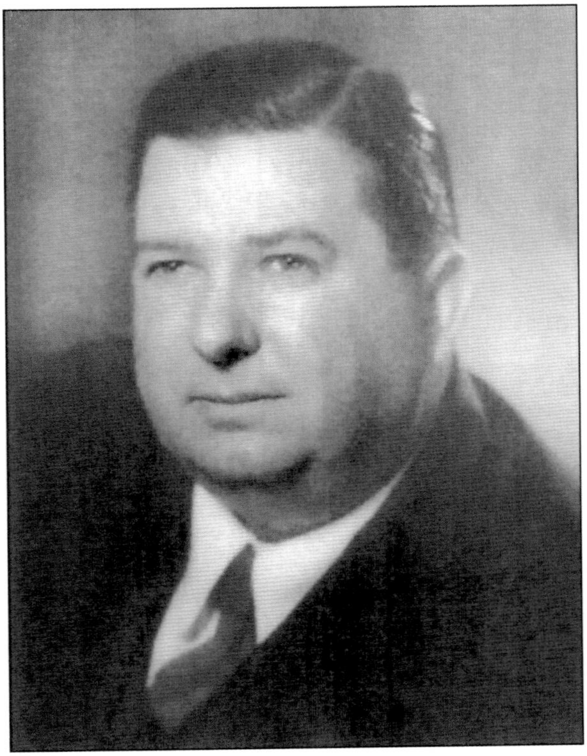

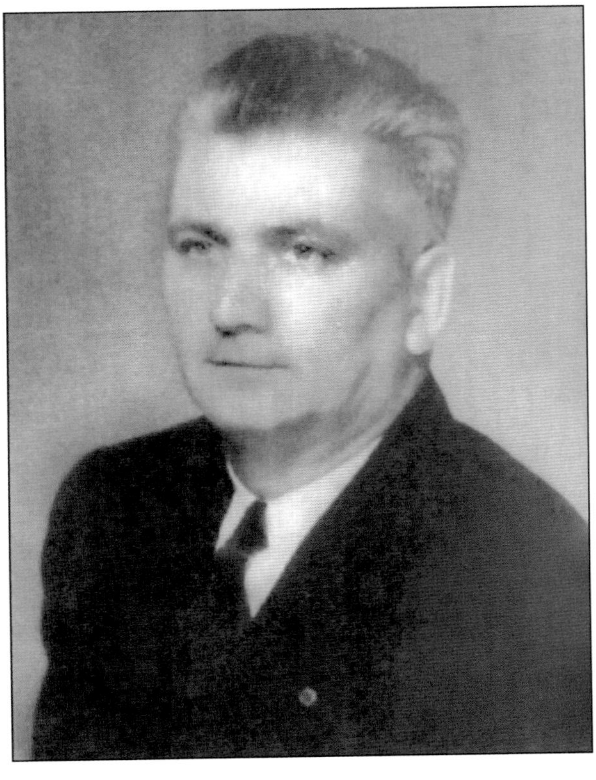

John L. Moore was recreation director and coach of the girls' and boys' basketball teams. Along with coaching the baseball teams, he served as Village Council president in 1944–1945. (Courtesy of Sam and Yvonne Grice.)

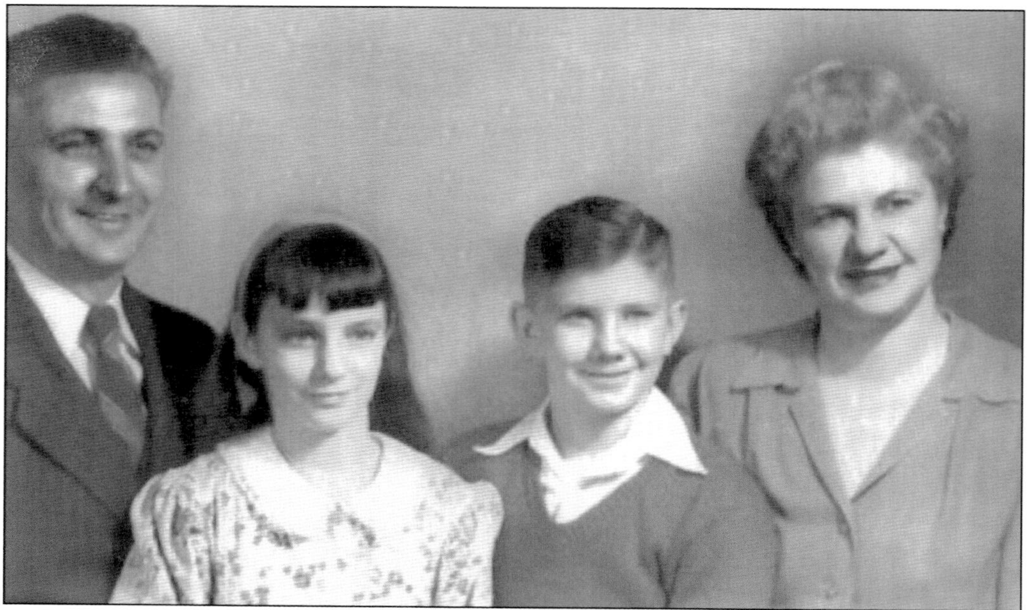

John L. Moore's family is shown above. From left to right are John L. Moore, daughter Barbara, son John Paul, and wife, Edith. The Moores moved to Bemiston in 1942. John was the recreation director and also coached the basketball and baseball teams. He called the square dances every Saturday night, which involved whole families, and was master of ceremonies at the annual Cotton Ball dances. (See chapter two for more on the Cotton Ball festivities.) Edith Moore was also active in the Bemiston Methodist Church, and the church library is named for her. The recreational center is named for John L. Moore. (Courtesy of John and Marlene Moore.)

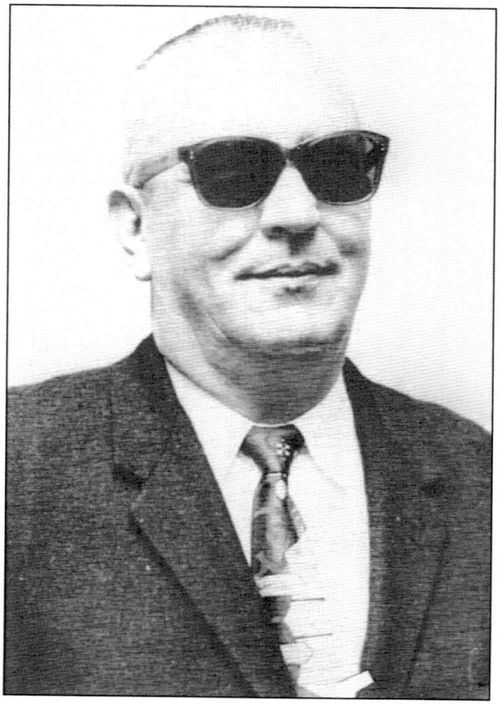

George T. Shaw was truly an inspiration to everyone he met. He was blinded in 1922 at the age of 10. A friend accidentally discharged a gun, which left him completely blind. His family moved to Bemiston to enroll him in the Alabama Institute for the Deaf and Blind. George mastered the demands of his new environment; he possessed leadership qualities and adjusted to his new environment, which proved to be an inspiration to his classmates. He was especially talented in music and taught as well as tuning pianos. He began teaching private lessons in his home in Bemiston. The Bemis Brothers Bag Company later employed him to teach the community children. He was also the pianist for the Bemiston Baptist Church until his death in 1964. (Courtesy of Barbara Shaw.)

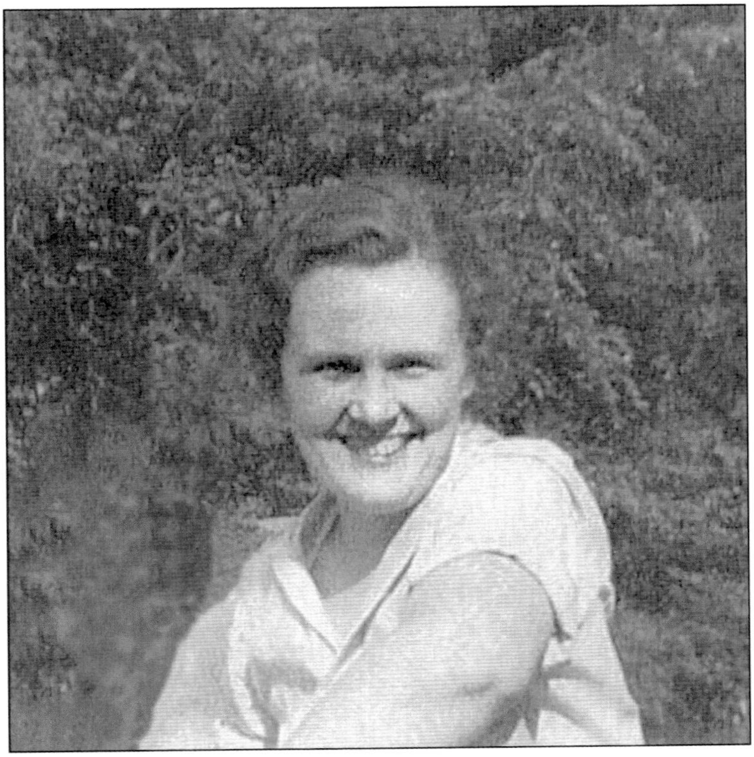

Vera Sue (Caughran) Cork was married to John D. Cork. She taught fourth grade at the R. L. Young Elementary School, and he was manager of the general store. They had two children, Frances Sue and John Jr. Vera's brother Claude and sister Virginia both worked for the village of Bemiston. (Courtesy of Frances Ross.)

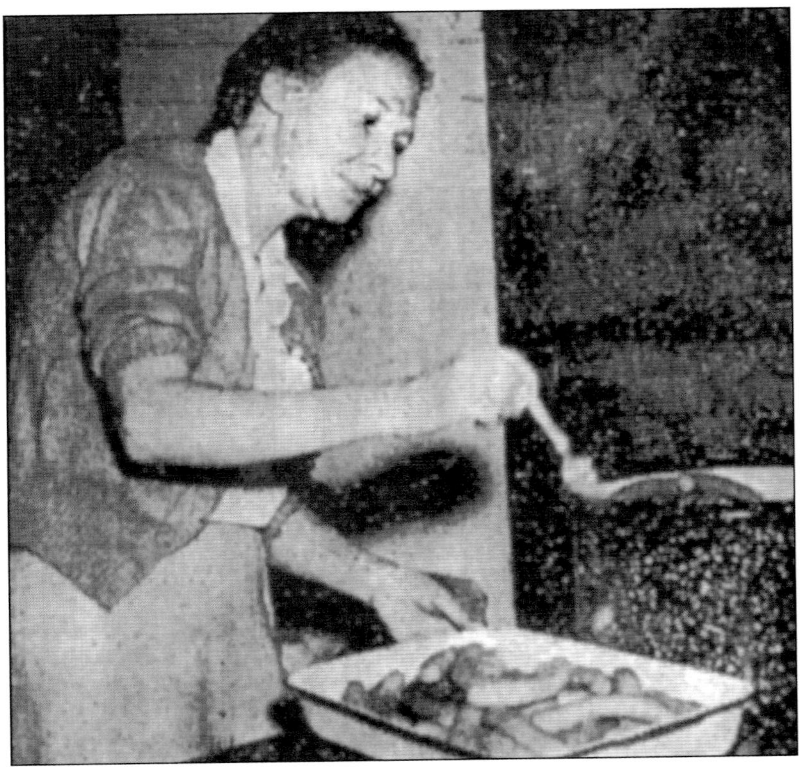

Minnie Bell Jacob is shown here cooking wieners for a community gathering. She was the first secretary to be hired in Bemiston. She said she waded in mud to get to the temporary headquarters to apply for work. She said, "I convinced them they could not get along without me." She started work on October 11, 1929, at the age of 16 and continued until retirement. (Courtesy of the *Parkway News*.)

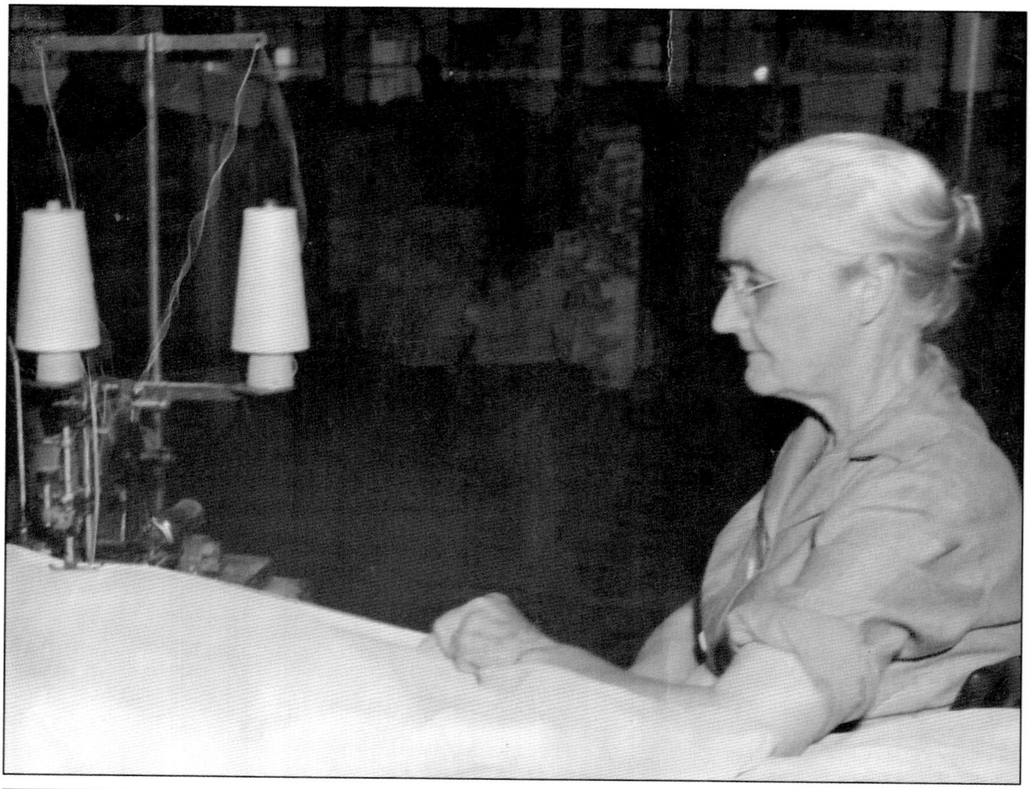

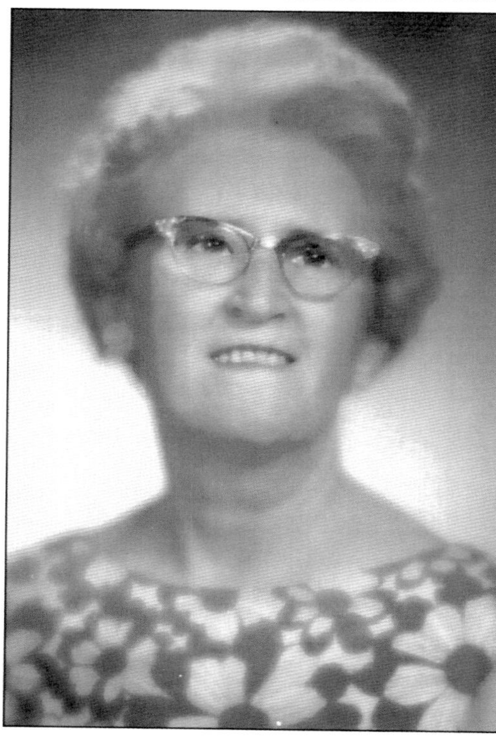

Lula "Ma" Baker started to work in 1931 as a seamstress sewing bags. She was the first woman to work in the Bemis Brothers Bag Company plant. She worked until her death in 1948. (Courtesy of J. W. Baker.)

Manilla T. Fulton came to Bemiston in 1946 as recreational director, the assistant to John L. Moore. She had three children, Fitzhugh, Robert, and Louise. She was involved in the drama club and also directed most of the school plays. She was instrumental in arranging and sponsoring the dances and other holiday festivities in the community. Manilla was also active in the Bemiston United Methodist Church. (Courtesy of John and Marlene Moore.)

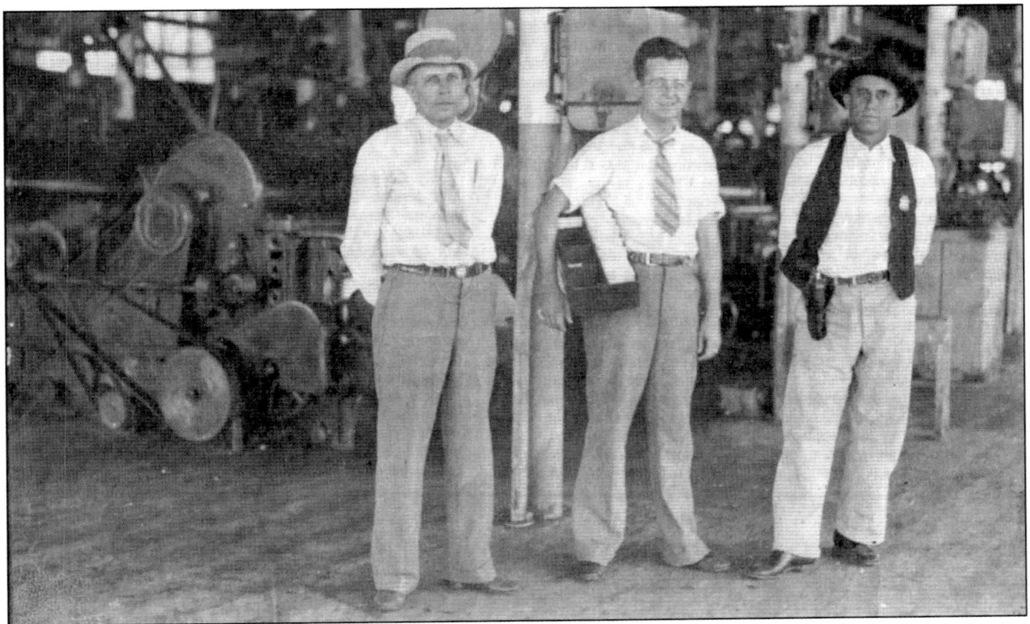

In the beginning, all salaries were paid in cash. This was because none of the employees had a bank account and had nowhere to cash a check. This picture shows, from left to right, W. B. Garner, department head; Jerry Dumas, paymaster; and Uell Lakey, security guard, on a 1931 payday. (Courtesy of Talladega Public Library.)

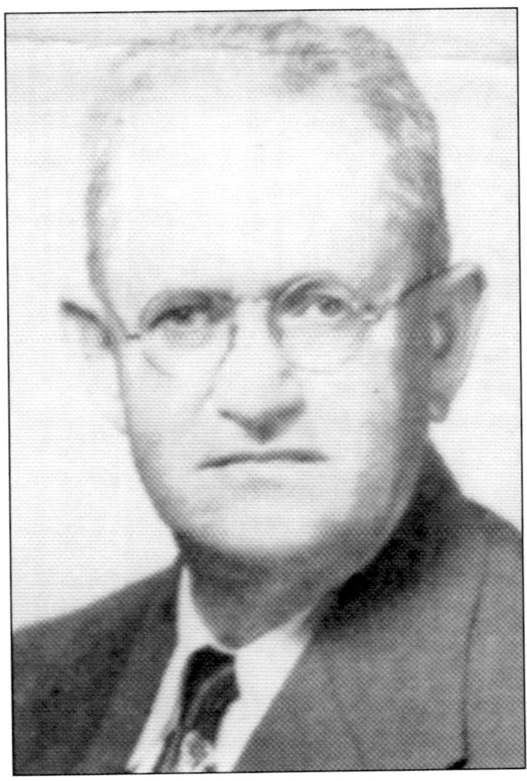

M. L. Pafford was a very special person and added a lot to life in Bemiston. Most of the pictures in this book would have to be attributed to him. Whenever there was anything going on in the village, whether it be a child's birthday party, a wedding, an award ceremony, or just children playing on the playground or a ball game, Pafford was there. Everyone addressed him as Mr. Pafford because he was truly a Southern gentleman. He came to the Bemis Brothers Bag Company in St. Louis in 1927, and when the Bemiston plant began operations in 1929, he came to Alabama. His first job was as a sweeper in the spinning department, and he started as staff photographer in 1944, where he remained until his retirement in November 20, 1952. (Courtesy of the *Parkway News*.)

BEMIS BRO BAG COMPANY

The Cat WITH NINE BILLION LIVES

First in a Series of Advertiser Stories

SOME trade marks are born on the drawing board, the product of careful thought. Some of them just sort of happen. The "Cat-In-The-Bag" trade emblem of Bemis Bro. Bag Co. is one of those that just sort of happened—66 or more years ago.

The cat destined to achieve this limited form of immortality lived, just as the Civil War was getting under way, in a home at 2132 Wash Street in St. Louis. She was owned by one Miss Annie Fyfe, a forelady in the cotton department of Bemis, Brother and Company—a bag manufacturing firm that had not yet celebrated its 25th year when, in 1882, Miss Fyfe brought her cat to the factory to live and catch the mice which abounded.

This cat—she probably had a name, but it is forgotten—made herself at home in the factory and became a common sight lying in wait for a mouse, basking in the warmth of the boiler room, or at play among the bolts and bales. One day she was exploring the inside of an empty bag lying on the floor and, upon emerging, she struck the pose which has become so familiar as the Bemis "Cat-In-The-Bag." For this brief pose was noticed by Judson Moss Bemis, founder of the company, and inspired the trade mark that has appeared countless millions of times on Bemis bags, on letterheads, in advertising—even in motion pictures, which were undreamed of when this tabby still lived.

After the peering-out-of-bag episode, the cat apparently decided her destiny had been fulfilled. First thoughtfully providing a litter of kittens to carry on with the mousing work, she departed one December night and was lost to human sight for several months. Only another cat could imagine where she had gone, how many of her nine lives she expended in the byways of St. Louis.

Finally, her solitary adventure at an end, the original Bemis cat returned to her first home and domesticity, showing up unannounced at the house at 2132 Wash Street. Here she peacefully lived in her declining years, making it a habit on cold nights to sleep in the oven of the old iron cookstove in the kitchen.

So much for the romantic history of the Bemis trade mark. As far as is known, the celebrated cat first appeared in an advertisement in the May 30, 1884, issue of The Northwestern Miller. The cat appearing in the early advertising was young; obviously a kitten bent on mischief. But in passing years she has matured and in the emblem as it is used today a sedate, dignified cat calmly looks out at the world from every Bemis advertisement and from most Bemis bags.

AMERICAN FERTILIZER — APRIL 29, 1950

This article, printed in *American Fertilizer* in 1950, explains the origin of the famous Bemis "Cat in the Bag" logo. (Courtesy of *American Fertilizer*.)

Two

Life in a Cotton Mill Village

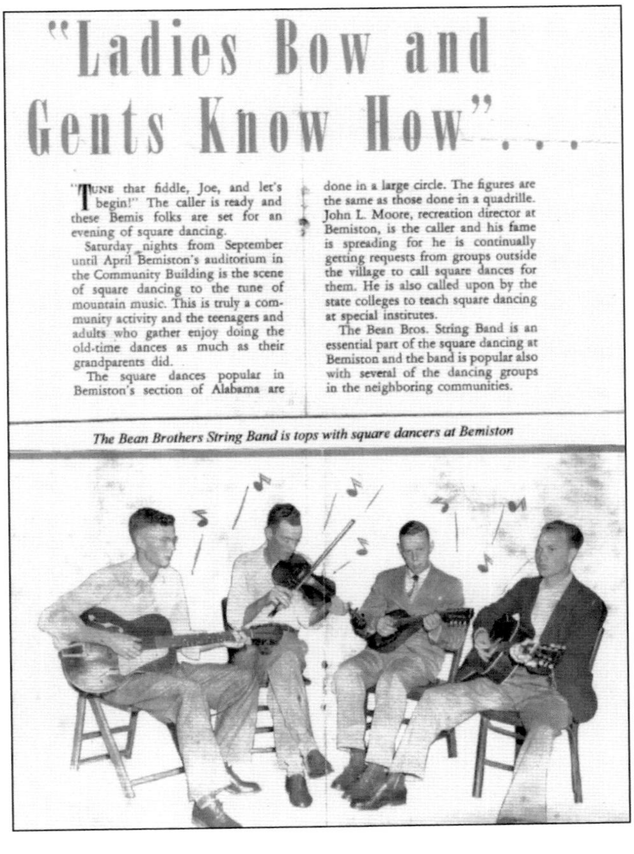

"Ladies Bow and Gents Know How"...

"Tune that fiddle, Joe, and let's begin!" The caller is ready and these Bemis folks are set for an evening of square dancing.

Saturday nights from September until April Bemiston's auditorium in the Community Building is the scene of square dancing to the tune of mountain music. This is truly a community activity and the teenagers and adults who gather enjoy doing the old-time dances as much as their grandparents did.

The square dances popular in Bemiston's section of Alabama are done in a large circle. The figures are the same as those done in a quadrille. John L. Moore, recreation director at Bemiston, is the caller and his fame is spreading for he is continually getting requests from groups outside the village to call square dances for them. He is also called upon by the state colleges to teach square dancing at special institutes.

The Bean Bros. String Band is an essential part of the square dancing at Bemiston and the band is popular also with several of the dancing groups in the neighboring communities.

The Bean Brothers String Band is tops with square dancers at Bemiston

"Ladies Bow and Gents Know How" was the calling of square dancing on Saturday nights. The Bean Brothers String Band was the favorite music when John Moore got his dancers together. (Courtesy of Willadean Marlaire.)

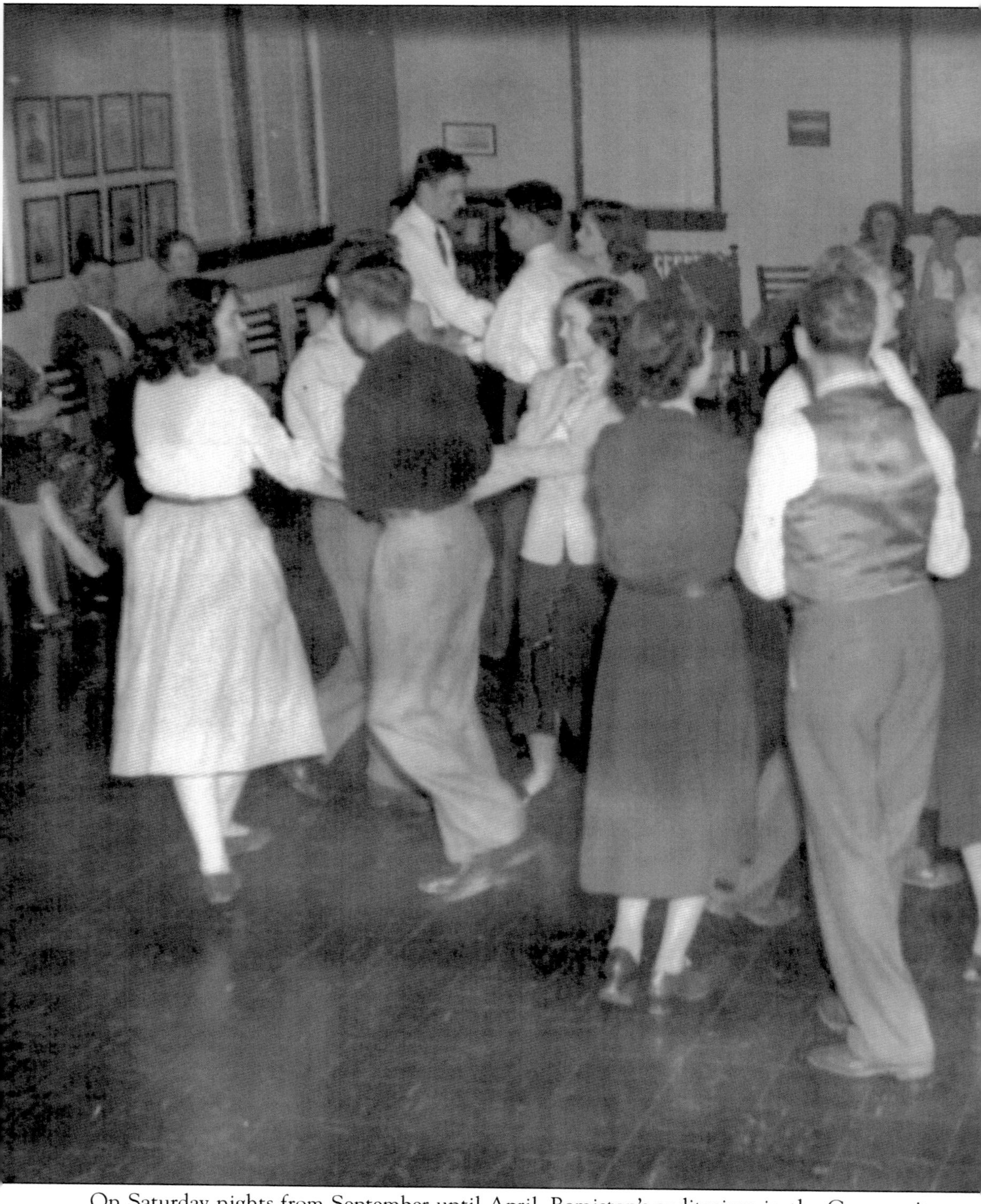

On Saturday nights from September until April, Bemiston's auditorium in the Community Building was the scene of square dancing to the Bean Brothers mountain music. This was truly a community activity where teenagers and adults gathered together to enjoy old-time dances just

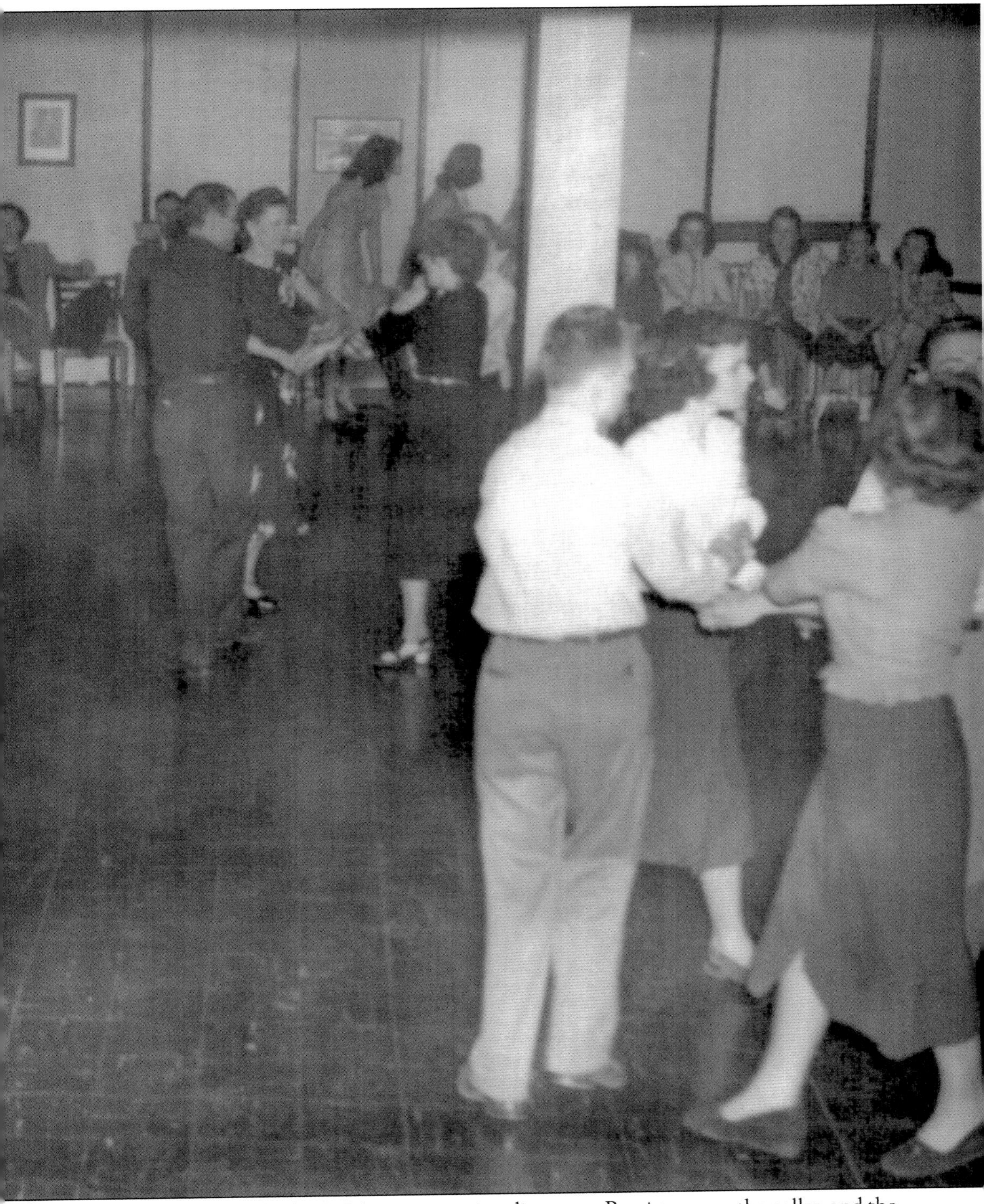

as their grandparents did. John L. Moore, recreation director at Bemiston, was the caller, and the dancers were performing the "Four Leaf Clover." (Courtesy of *Bemistory* magazine.)

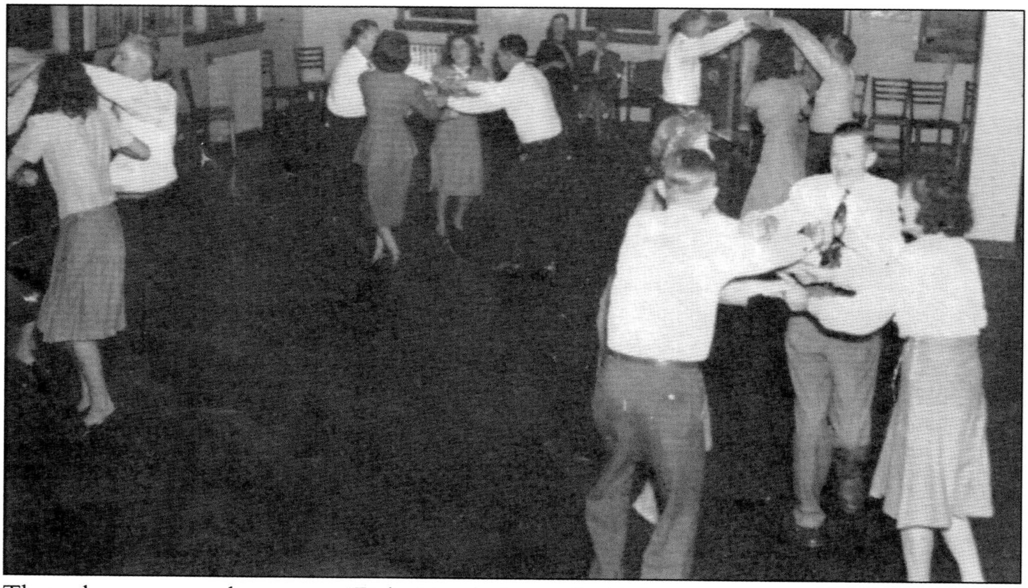

These dancers were dancing to "Eight Hands Across," which was popular with all ages because it was easy to follow, and everyone enjoyed it. (Courtesy of *Bemistory* magazine.)

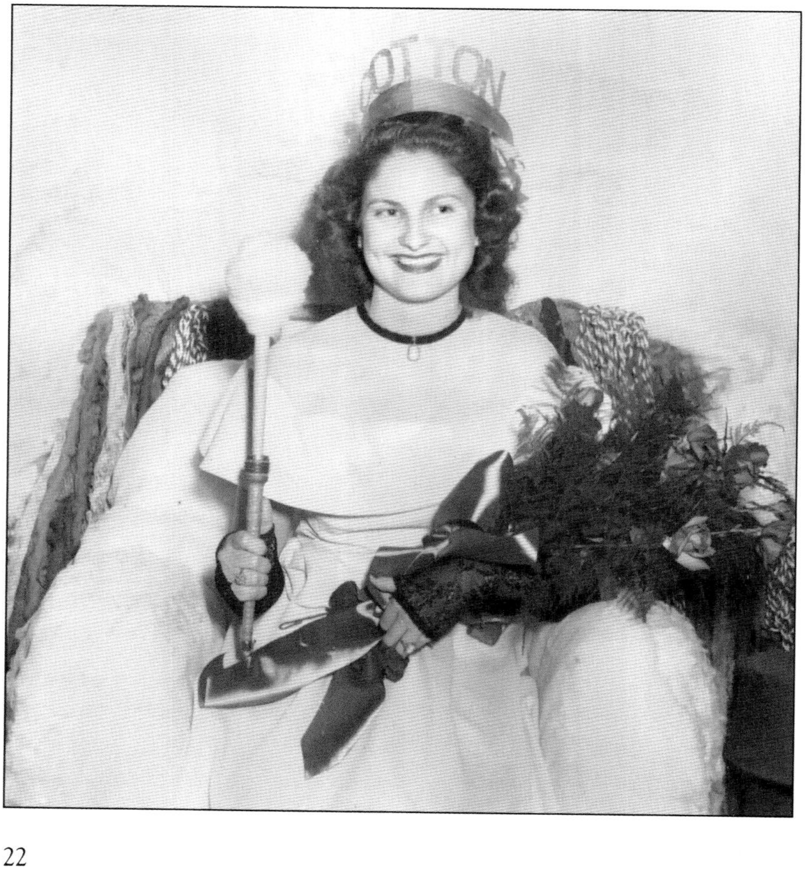

Ruth Brownlow was the first Bemiston Cotton Queen in 1948. Ruth was the daughter of Charlie and Willie Brownlow. She was payroll clerk in the main office. Ruth was also a member of the Bemiston Kittens' basketball team. (Courtesy of J. W. Baker.)

Josie Williams was crowned the Cotton Queen in 1949. She was the daughter of Samuel and Maybell Williams, who were also employees of the Bemis Brothers Bag Company. (Courtesy of Josie Williams.)

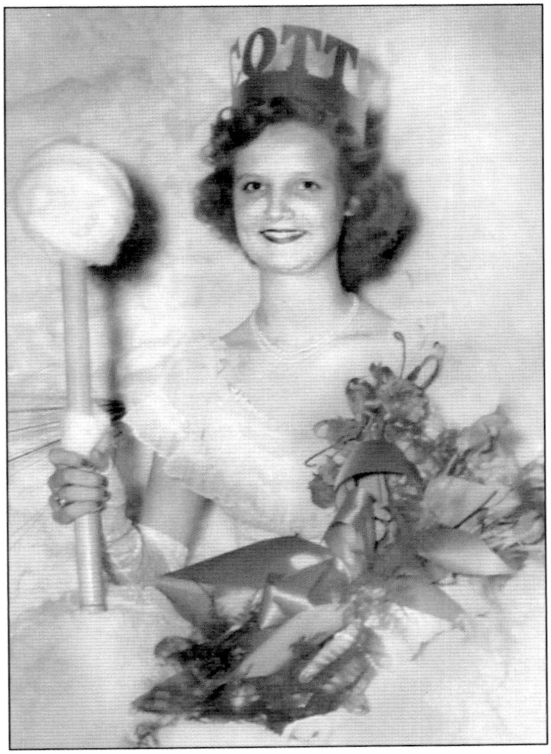

Willadean Vickers was crowned the Cotton Queen in 1951. Roxie Poulson, a former queen, is shown here passing the tiara. Willadean played piano and was a member of the Baptist Church choir. She was also a cheerleader for Talladega High School. (Courtesy of Willadean Marlaire.)

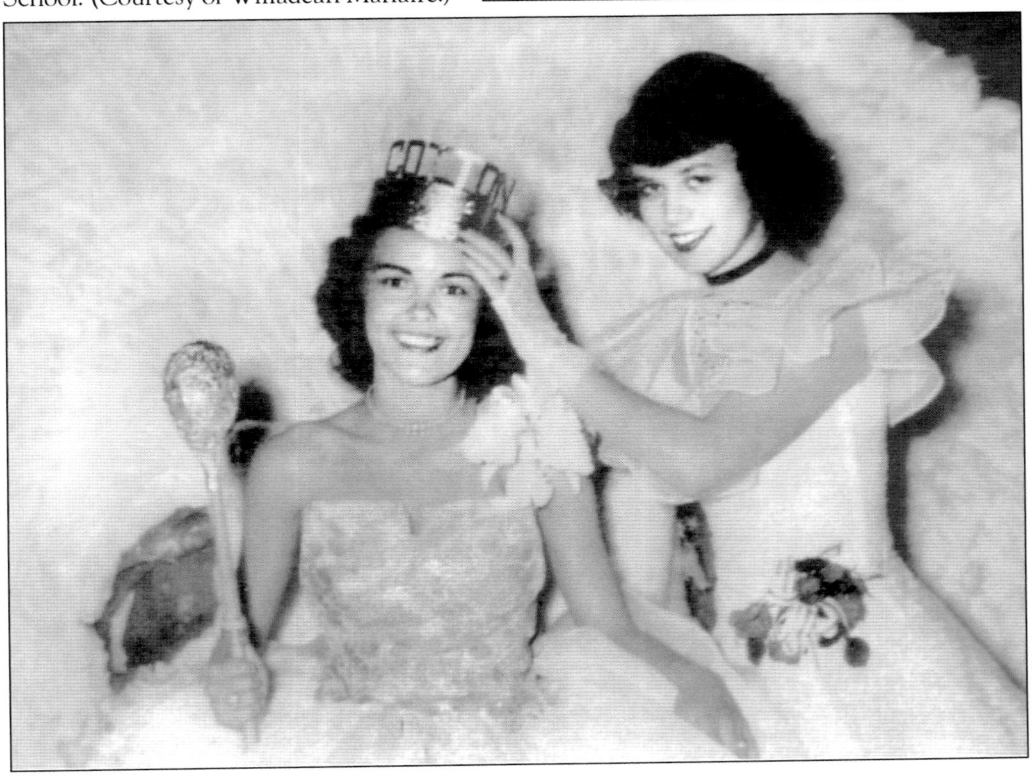

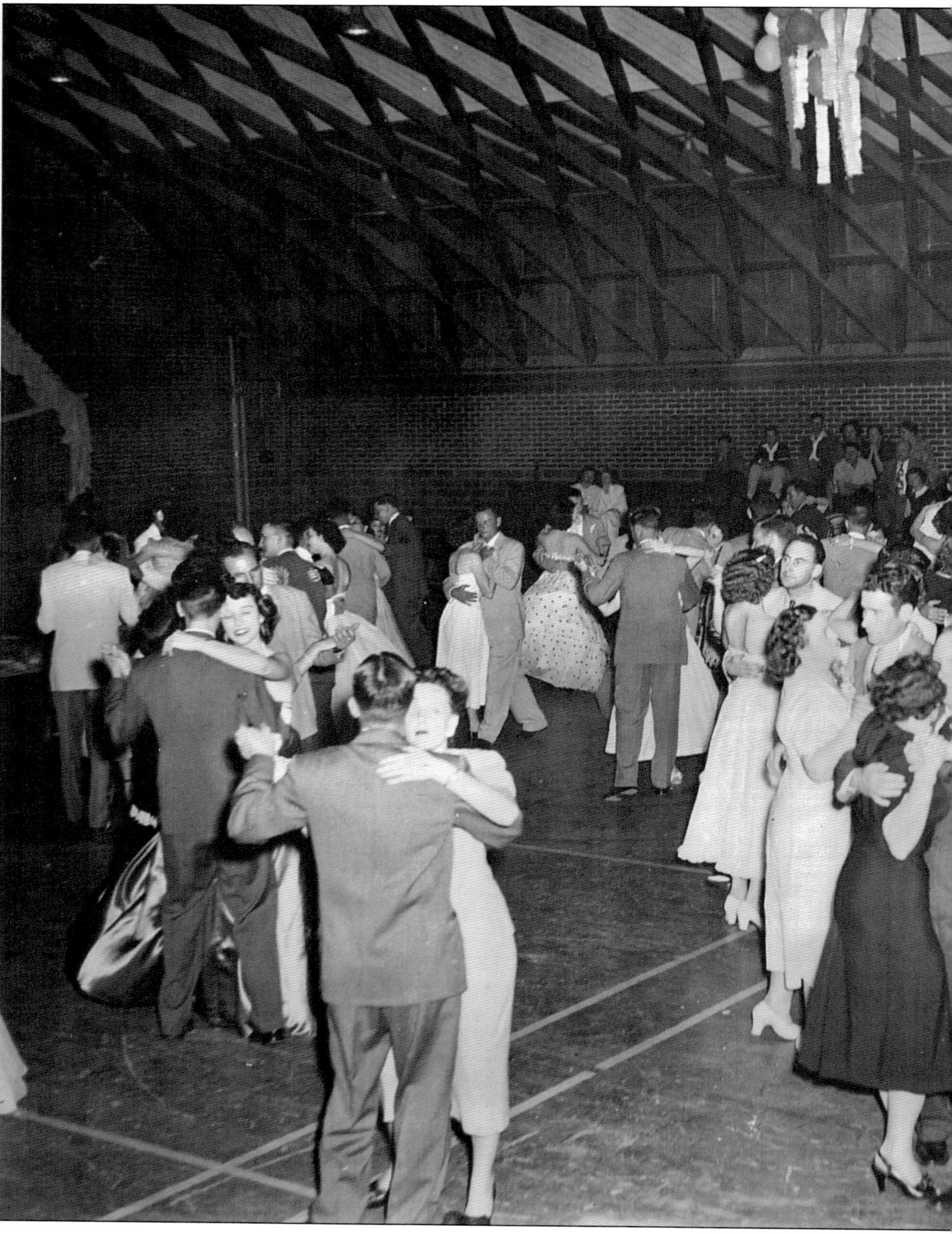

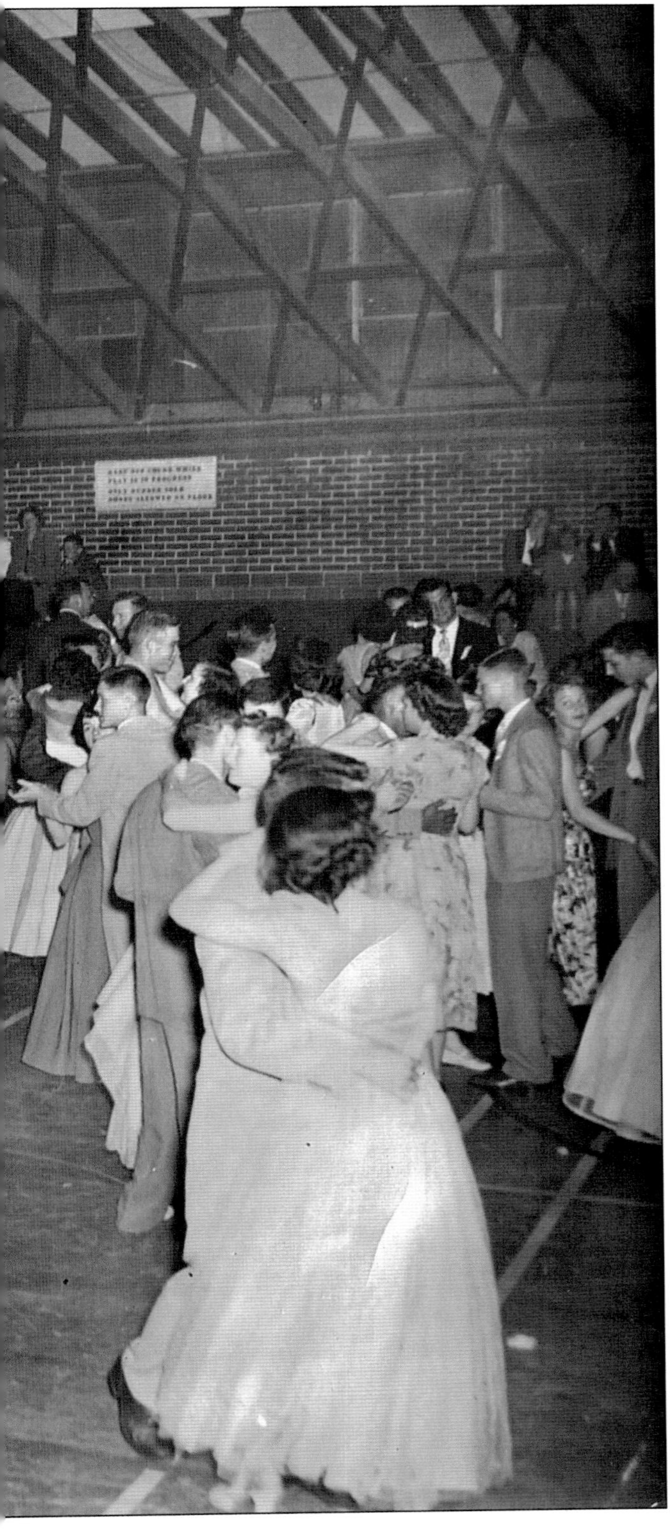

After the Cotton Queen was crowned, a formal dance was held in the gymnasium with a live band and evening clothes. The music was by the Milford Hodges Orchestra. It was the highlight of the spring season, and everyone participated, both young and old. The first number was "Dixie," and when "Stars Fell on Alabama" played, it was time to leave. (Courtesy of the *Parkway News*.)

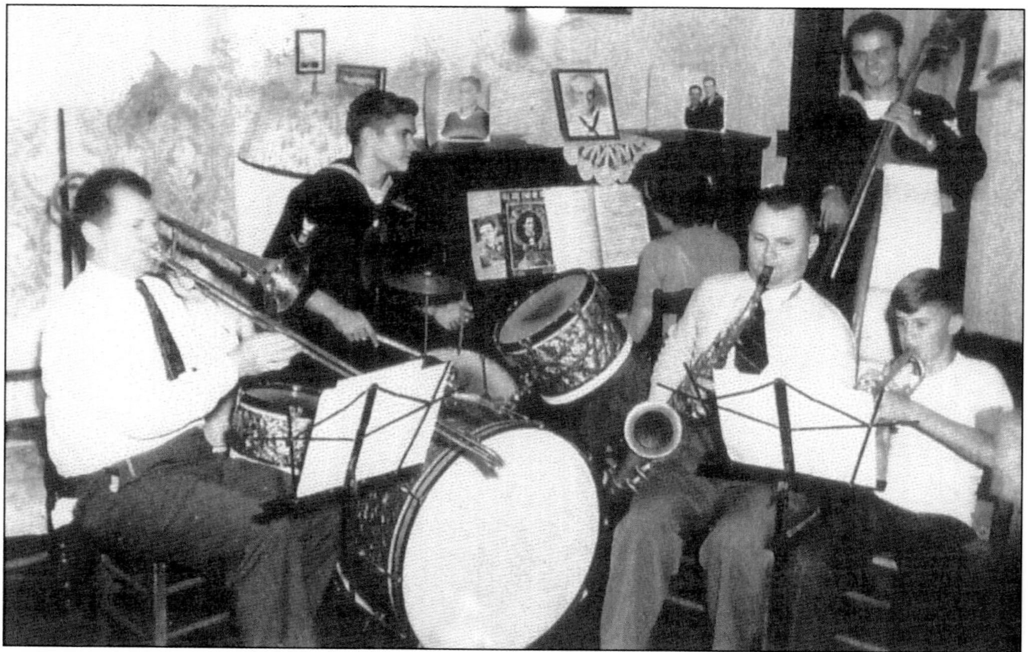

Village Jazz Band members are, from left to right, Ralph Beckett (trombone), Saxon Vickers (drums), Imogene Costner (piano), S. R. Phillips (saxophone), Joe Wayne Ingram (clarinet), and (standing) Hershel Vickers (bass fiddle). They were always available and willing to play for any affair the community might have. (Courtesy of Willadean Marlaire.)

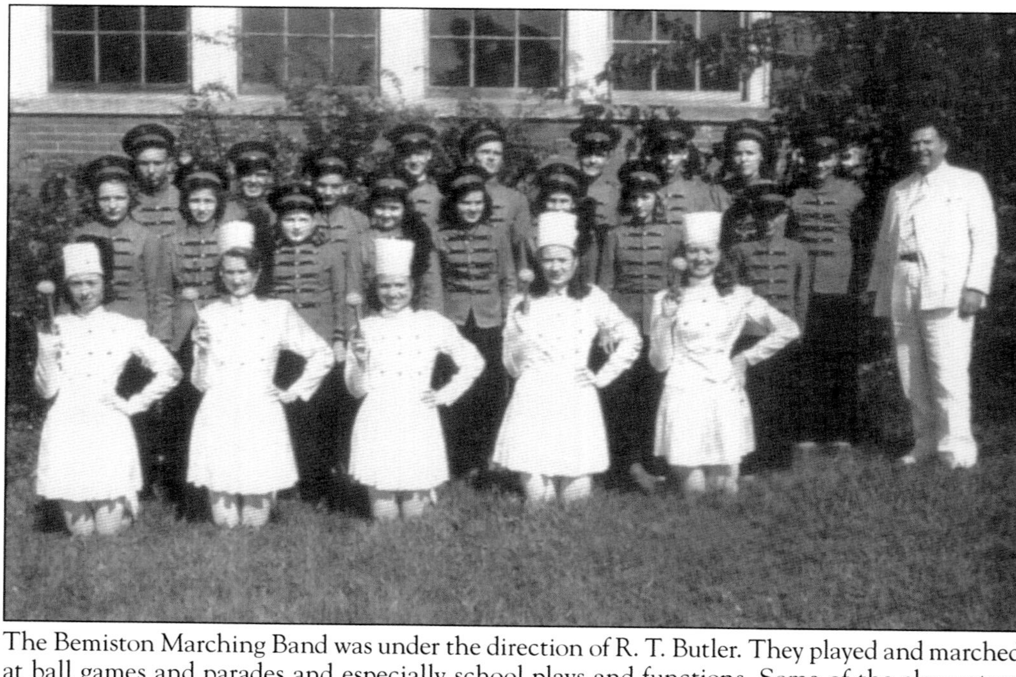

The Bemiston Marching Band was under the direction of R. T. Butler. They played and marched at ball games and parades and especially school plays and functions. Some of the elementary students had mastered an instrument well enough to qualify for the marching band. (Courtesy of Willadean Marlaire.)

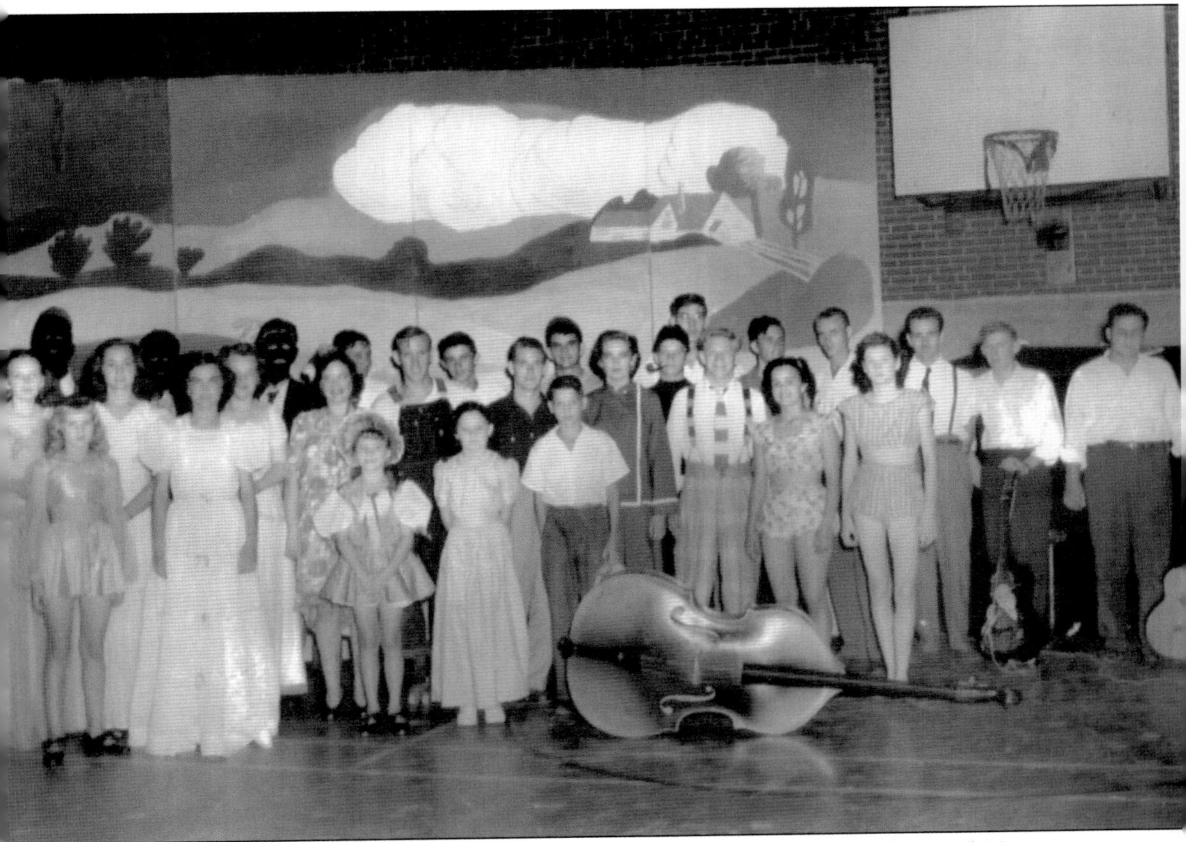

For the Variety Floor Show in 1947, cast members shown are, from left to right: (first row) Virginia Patterson, Harriet Wells, Mary Peyton, and Jan Patterson; (second row) Dorothy Wallace, Mildred Spencer, Sara Wallace, Virginia Benefield, Frank Ford, Harvey Stewart, Barbara Duncan, Hoover Atchley, Jean Vickers, and Betty Estes; (third row) Robert Fulton, S. R. Phillips, Charles Sprayberry, Leon White, Joe Wayne Ingram, Thurman Baker, Reginald Rogers, Tommy Duncan, J. D. White, Luther Miller, Dan Wallace, Hubert Shropshire, and Melvin White. (Courtesy of John Moore.)

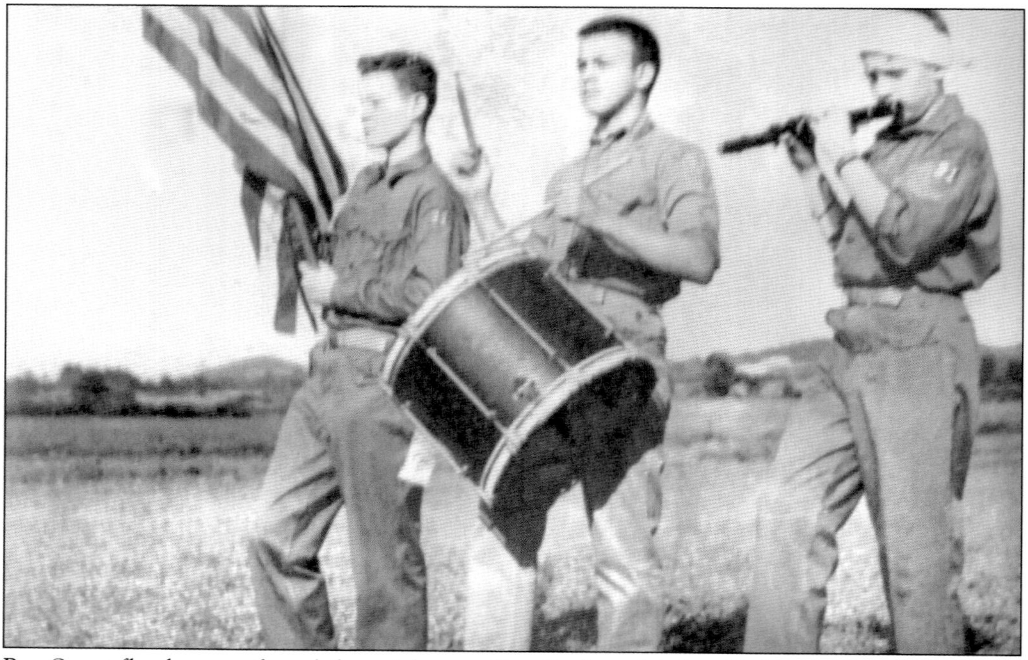

Boy Scout flag bearers, from left to right, are Don Poulson, Mickey Vickers, and Myron Waites, who also marched in parades and other outings of a patriotic nature. They were under the direction of Ralph Beckett, who was director of the marching band and helped with the Scout troop they represented. (Courtesy of the *Parkway News*.)

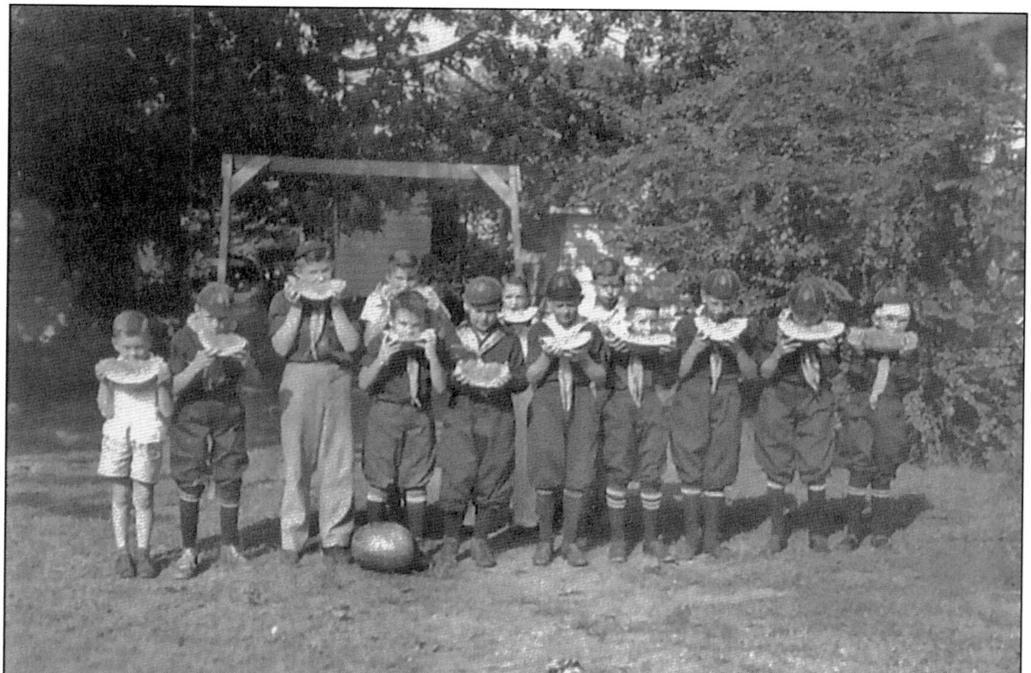

Cub Scouts were enjoying a watermelon outing. For obvious reasons, it is difficult to identify any of them. (Courtesy of Yvonne Grice.)

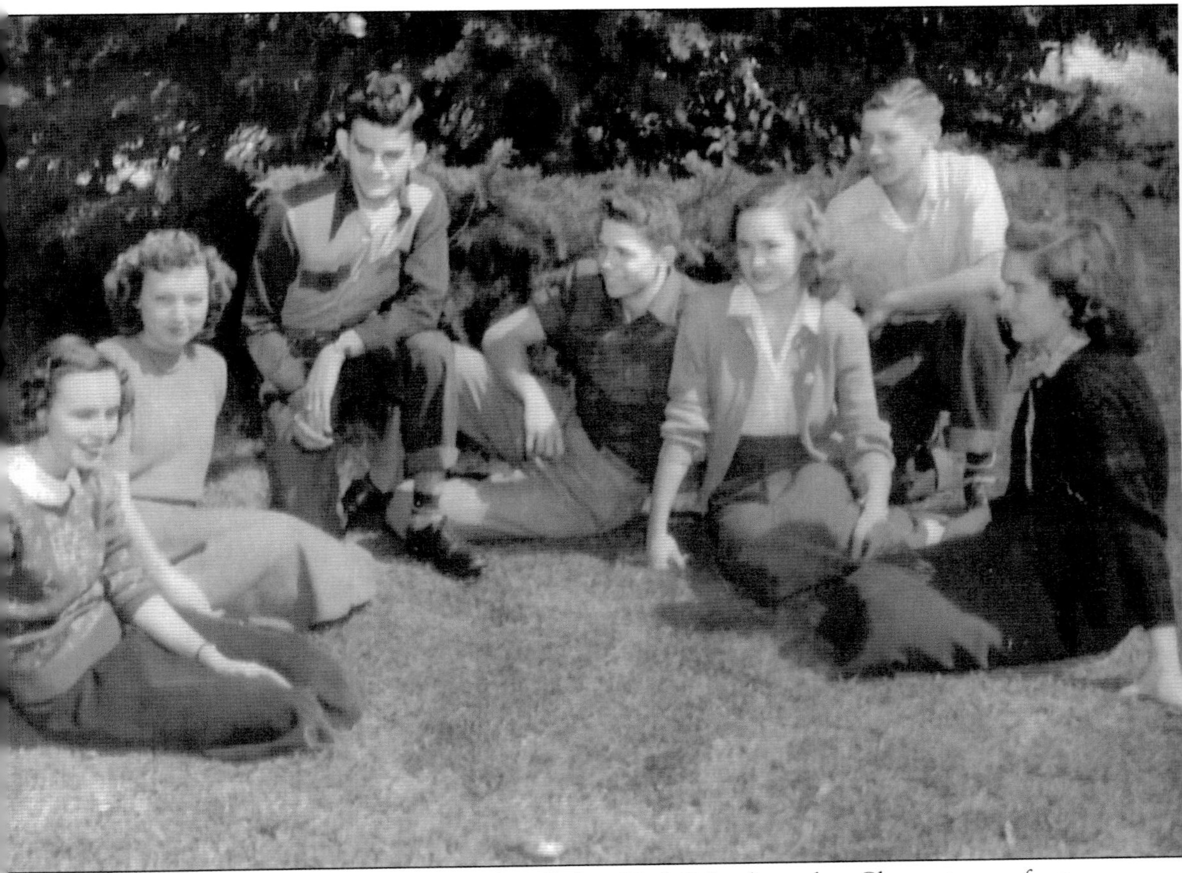

This group completed kindergarten through Talladega High School together. Classmates are, from left to right, Bobbye Jo Baker, Imogene Brown, Thurman Baker, Harold Cottle, Mildred Spencer, Aaron Browning, and Barbara Ann Duncan. Most of this group remain in close contact with each other and still attend class reunions when possible. (Courtesy of Bobbye Trammell.)

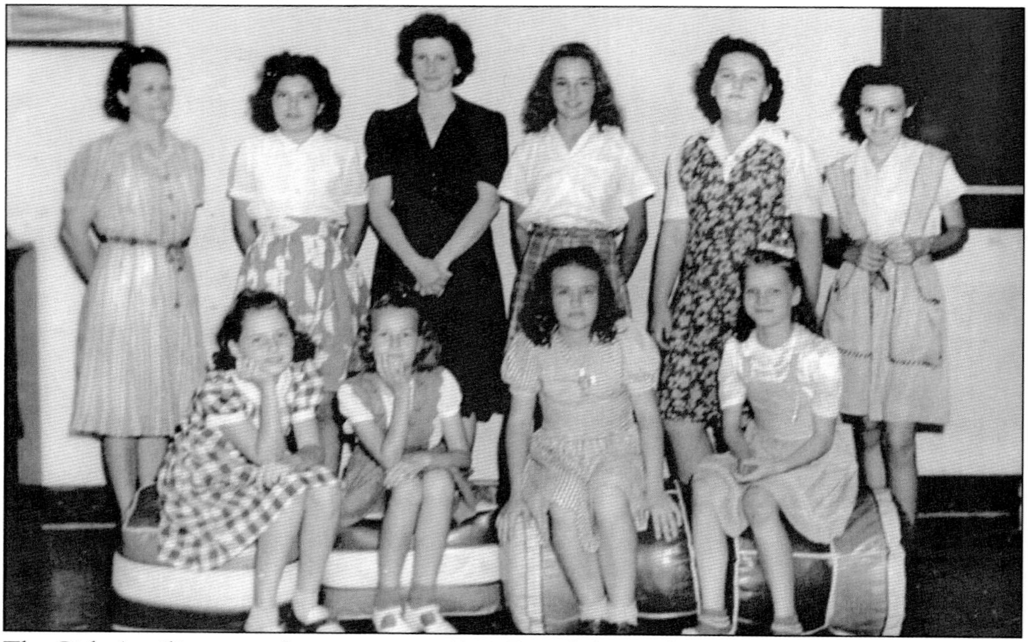

The Girls Auxiliary attends a meeting in 1944. From left to right are (first row) Gail Wood, Faye Patjens, Jeanette ?, and Marlene Patterson; (second row) Lavada Roberts (leader), Mary Noah, Ollie Pearl Forbus (leader), Mildred Spencer, Mildred Burnam, and Bobbye Jo Baker. (Courtesy of Bobbye Trammell.)

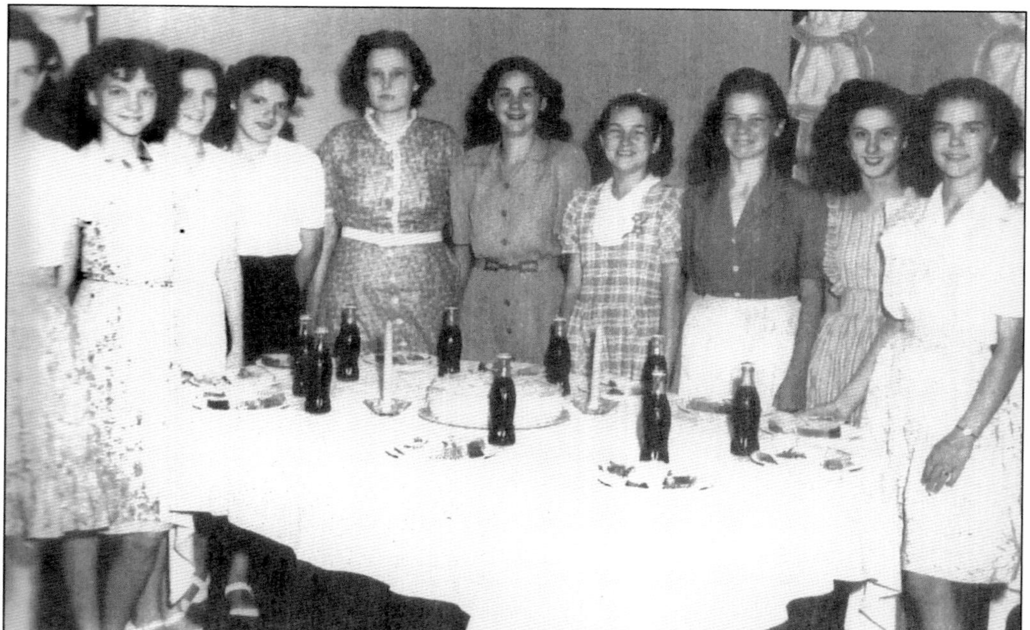

The Girls Auxiliary is enjoying a party in 1947. Members are, from left to right, Dot Duncan, Marlene Patterson, unidentified, Mary Noah, Esther Ellison, Annette Phillips, Faye Patjens, unidentified, Pauline Williams, and Willadean Vickers. The party is hosted by Marlene Patterson at her parents' home. (Courtesy of Willadean Marlaire.)

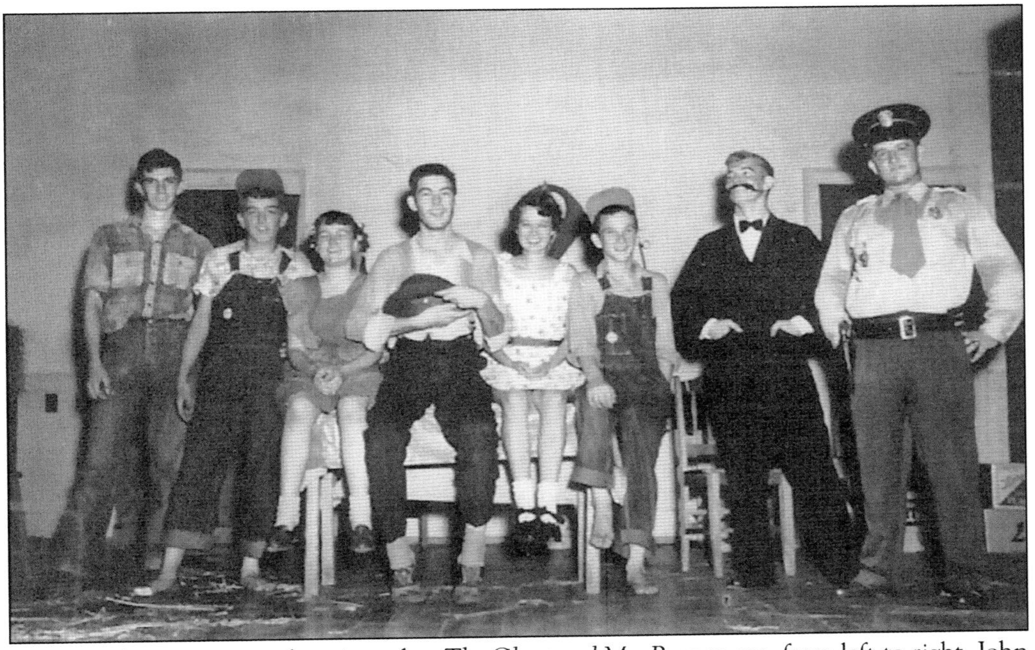

Parkway Players cast members in a play, *The Ghost and Mr. Penney*, are, from left to right, John Moore, Clyde Williams, Faye Patjens, Tommy Duncan, Roxie Poulson, Elgin Robinson, Lamar Roberts, and Joe Neal Sprayberry. This group performed at other locations and also had a broadcast on the local radio station. Manilla Fulton directed the play. (Courtesy of John Moore.)

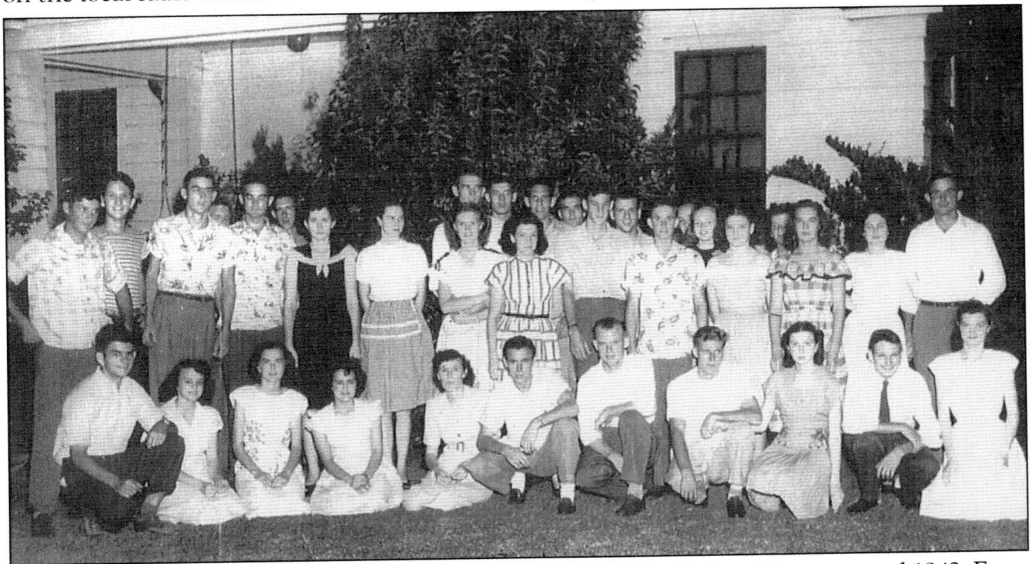

This Sunday school party was held for both churches at the Ila Vickers House around 1942. From left to right are (first row) Thurman Baker, Yvonne Vickers, Willadean Vickers, Jean Vickers, Daphene Baker, J. W. Baker, Bill Garrett, Harvey Stewart, unidentified, Jimmy Brownlow, and Peggy Cline. Also pictured, in no particular order, are Sam Grice, Nolen Hamlin, Lamar Roberts, Sallie Hutton, Geraldine Colvard, Betty Ingram, Sue Peters, Floyd Barton, Billy Hamlin, Tommy Duncan, Mildred Spencer, Dot Wallace, Barbara Duncan, Ruth Brownlow, and Stewart Ellison. Some are unidentified. (Courtesy of Willadean Marlaire.)

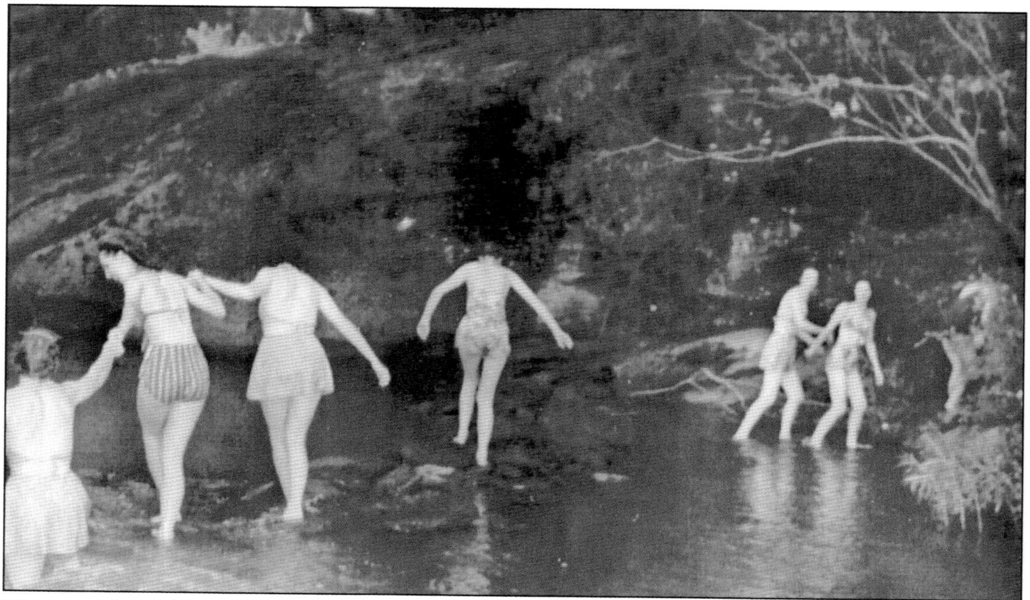

This was the girls' day out at the swimming hole at Talladega Creek. Sometimes after a hard day's work at the office, nothing can be more restful than relaxing in the cool water of a clear creek to let the rest of the world go by. (Courtesy of J. W. Baker.)

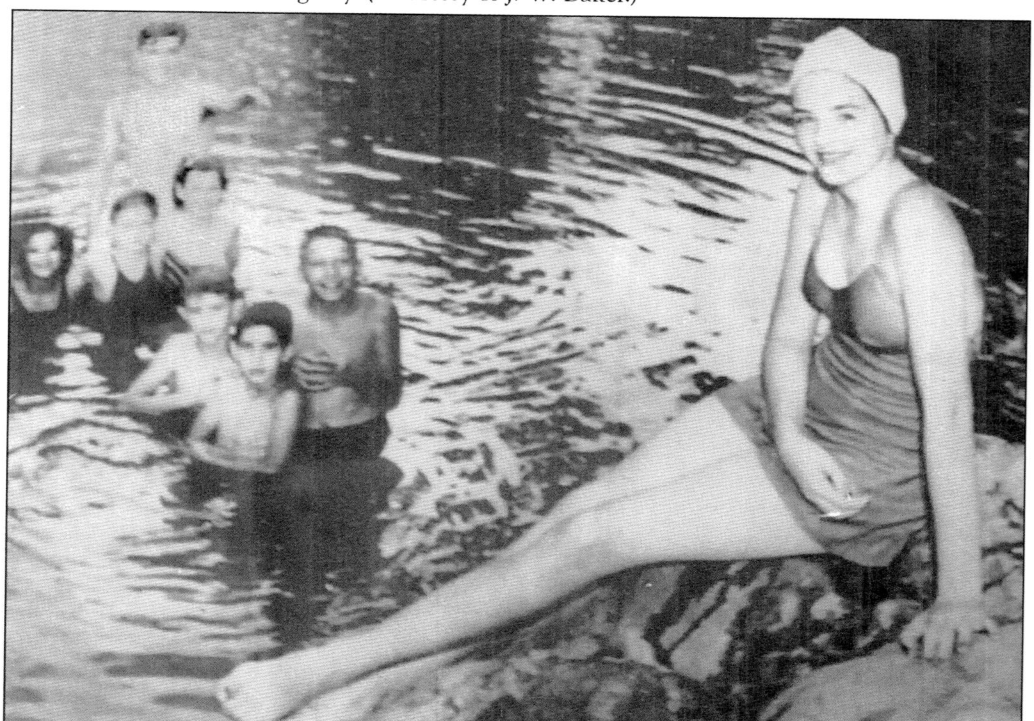

This group of young boys was admiring the view as Doris Ann Drake suns on the big rock at the swimming hole. They do not seem to be enjoying swimming as much as they do watching the view. (Courtesy of *Bemistory* magazine.)

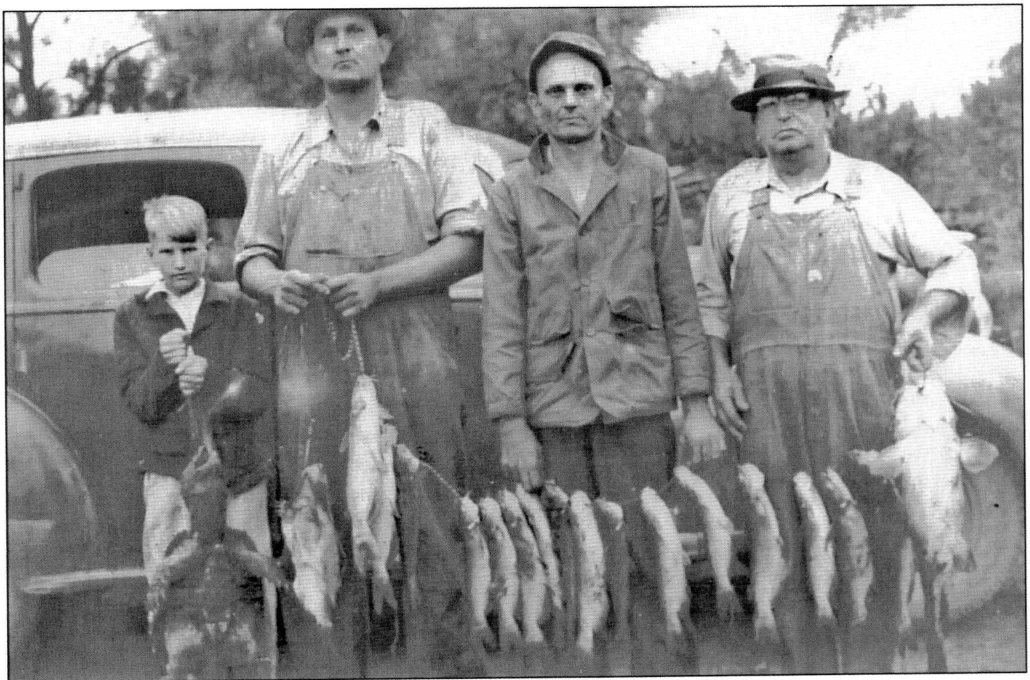

These fishermen had a good day. From left to right are Frank Bone Jr., Frank Bone, Theodore "Buddy Brown," and Henry "Grandpa" Holcombe. Not only did the men seem to have good luck, but Frank Jr. did not do so badly by catching the big turtle. (Courtesy of Johnny and Betty Brown.)

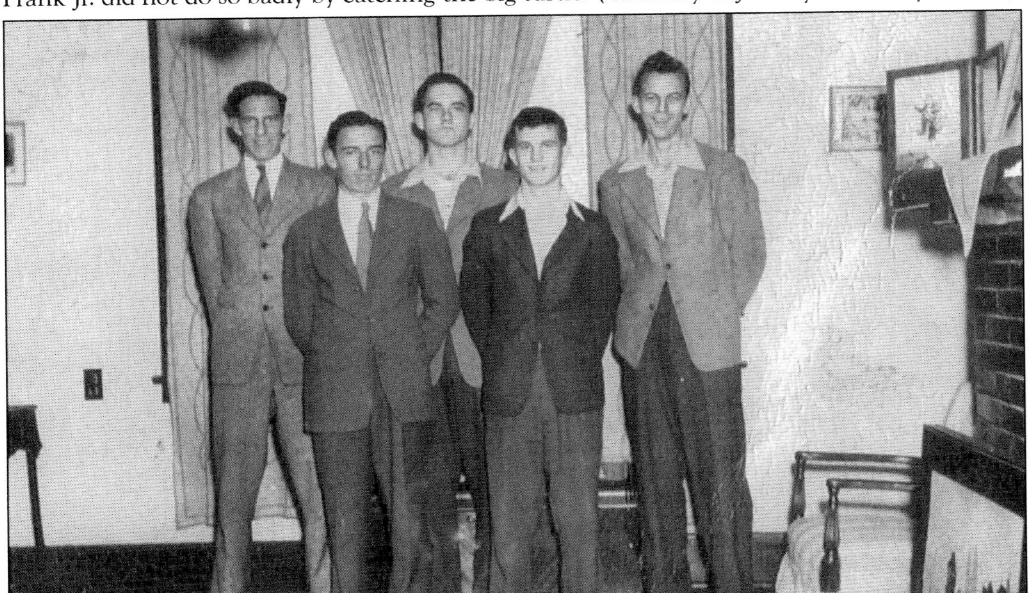

Good friends are shown here enjoying each other's company. Every weekend, these fellows were together just to enjoy the fellowship. They had been friends since childhood, and someone thought to bring a camera. They are, from left to right, (first row) J. W. Baker and Charlie Scroggins; (second row) Floyd Barton, Nolen Hamlin, and Richard Brown. (Courtesy of Bobbye Trammell.)

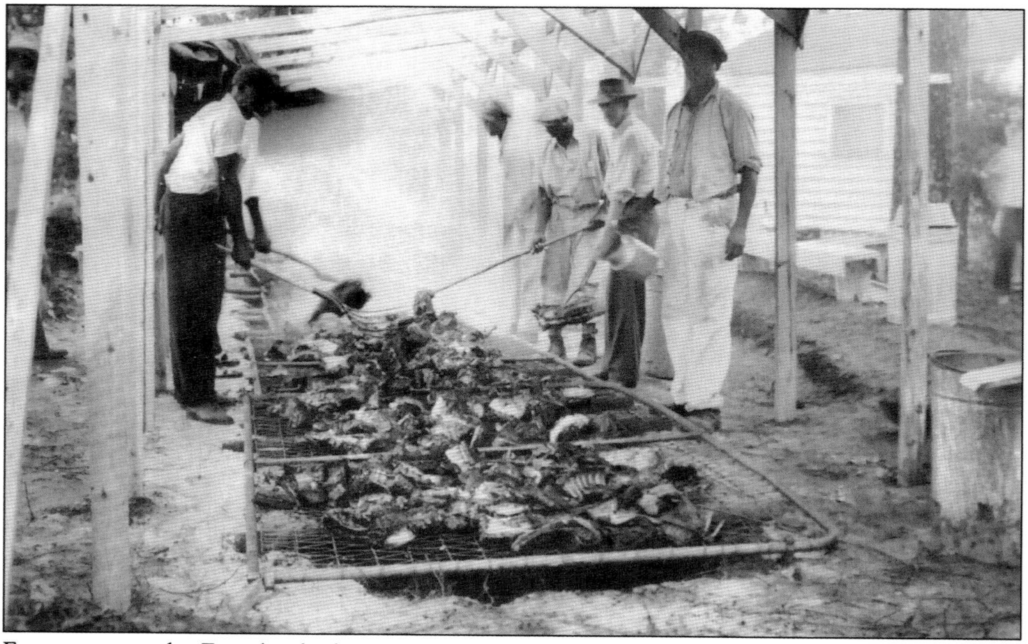

Every year on the Fourth of July, Bemiston honored the employees' families with a day of food and fun. Shown in this picture are the workers at the grilling pit getting ready for ball games, eating, and dancing, horseshoes, sack races, and good fellowship with their friends. (Courtesy of J. W. Baker.)

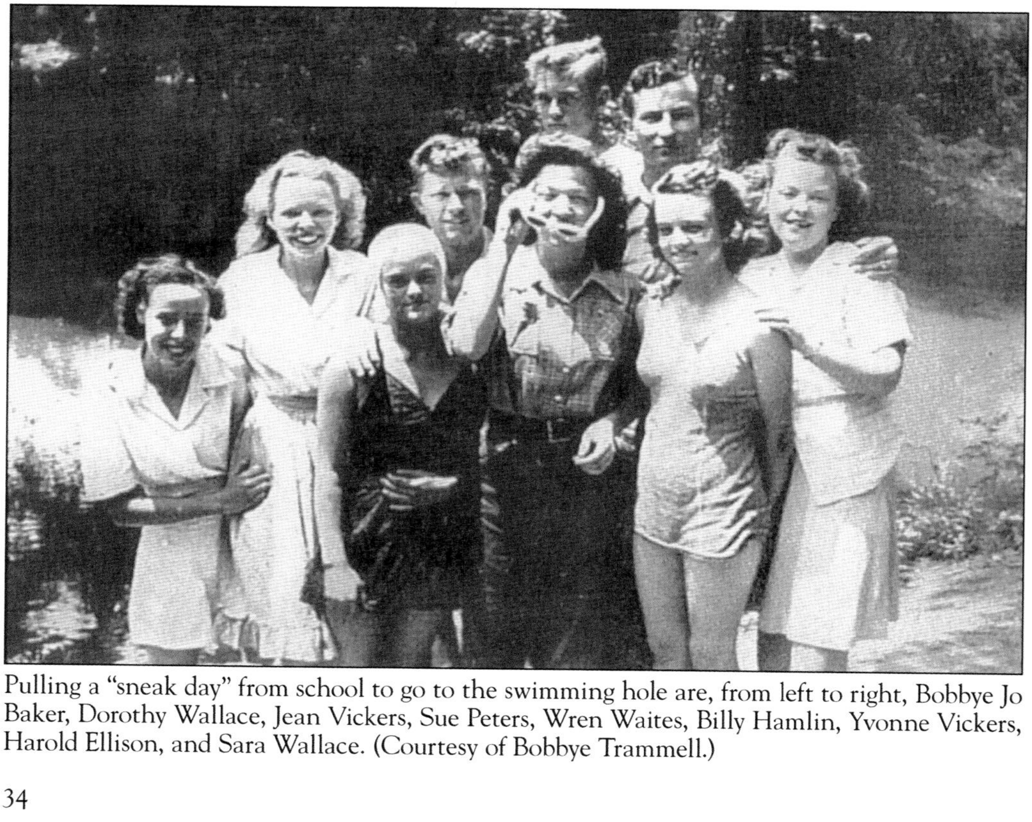

Pulling a "sneak day" from school to go to the swimming hole are, from left to right, Bobbye Jo Baker, Dorothy Wallace, Jean Vickers, Sue Peters, Wren Waites, Billy Hamlin, Yvonne Vickers, Harold Ellison, and Sara Wallace. (Courtesy of Bobbye Trammell.)

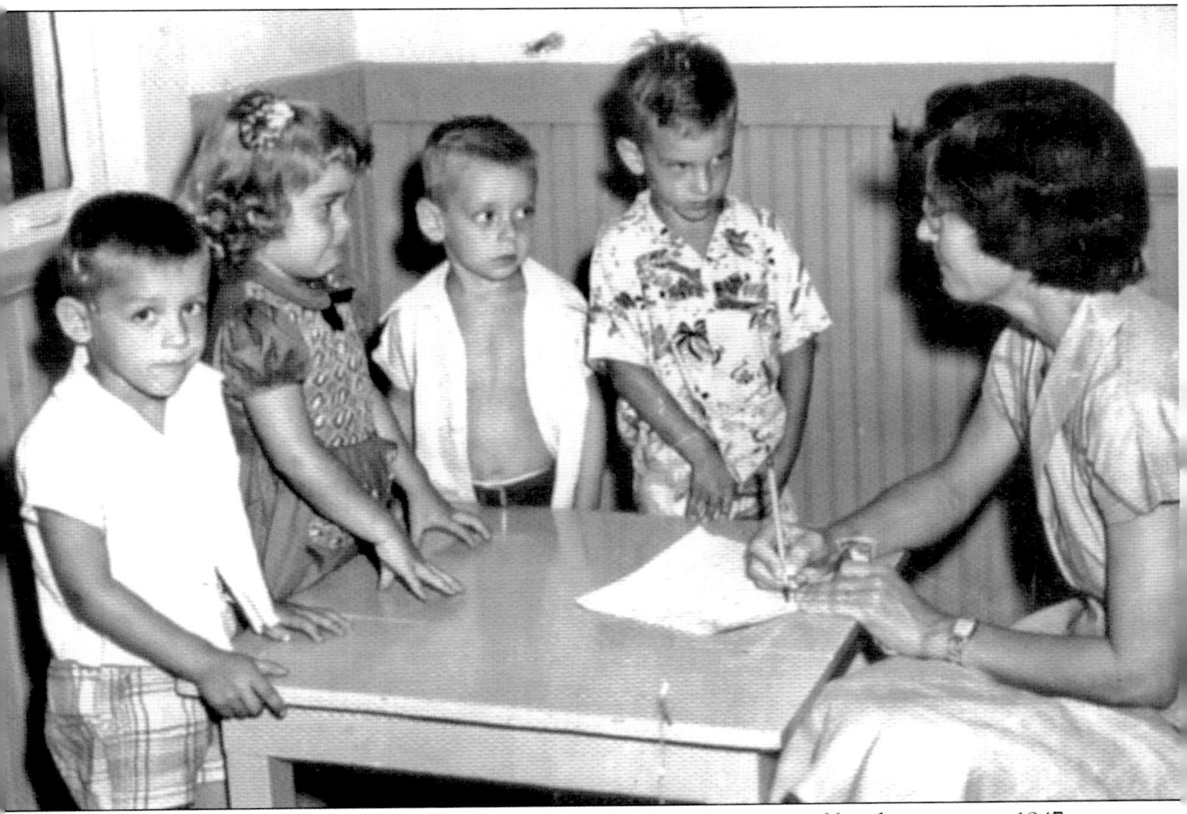

Louise Spencer is shown here registering students for their first year of kindergarten in 1947. The two children standing in the middle are Charlotte Staples and Byron Taff; the others are unidentified. Louise Spencer and Lavada Roberts were the teachers, and they always looked forward to the new students. (Courtesy of Willadean Marlaire.)

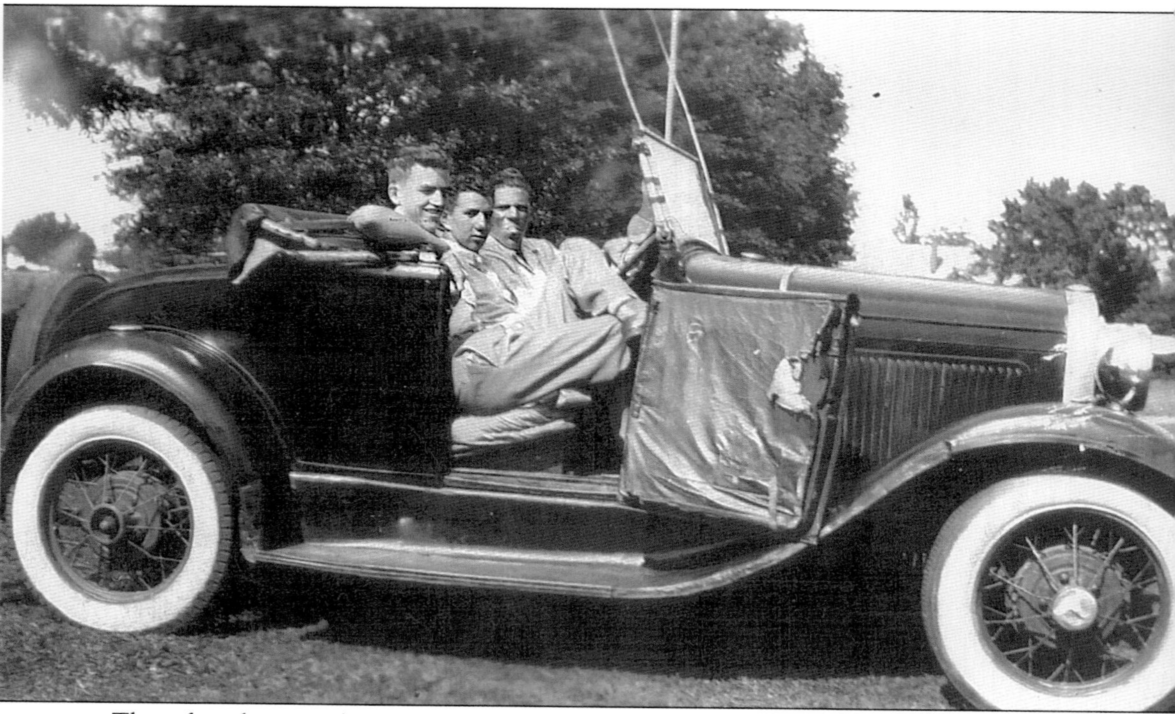

Three friends get ready for an afternoon drive in Clifford Barton's newly acquired Ford Model A convertible. Pictured from left to right are Sam Grice, Alfred Mitchell, and Clifford Barton. They did not have room for any more passengers—even if they can get it to start. (Courtesy of Bobbye Trammell.)

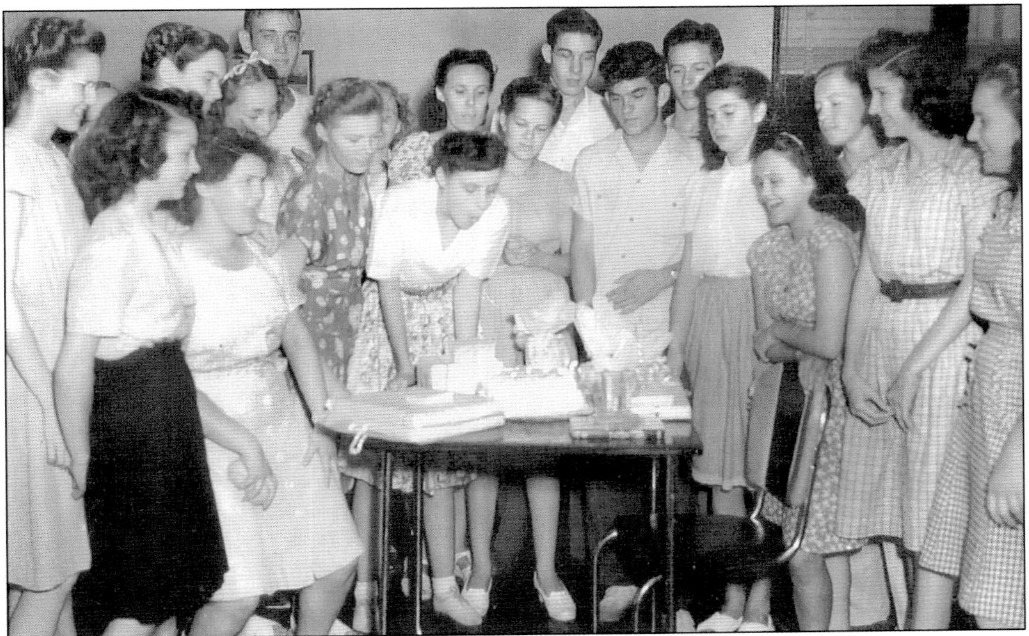

Bobbye Jo Baker was honored on her 16th birthday with a surprise party at the Community Building. Pictured with the honoree are, in no particular order, Yvonne Vickers, Geraldine Colvard, Virginia Benefield, Barbara Duncan, Mildred Spencer, Billy Hamlin, Betty Ingram, Daphene Baker, Martha Sue Benefield, Tommy Duncan, Thurman Baker, Annette Phillips, Jean Vickers, Charles Sprayberry, Maurice Patterson, Dot Duncan, and Betty Gambrell. (Courtesy of J. W. Baker.)

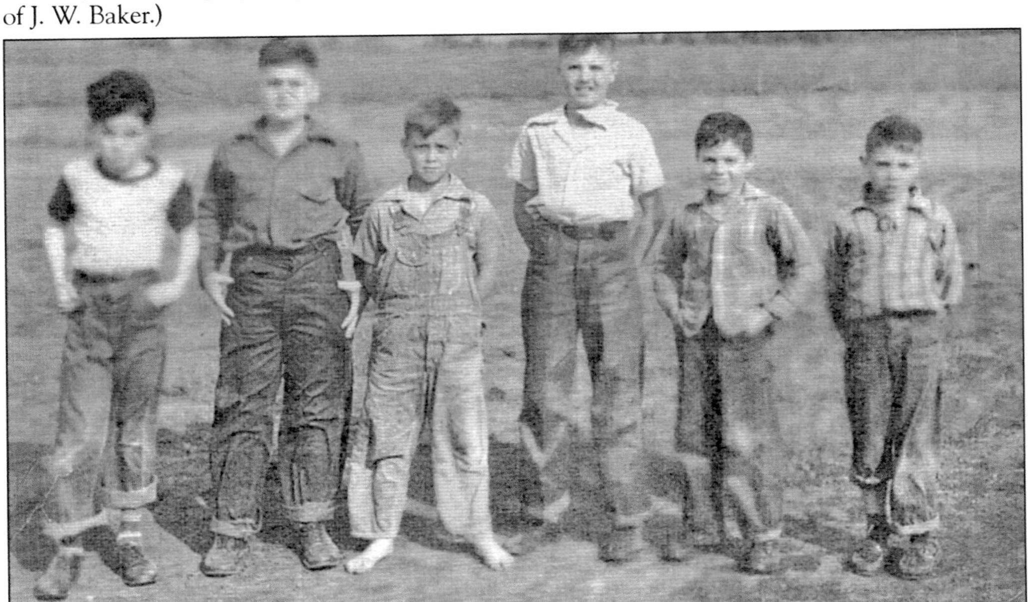

The young boys shown here are enjoying the day. From left to right are Myron Waites, Joe Charles Cooley, Mickey Vickers, Lamon Bowen, Alden Limbaugh, and an unidentified friend. It is hard to tell if it is a summer day or a fall day. Some are wearing flannel, and one is barefoot. (Courtesy of Yvonne Grice.)

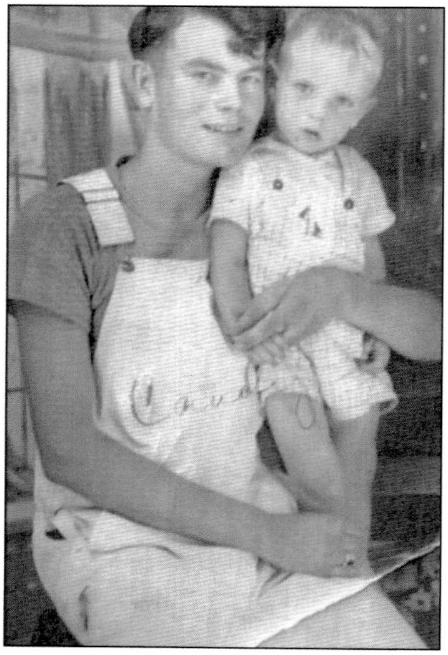

Shown in the picture here are J. W. Knight (left) and Tommy Ray Baker. Tommy's dad, John Alvin Baker, was killed in action in the South Pacific on June 1, 1945. This photograph was taken soon after in June 1945. (Courtesy of J. W. Knight.)

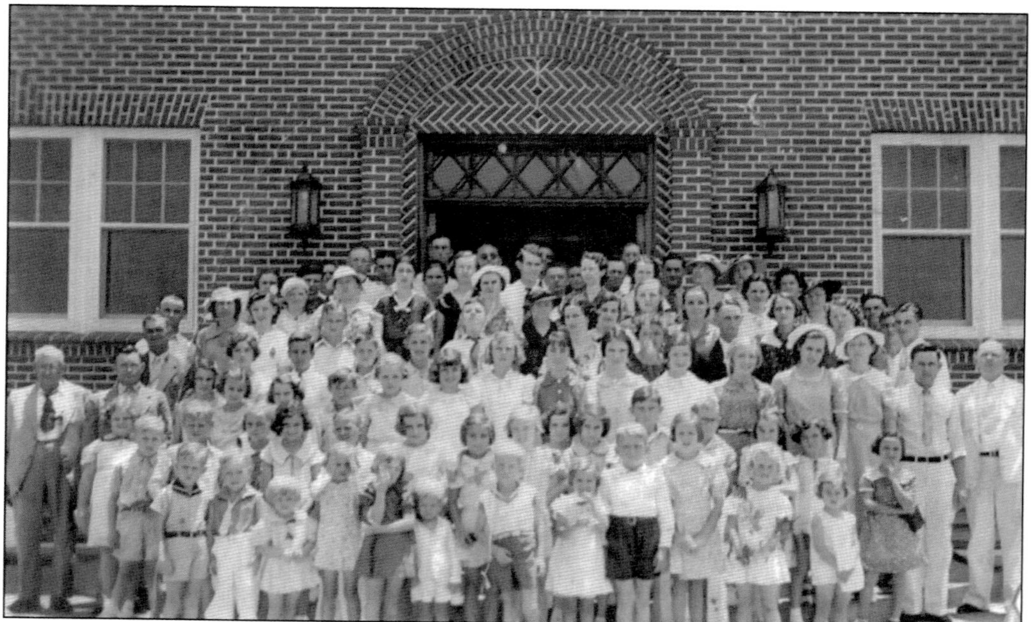

This photograph shows congregations of both the Bemiston United Methodist Church and the Bemiston Baptist Church. The churches met together at the R. L. Young Elementary School. Baptists would hold services on Sunday morning and the Methodists on Sunday night. The next Sunday services would be reversed. Later a village house was provided by the Bemis Brothers Bag Company for both congregations. In the early 1950s, the Bemis company gave each church family property to build on and matched the money they raised to help build the churches. The Bemiston Baptist Church was built in 1951, and the Bemiston United Methodist Church was built in 1956. This picture was taken in the front of the Bemiston Community Building in 1939. The ministers are shown on each end of the third row. On the left is a Reverend Jordan, and on the right is Rev. W. A. Wiggins. (Courtesy of Wren Herd Owens.)

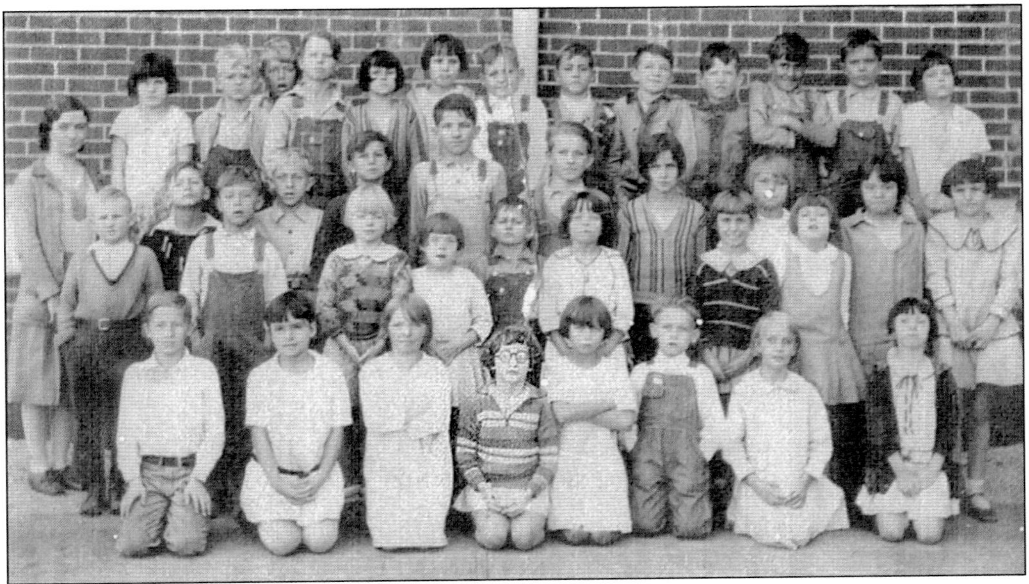

Shown here is the second-grade class at the R. L. Young Elementary School in 1930. The teacher, a Mrs. Brown, is on the far left. The school was built in 1929, and this class was probably the first class to attend. Among those pictured are, in no particular order: Mary Doris Adams, Daffeane Baker, Montez Evans, Evelyn Goggins, Lorene Haywood, Mary Herring, Della Hicks, Elizabeth Humphries, Isabell Jarvis, Gladys Limbaugh, Helen Limbaugh, Wilmer Minter, Robineal McEachern, Thelma Smith, Peggy Ann Smith, Vinnie Vaden White, Reba Williams, Jeanette Ellison, Joe Bailey, Paul Bain Jr., Clarence Burdette, Fay Cook, Charles Ellison, Preston Howell, James Huckaba, Dura Keahey, Edward Keahey, Thurston Key, Edward Newton, Gordon Richardson, Dave Smith, Jim Smith, Cecil Fincher, and J. C. Hatter. (Courtesy of R. L. Young Elementary School.)

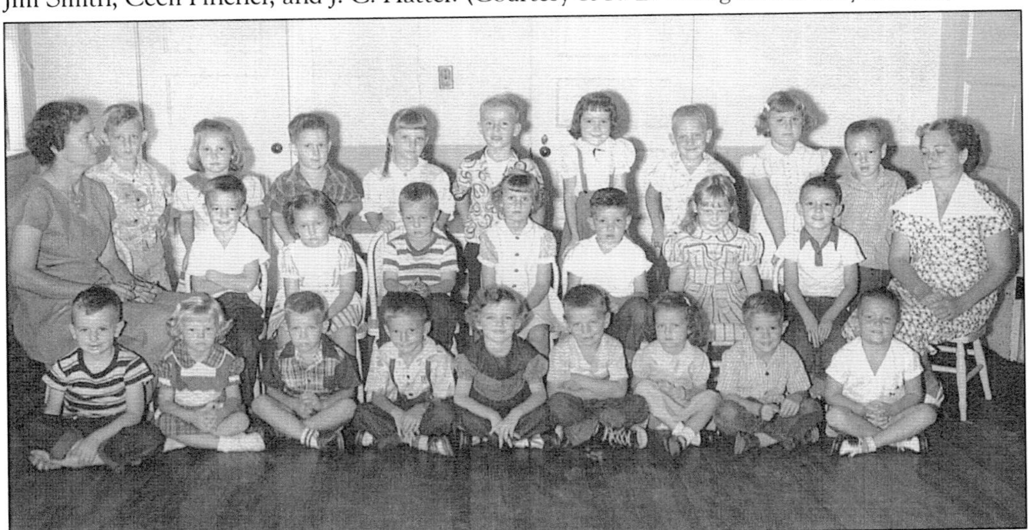

The 1954–1955 kindergarten class included, from left to right, (first row) Frankie Stewart, Linda Parton, Dan Burrell, Melvin Mitchell, Patty Garrett, Ronnie Gilbert, Linda Horn, and Phil Fessender; (second row) Ricky Robison, Diane Sargent, Greg Caldwell, Bonnie Smith, Shirley Cooper, and Bobby Lumpkin; (third row) Ray Burrell, Nancy Shaddix, ? Hughston, Ronnie Martin, Jeanine Clark, ? Matson, and Joyce Howard. (Courtesy of Mildred Brownlow.)

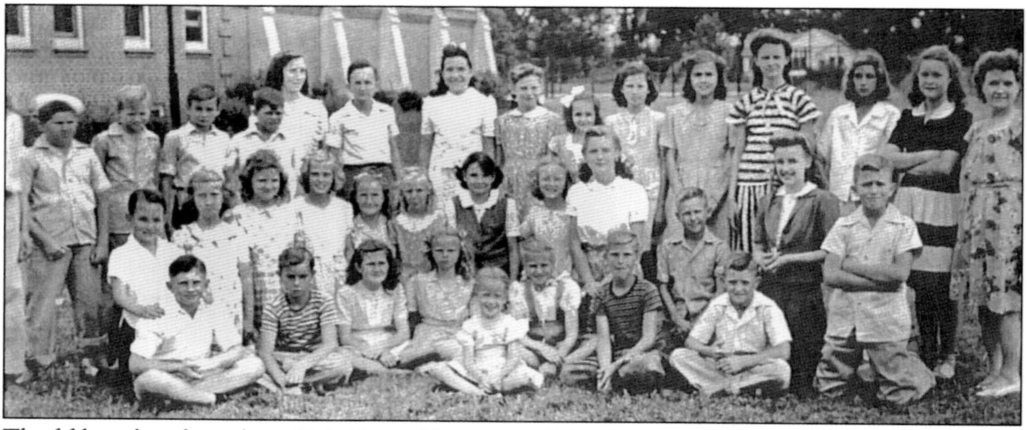

The fifth and sixth grades at R. L. Young Elementary School enjoy a *c.* 1942 picnic. From left to right are (first row) John Paul Moore, Kenneth Daniel, Margaret Nunn, Virginia Hall, unidentified, Sylvia Gaines, Virginia Ruth Patterson, Roy Gravette, and Donald Roberts; (second row) Elgin Robinson, Faye Anderson, Mary Ann Brownlow, Jeanette Hanner, Melva Ann Benefield, unidentified, Earlene Gallman, Billie Mae Martin, Wallace Gene Morris, Jean Brady, and unidentified; (third row) unidentified, Bert Garner, unidentified, Wilmer Casey Preston, Gerald White, Mary Payton, Donald Barton, Edith Mitchell, Betty Estes, Willadean Vickers, Christine Evans, unidentified, Flo Brewer, and ? Smith (teacher). (Courtesy of Jean Brady.)

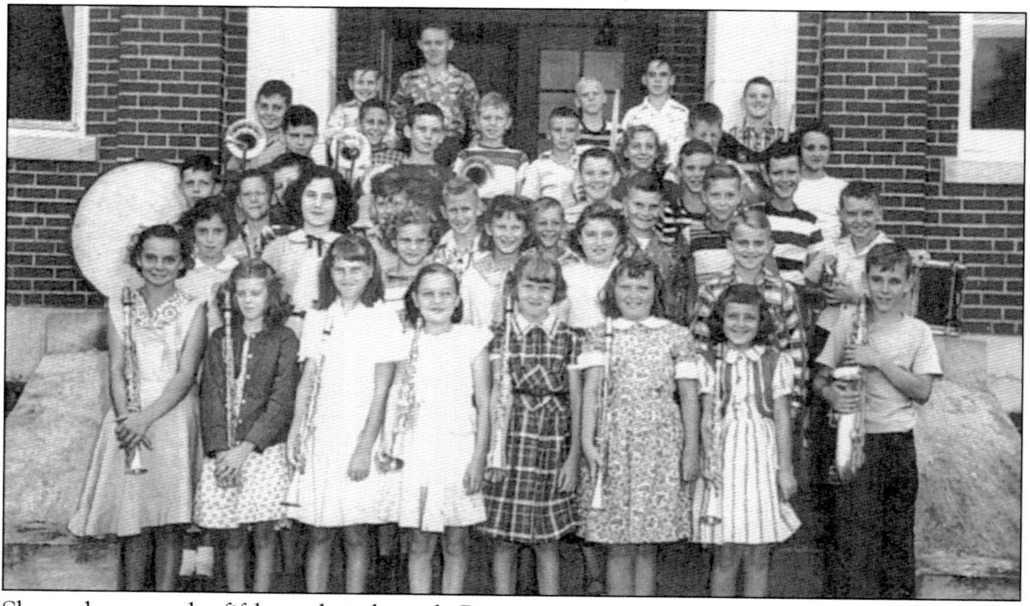

Shown here are the fifth- and sixth-grade Bemiston music students at R. L. Young Elementary School. From left to right are (first row) Dorothy Cosby, Edna Mae Ford, June Shropshire, Donna Dye, Sara Forrest, Sue Anderson, Faye Smith, and Larry Barton; (second row) Gay Baker, Barbara Hawkins, Faye Turner, DeLois Key, Gloria Morgan, Kenneth Olivet, and James Parton; (third row) N. L. Cosby, Phillip Willis, Larry Thornburg, Glenn Cosby, Clifford Jennings, and Edward Forrest; (fourth row) Dorman Hughston, Bob Garner, Wayne Cheatwood, Terry Tomlin, Ernest Mitchell, Wayne Bowen, Jerry Holcomb, Wayne Folsom, and Faye Malone; (fifth row) Dan Nabors, Richard Sewell, Jonny Mack Brown, Kenneth Patterson, Bob Nunn, and Lynn Lawson. (Courtesy of *Parkway News*, October 1950.)

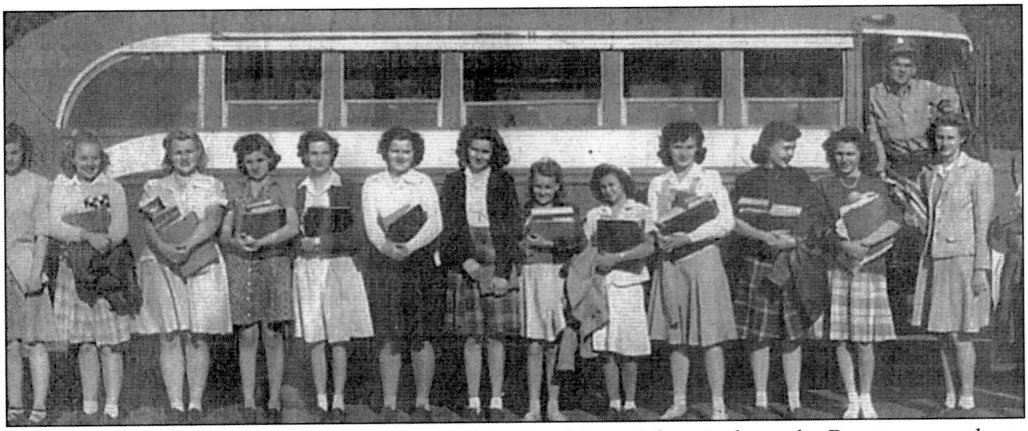

Shown here are the girls waiting to get on the school bus. After sixth grade, Bemiston students had to ride the bus to Talladega High School in the city of Talladega, Alabama. Talladega High School was approximately 3 miles from Bemiston. There were no boys in this picture because the boys and girls rode separate buses. (Courtesy of *Bemistory* magazine.)

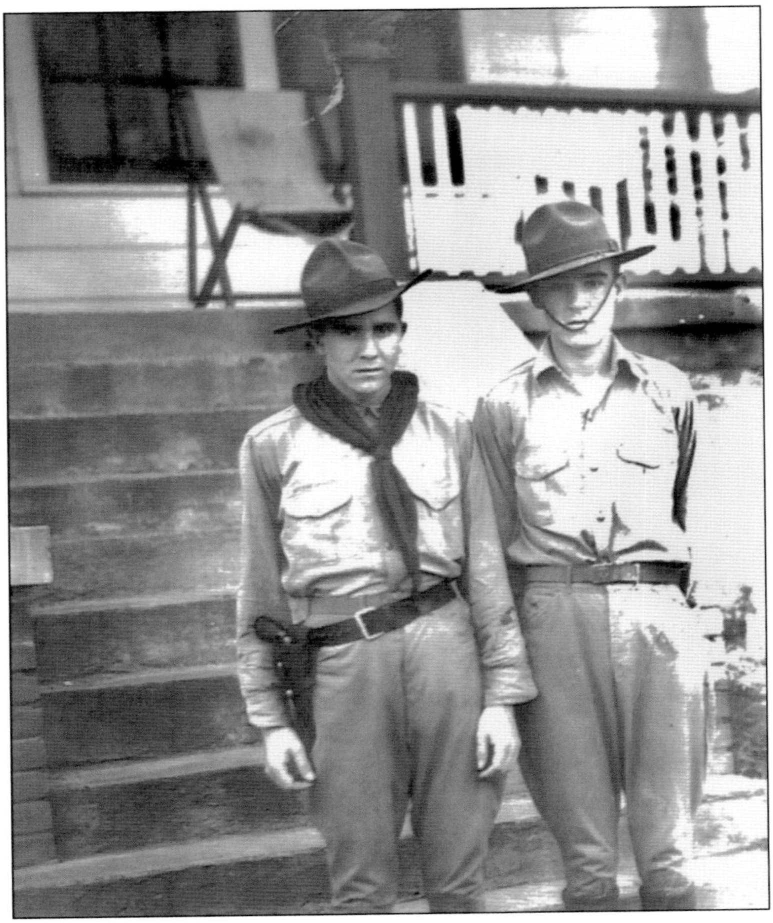

Boy Scouts proudly showcase their uniforms in 1936. Scouts are Jim Smith (left) and John Alvin Baker. No, that is not a real gun Jim has on his side, hopefully. Jim worked in the plant, and John Alvin worked in the general store. (Courtesy of Jean Ipavec.)

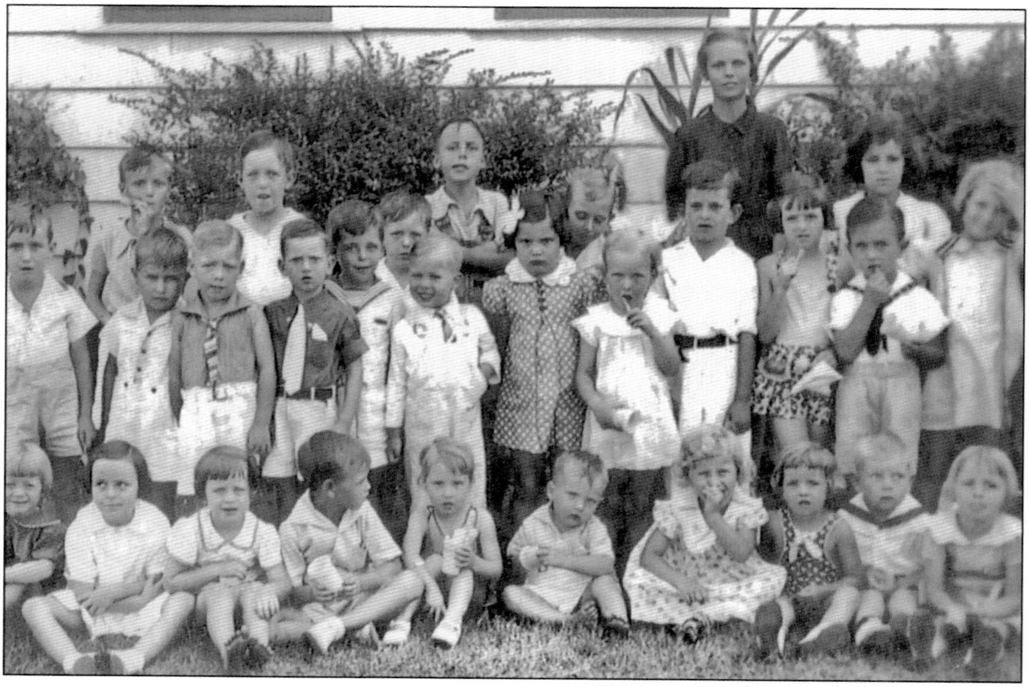

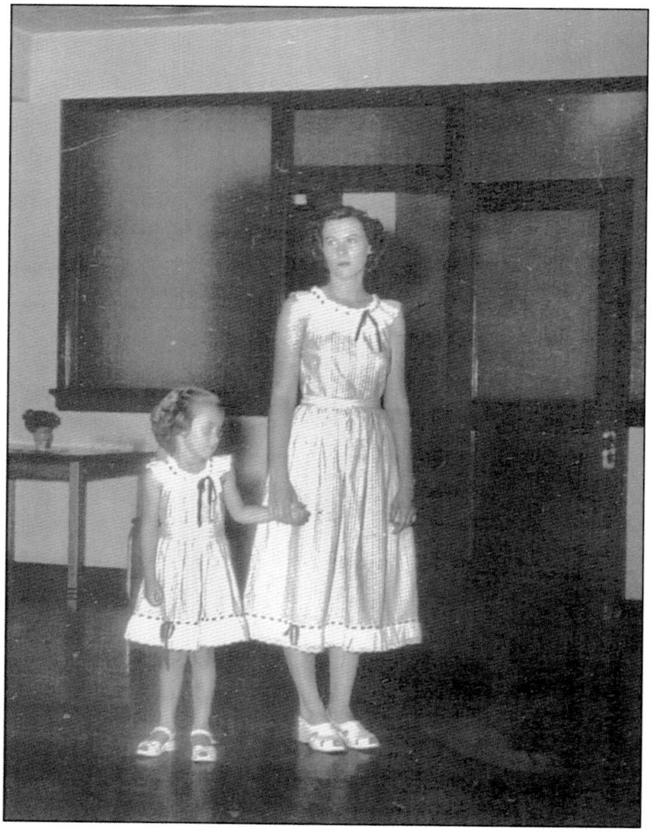

At Mary Noah's sixth birthday party in 1936 are, from left to right, (first row) unidentified, Bobbye Jo Baker, Evelyn ?, Lamar Anderson, Joyce Hindmon, Elgin Robinson, Rudene Burdette, Patsy Drake, Joe Mel Smith, and Jean Brady; (second row) Elois Williams, Jack Williams, unidentified, Bobby Jones, Roland Patterson, Lamar Butts, Mary Noah, Faye Anderson, Thurman Baker, Doris Ann Drake, Donald Barton, and Frances Smith; (third row) Merlyn Osbourne, Julius Jones, J. W. Baker, unidentified, Harold ?, Annie Laura Shaw, and Juanita Knott. (Courtesy of J. W. Baker.)

Marybelle Vickers and daughter Amy model in a fashion show wearing dresses made by Marybelle. These dresses had to be made from Bemis cotton bags to enter the contest. (Courtesy of J. W. Baker.)

Ferial Forbus is shown modeling a dress made by her mother, Ollie Pearl Forbus. Many mothers in the village made their families' clothing, but these were made from Bemis cotton. (Courtesy of J. W. Baker.)

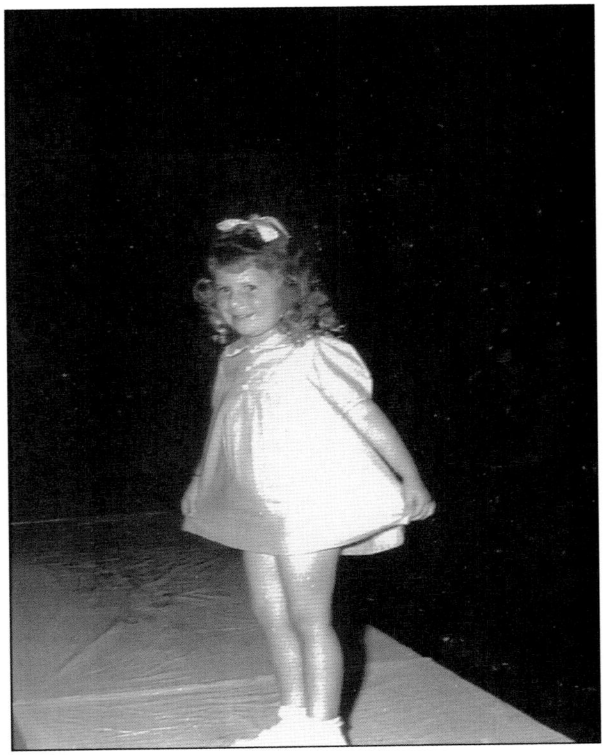

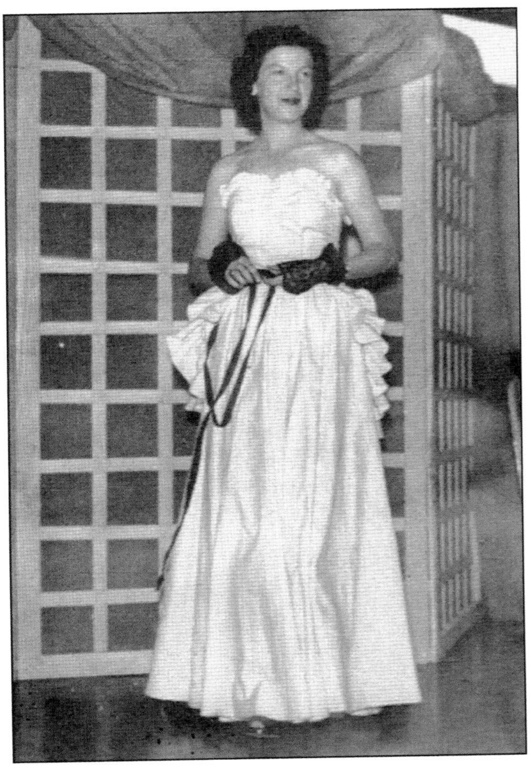

Sue Peters is wearing a beautiful formal dress design from the National Cotton Council. Sue was employed in the Bemiston Main Office. (Courtesy of *Bemistory* magazine.)

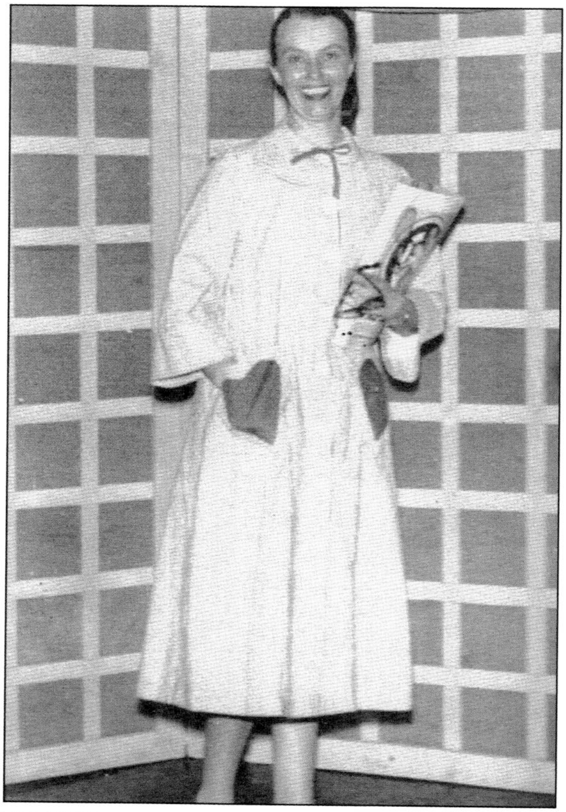

Cathel Clark is modeling a stunning striped brunch coat. It was also a design from the National Cotton Council. Clark was employed in the Bemiston Main Office. (Courtesy of *Bemistory* magazine.)

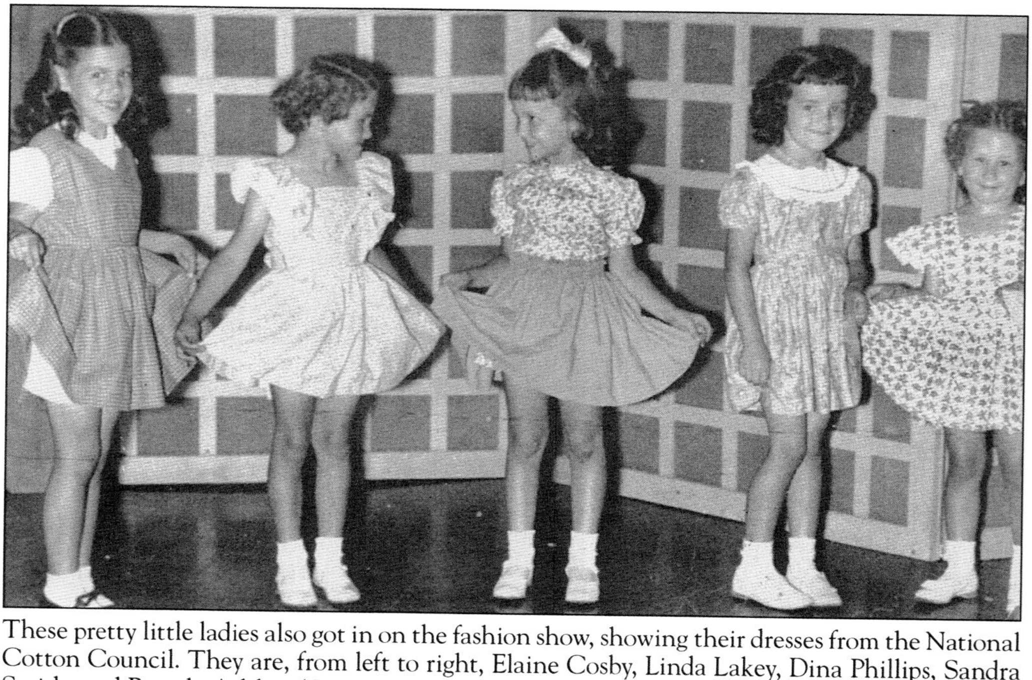

These pretty little ladies also got in on the fashion show, showing their dresses from the National Cotton Council. They are, from left to right, Elaine Cosby, Linda Lakey, Dina Phillips, Sandra Smith, and Brenda Ashley. (Courtesy of *Bemistory* magazine.)

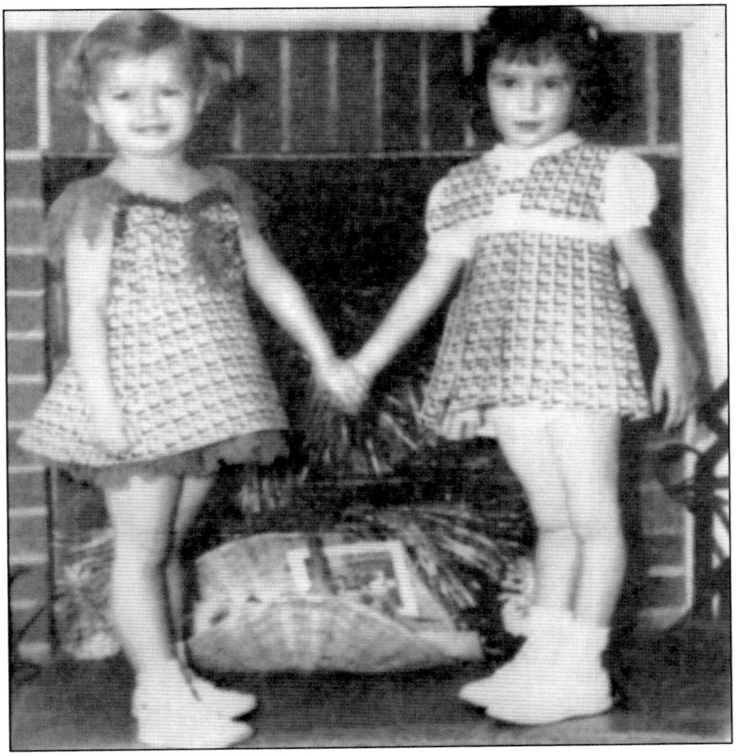

These two cuties are wearing dresses for their fashion show made from Christmas seals. They are Emily Coker (left), daughter of Oliver and Beth Coker of Talladega, and Jeanine Clark, daughter of Hoyt and Mary Lee Clark of Bemiston. Jeanine's dress was made by her mother, and Emily's was made by her aunt, Anne Tyler. Proceeds from the sale of Christmas seals went to fight tuberculosis. (Courtesy of the *Parkway News*.)

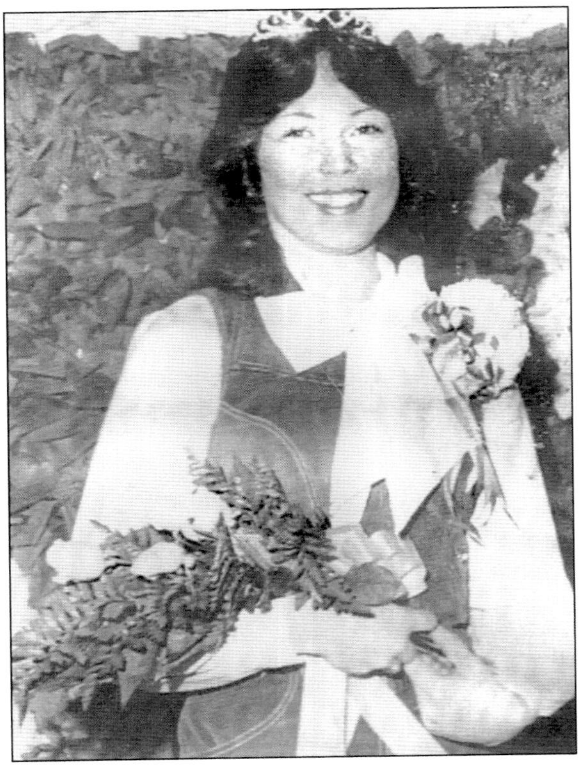

Pretty Lisa Freeman is the daughter of James and Allene Freeman. In addition to being homecoming queen, Lisa was elected as a Girls' State representative, editor of the school newspaper, head varsity cheerleader, and recipient of the Sally Steed Memorial Award, which exemplifies character and best all-around student. (Courtesy of the *Bemis Echoes*.)

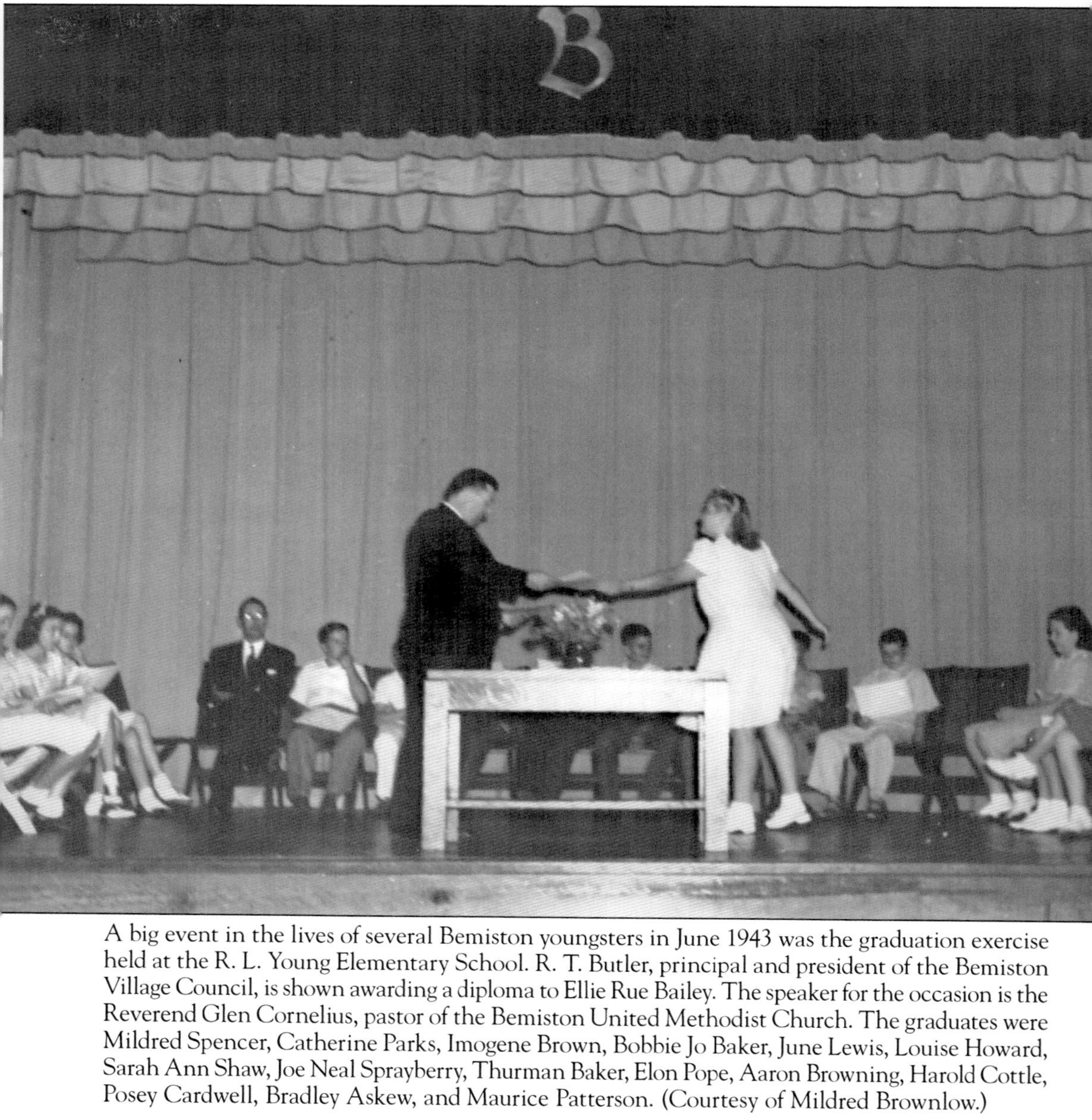

A big event in the lives of several Bemiston youngsters in June 1943 was the graduation exercise held at the R. L. Young Elementary School. R. T. Butler, principal and president of the Bemiston Village Council, is shown awarding a diploma to Ellie Rue Bailey. The speaker for the occasion is the Reverend Glen Cornelius, pastor of the Bemiston United Methodist Church. The graduates were Mildred Spencer, Catherine Parks, Imogene Brown, Bobbie Jo Baker, June Lewis, Louise Howard, Sarah Ann Shaw, Joe Neal Sprayberry, Thurman Baker, Elon Pope, Aaron Browning, Harold Cottle, Posey Cardwell, Bradley Askew, and Maurice Patterson. (Courtesy of Mildred Brownlow.)

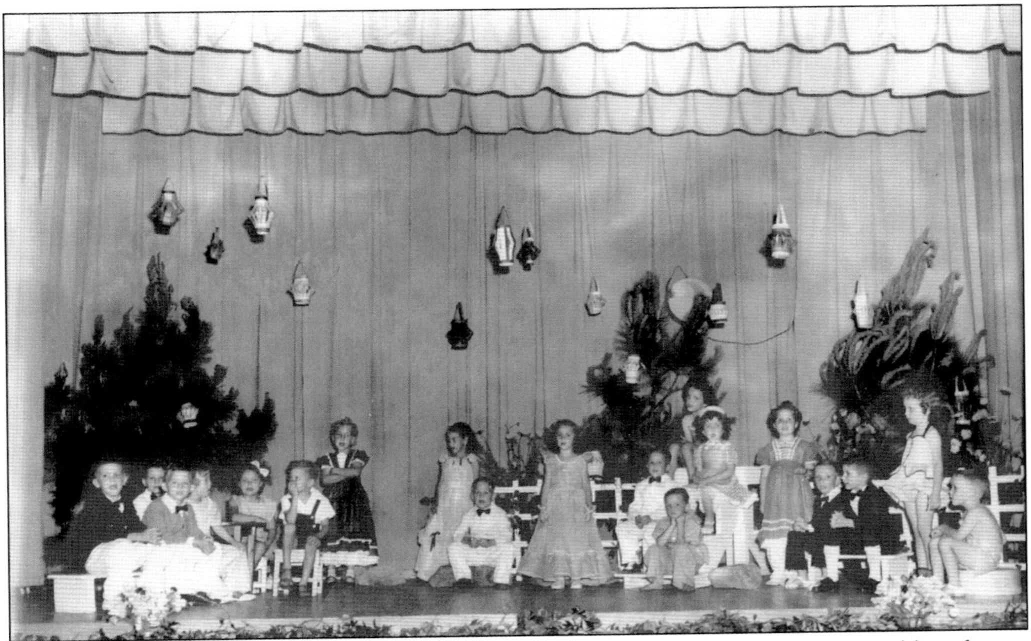

This is the 1948 kindergarten class graduation picture. Every year, the children would perform a last time as kindergarteners. Among those pictured are Skip Smithwick, Amy Vickers, Tommy Baker, Bob Shaddix, and Donald Baker. The kindergarten was a part of R. L. Young Elementary School, and the teachers were Louise Spencer and Lavada Roberts (not shown). (Courtesy of Mildred Brownlow.)

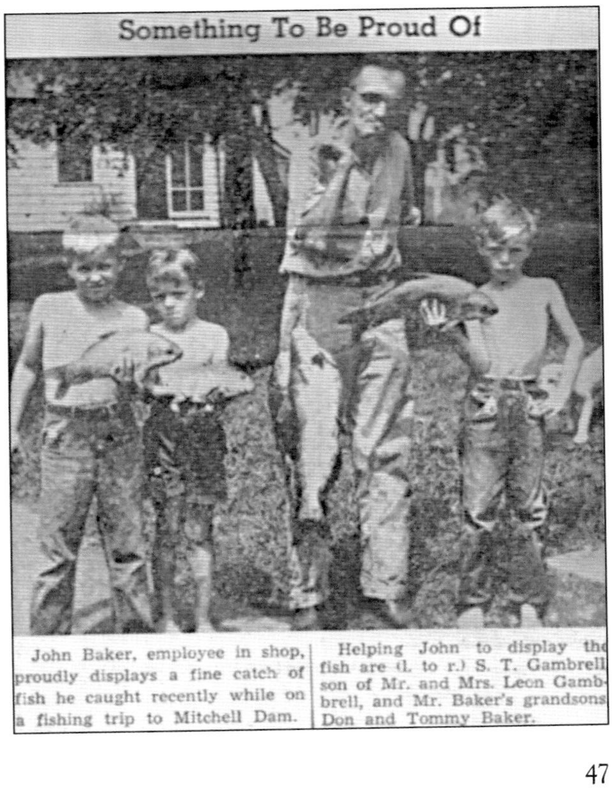

Something To Be Proud Of

John Baker, employee in shop, proudly displays a fine catch of fish he caught recently while on a fishing trip to Mitchell Dam.

Helping John to display th fish are (l. to r.) S. T. Gambrell son of Mr. and Mrs. Leon Gambbrell, and Mr. Baker's grandsons Don and Tommy Baker.

From left to right, John Baker, along with S. T. Gambrell, son of Leon and Thelma Gambrell; and John's grandsons, Don and Tommy Baker; proudly display their catch for the day after fishing in July 1951 at Mitchell Dam. (Courtesy of Willene Hughston.)

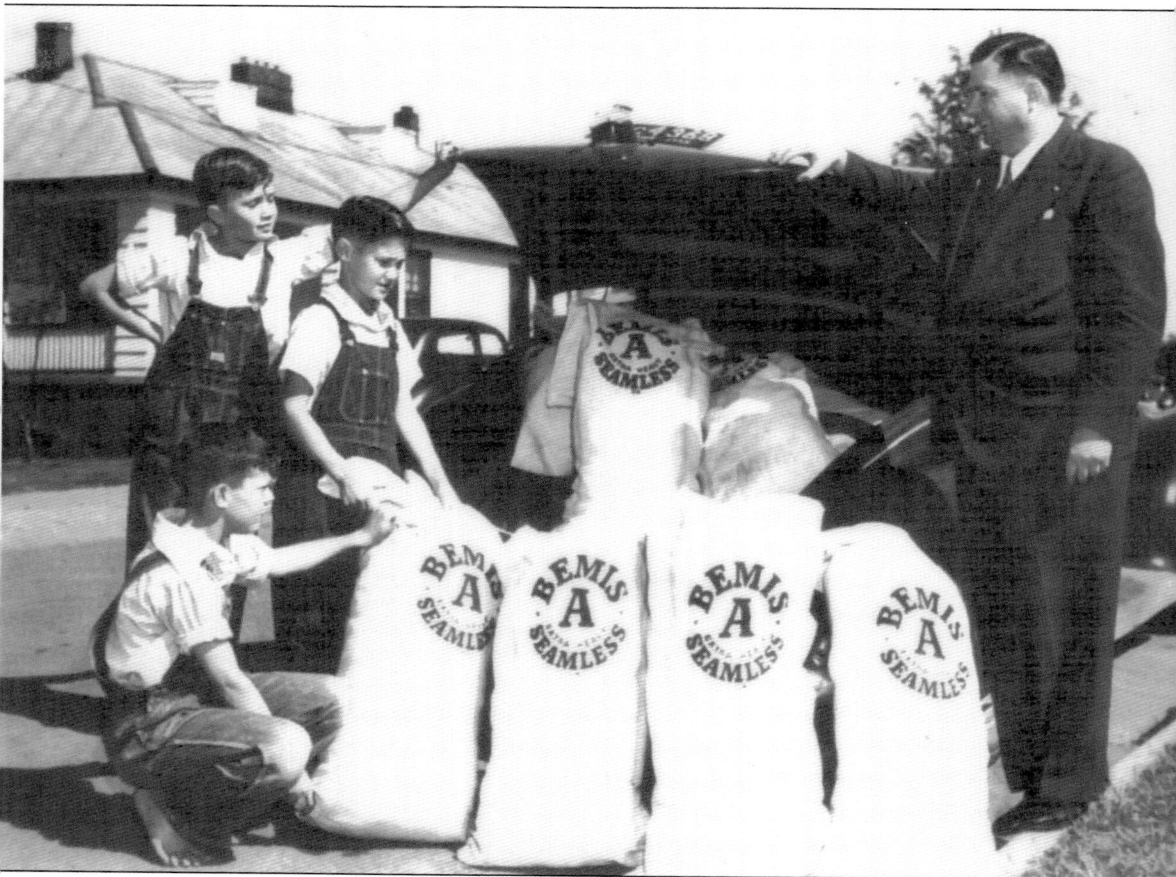

R. T. Butler, principal of the R. L. Young Elementary School, is helping these boys unload the Bemis bags full of collected clothing for the needy. The boys, from left to right, are Gerald White (kneeling), Max Morris, and Jack Spencer. This was an annual project for the school. (Courtesy of Mildred Spencer.)

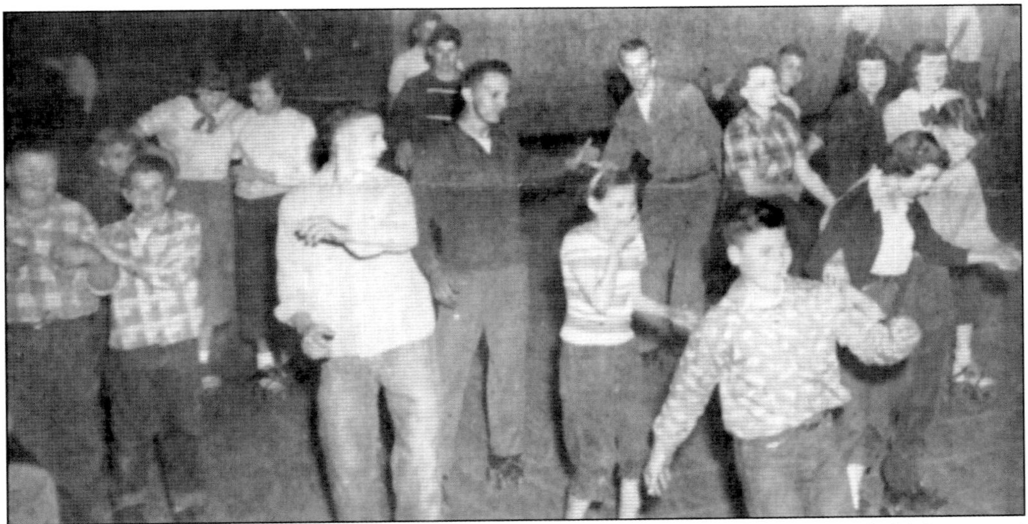

This picture shows a typical day of one of the favorite activities of both young and old. It seemed that everyone enjoyed roller skating in the gymnasium. When basketball season was over, the gymnasium was available for skating three afternoons a week. Since this was the only skating facility in the city, it was a very busy place. (Courtesy of the *Parkway News*.)

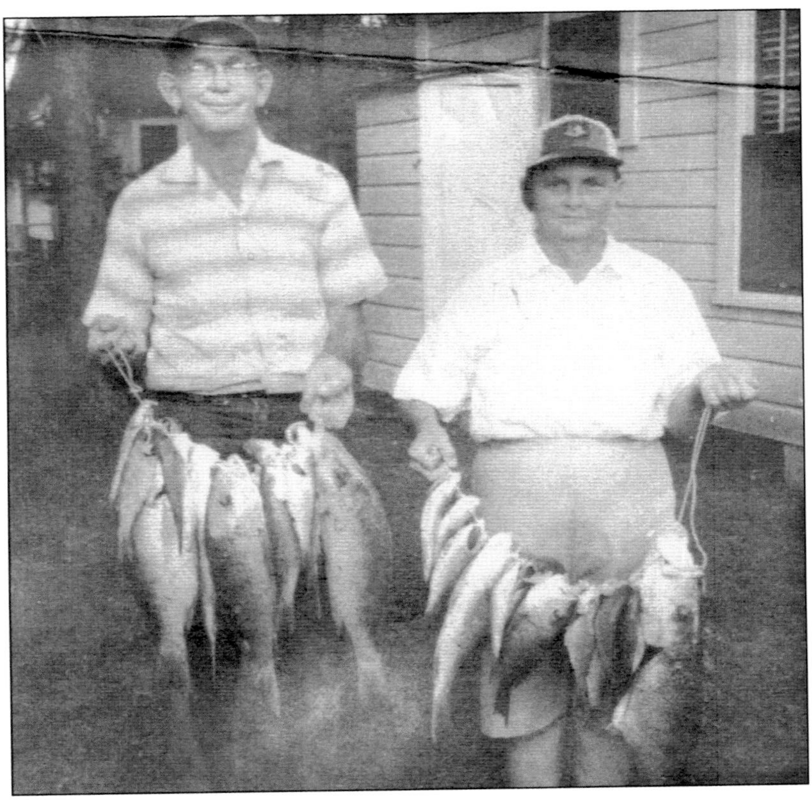

Verbon "Pluto" and Ruth Watkins display a string of red snapper they caught while on vacation in Panama City, Florida. Verbon and Ruth were known as avid fishermen, and this time they caught 40 pounds of fish. (Courtesy of the *Bemis Echoes*.)

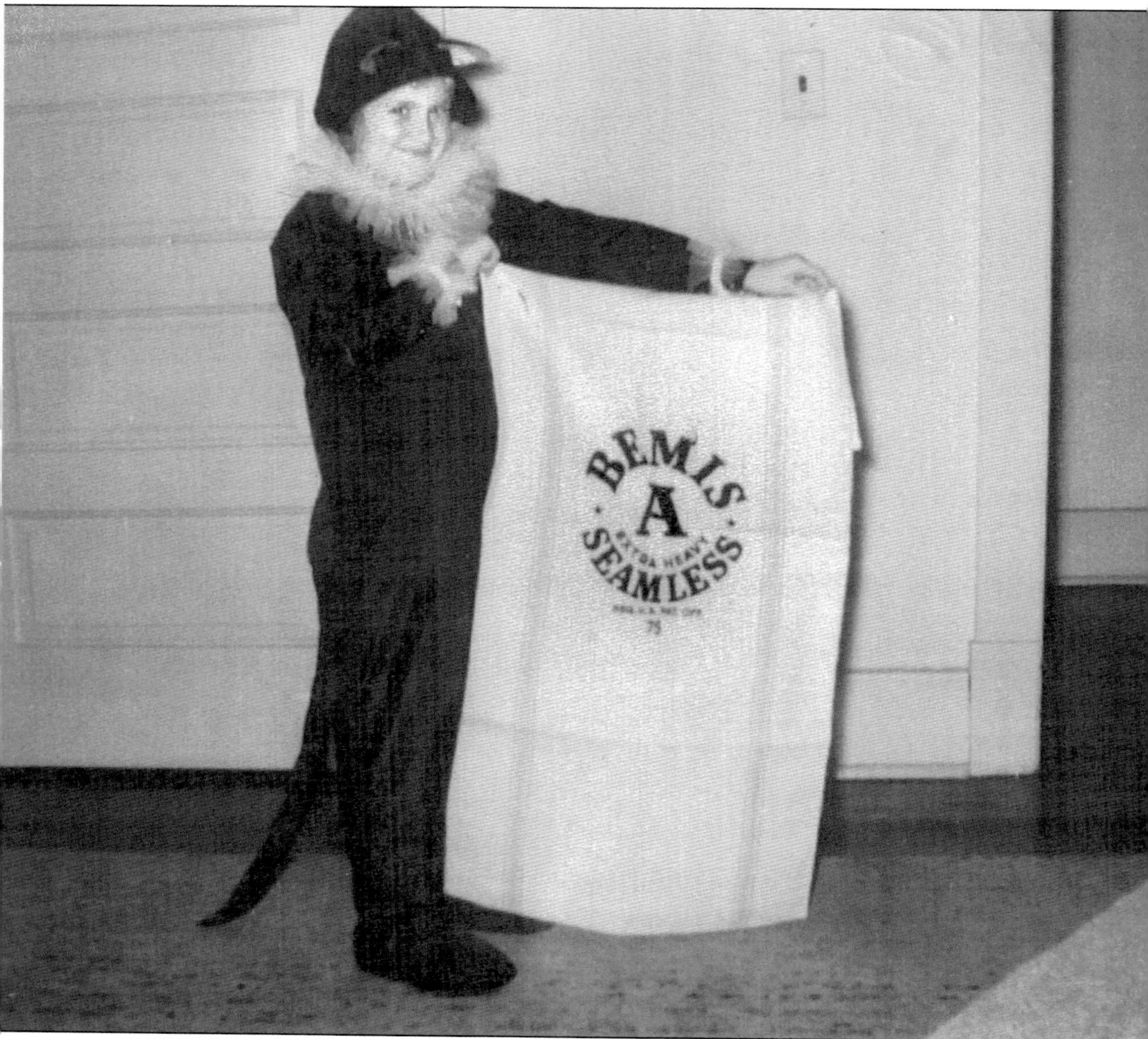

Cathy Brownlow is all dressed up in her cat outfit, ready for trick or treat on Halloween. She has her bag ready and is obviously expecting a large amount of treats. (Courtesy of Mildred Brownlow.)

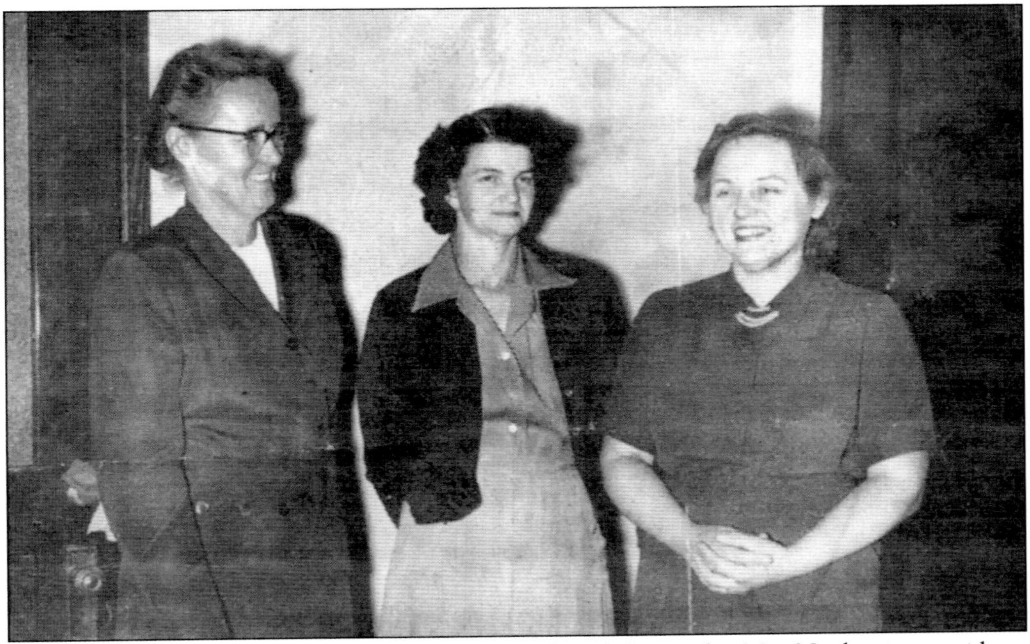

Home Demonstration Club officers in 1953 were, from left to right, Mae Noah, vice president; Effie Rogers, secretary; and Ruby Spencer, president. (Courtesy of the *Parkway News.*)

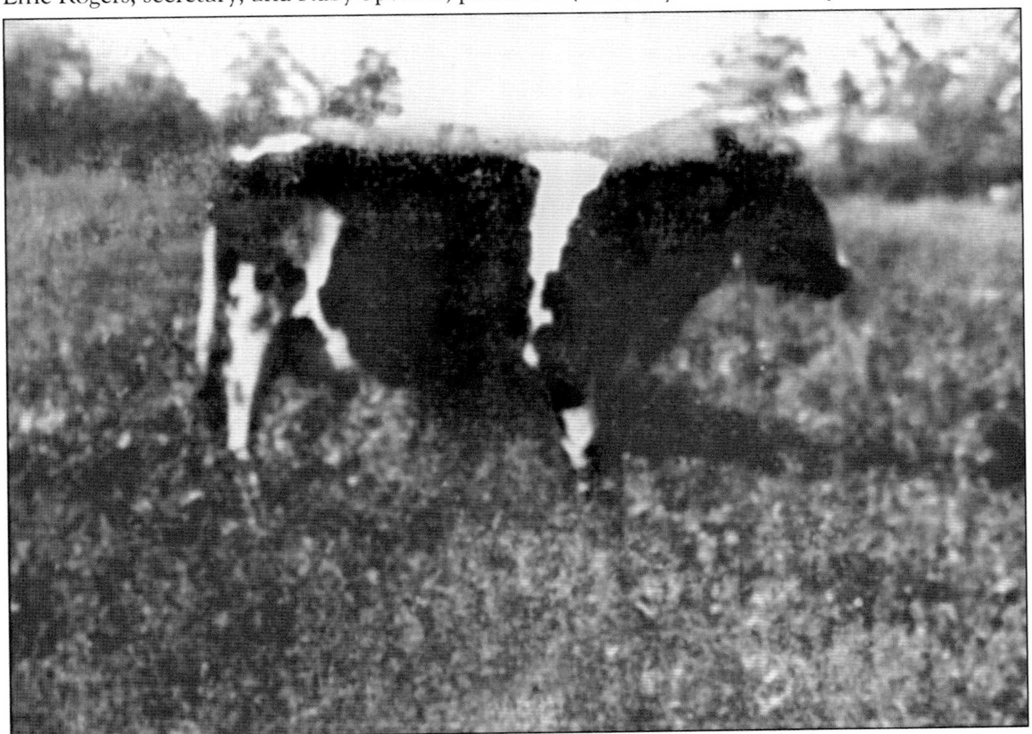

Meet Susie Dolly Ormsby, SX (top grade), who is a member of the One-Hundred Thousand Pounds Club of the Holstein-Friesian Association of America. She has produced more than 100,000 pounds of milk and has a certificate to prove it. (Courtesy of the *Parkway News.*)

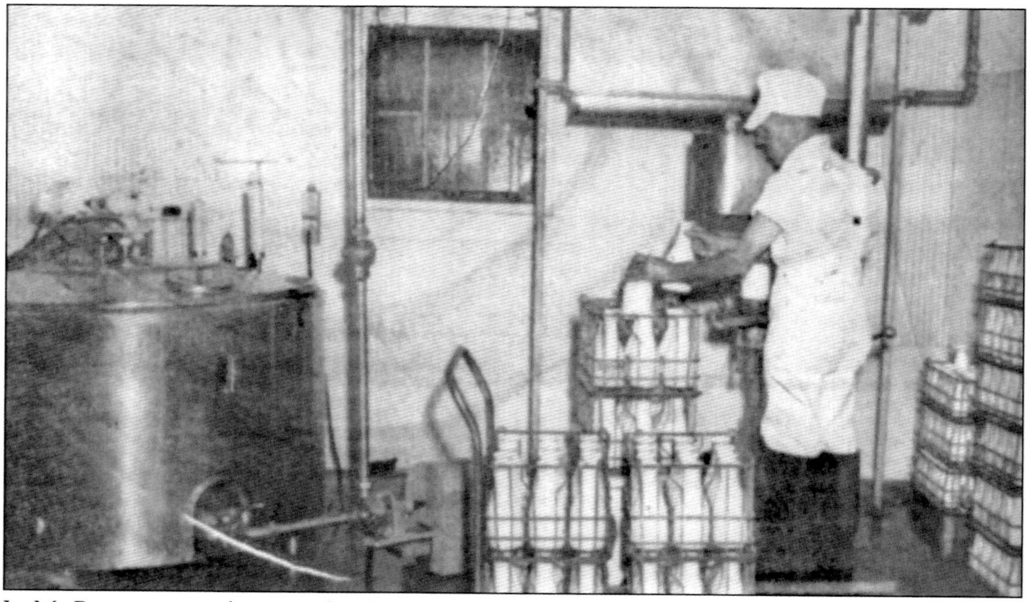

L. M. Patjens is working in the Bemiston Dairy. Patjens was responsible for processing and delivering the milk to the residents. He came to Bemiston in 1942 and worked in the dairy until his retirement. The bottling and capping machine and the milk cooler were also in this building. Patjens said he pasteurized 140 gallons this day. (Courtesy of the *Parkway News*.)

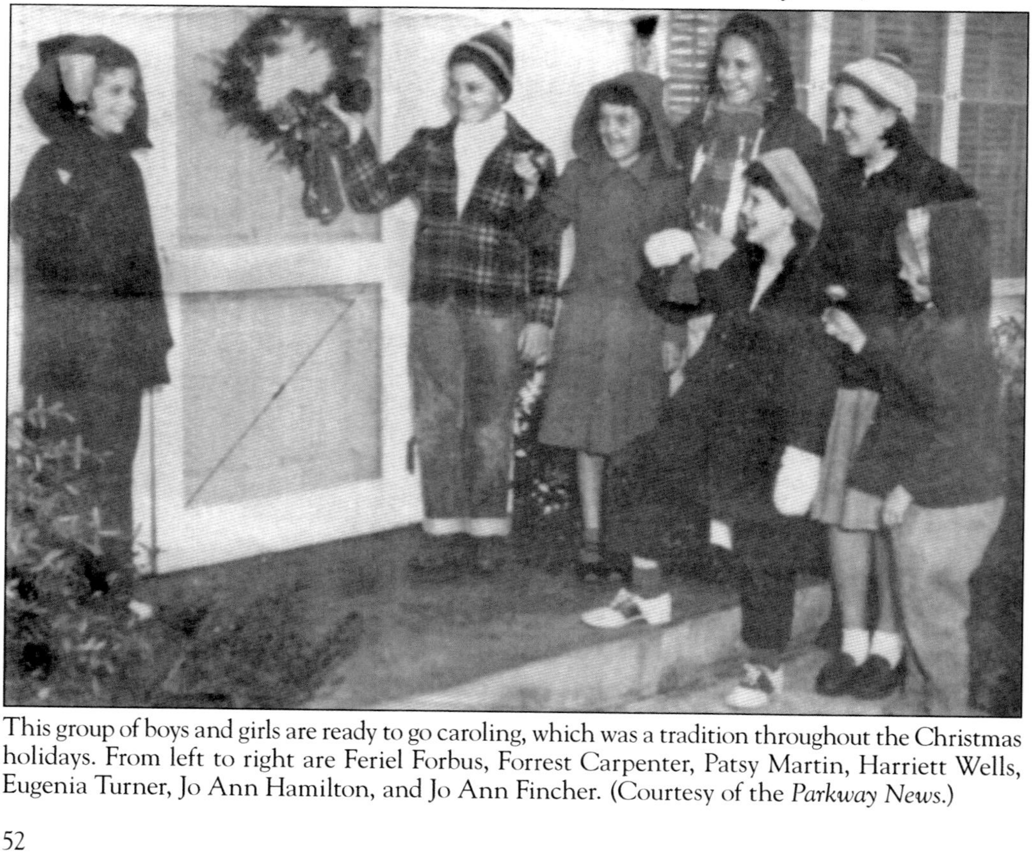

This group of boys and girls are ready to go caroling, which was a tradition throughout the Christmas holidays. From left to right are Feriel Forbus, Forrest Carpenter, Patsy Martin, Harriett Wells, Eugenia Turner, Jo Ann Hamilton, and Jo Ann Fincher. (Courtesy of the *Parkway News*.)

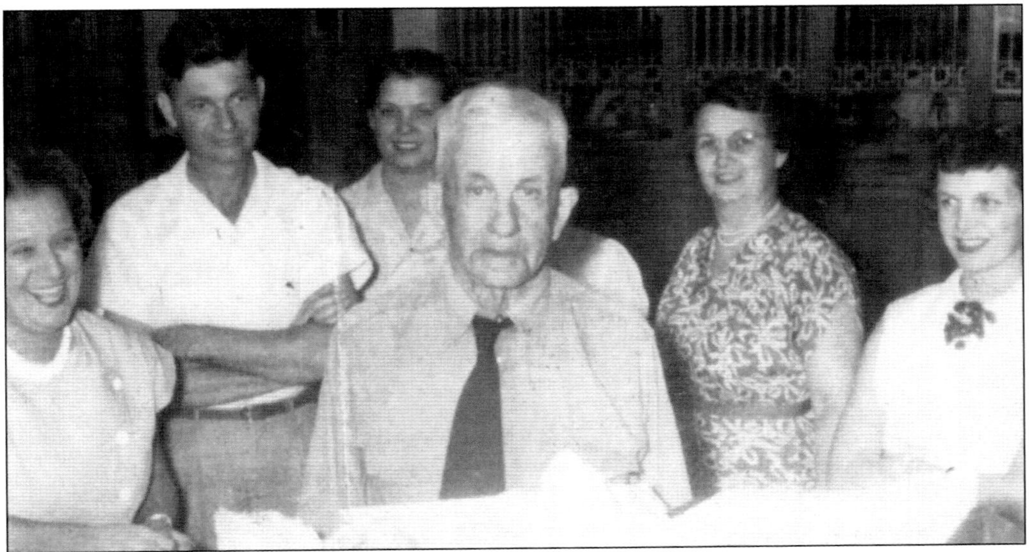

Bemiston Main Office employees give Robert Davis (center), better known as "Uncle Bob," an 81st birthday gift. Uncle Bob had his own column where he was always giving the readers some of his "sage" wisdom. In the picture with him are, from left to right, Willene Senn, Theron Bagwell, Louise Hardin, Marjorie Cooley, and Doris Gray. (Courtesy of the *Parkway News*.)

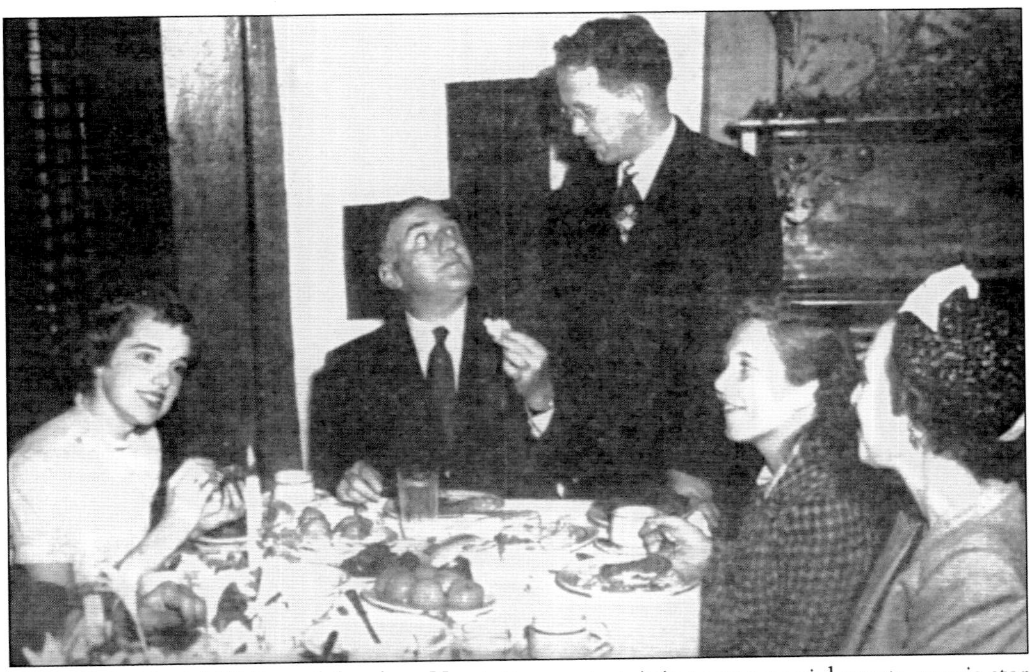

Janice (Mrs. R. A.) Wells and daughter Harriett are entertaining some special guests, movie star William Bendix and Sue Hussey, a local girl, who played a part in a movie with Lash Larue after his visit to the Talladega Turkey Festival. From left to right are Sue Hussey, William Bendix, Purefoy Hotel owner Ed Hyde, Harriett, and Mrs. Wells. (Courtesy of the *Parkway News*.)

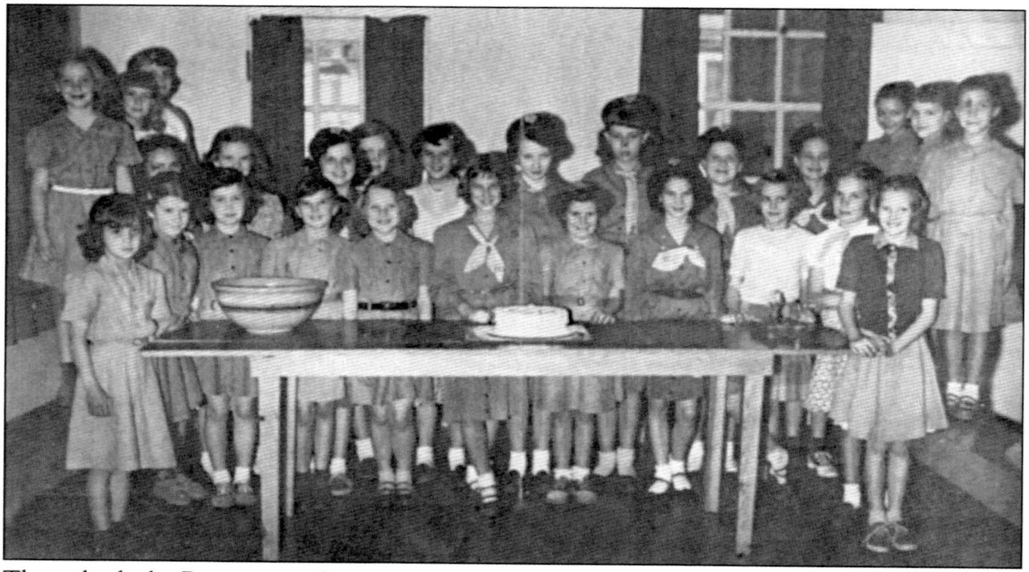

This is both the Brownies and Girl Scouts meeting in their new "Little House." As one can see, both troops are proud of this new meeting place. (Courtesy of the *Parkway News*.)

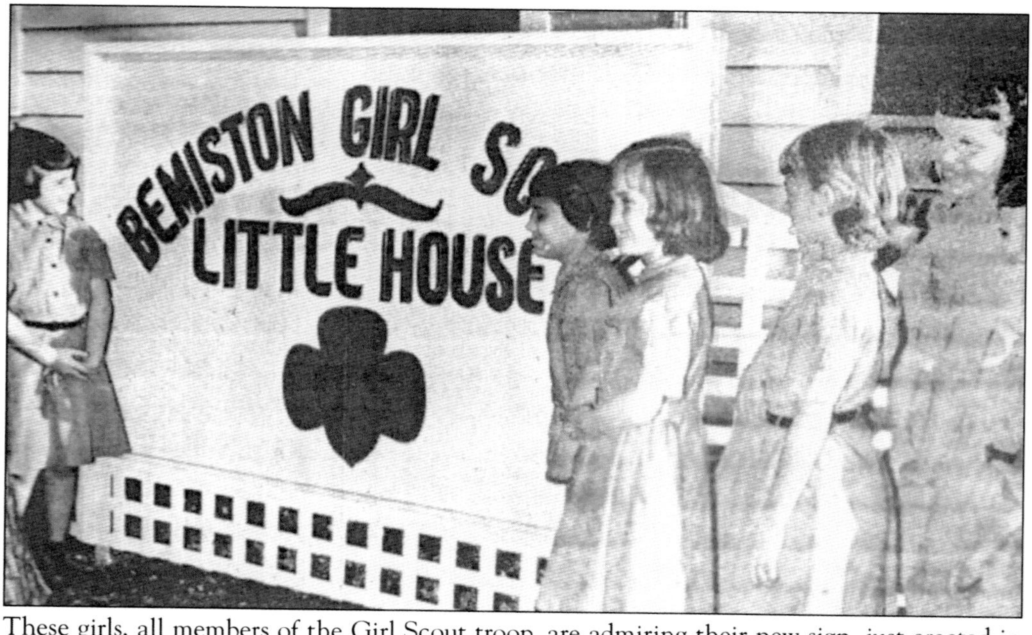

These girls, all members of the Girl Scout troop, are admiring their new sign, just erected in front of their "Little House," where they hold their meetings. They also have a furnished kitchen to teach them how to prepare and serve meals. They are, from left to right, June Lane, Babs Waits, Sandra Daniel, Sara Holcomb, Jennie Sue Williams, and Shirley Tomlin. (Courtesy of the *Parkway News*.)

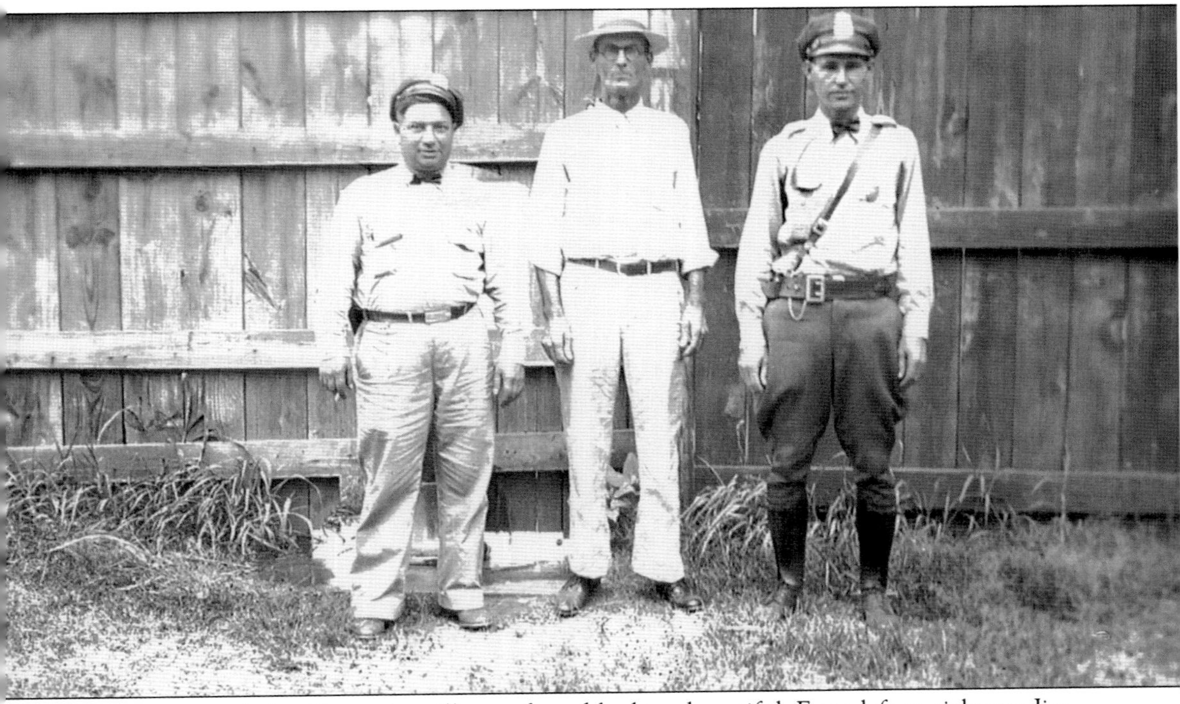

These three men helped keep the village safe and looking beautiful. From left to right are Jim Corby, keeper of the entrance gate; Walt Grice, village superintendent; and Clinton Spencer, who was in charge of the Bemis farms and dairy and who also worked part-time for the sheriff's department. (Courtesy of Mildred Brownlow.)

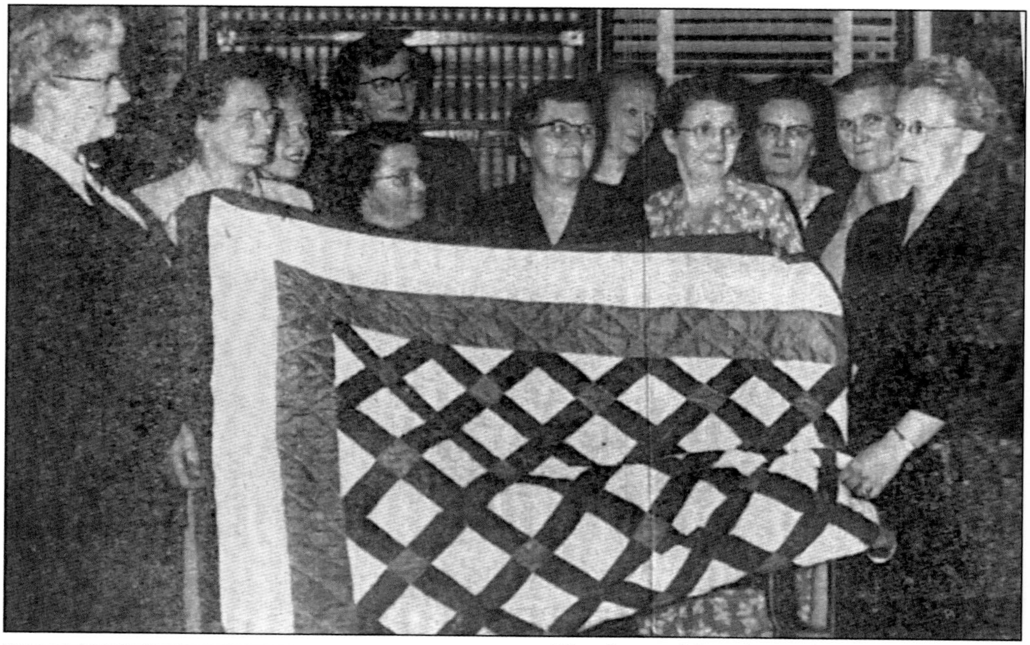

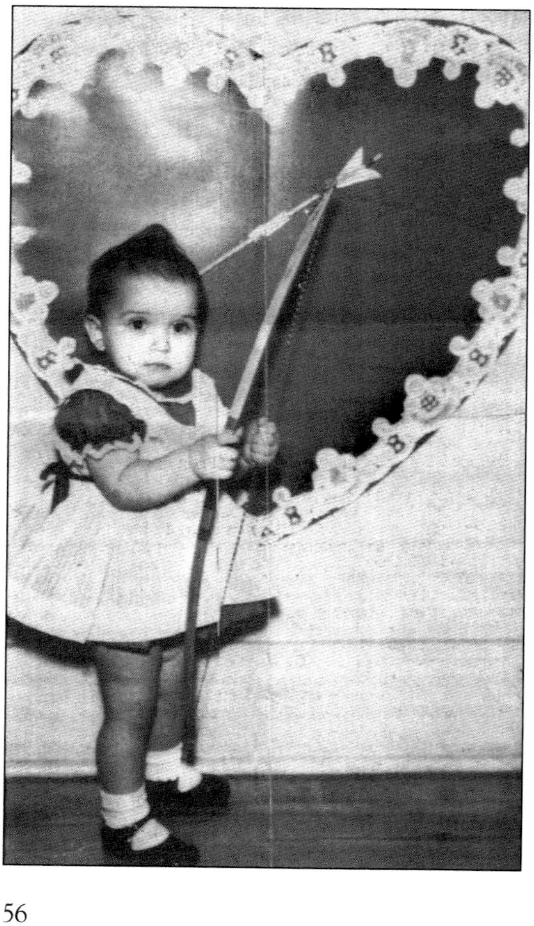

This beautiful quilt was known as a Serviceman's Quilt and had 90 servicemen's names embroidered on it in blue thread. The quilt was made by the Woman's Society of Christian Service. It netted the society $126.68 and was turned over to the Bemiston United Methodist Church. The quilt was donated to the church parsonage. The colors were all red, white, and blue. (Courtesy of the *Parkway News*.)

One-year-old Phyliss Ann Baker is shown getting ready to shoot her arrow into the heart for Valentine's Day. Phyliss is the daughter of J. W. and Betty Baker, and the granddaughter of John and Minnie Baker and Leon and Thelma Gambrell. All were employed at the Bemis Brothers Bag Company. (Courtesy of the *Parkway News*.)

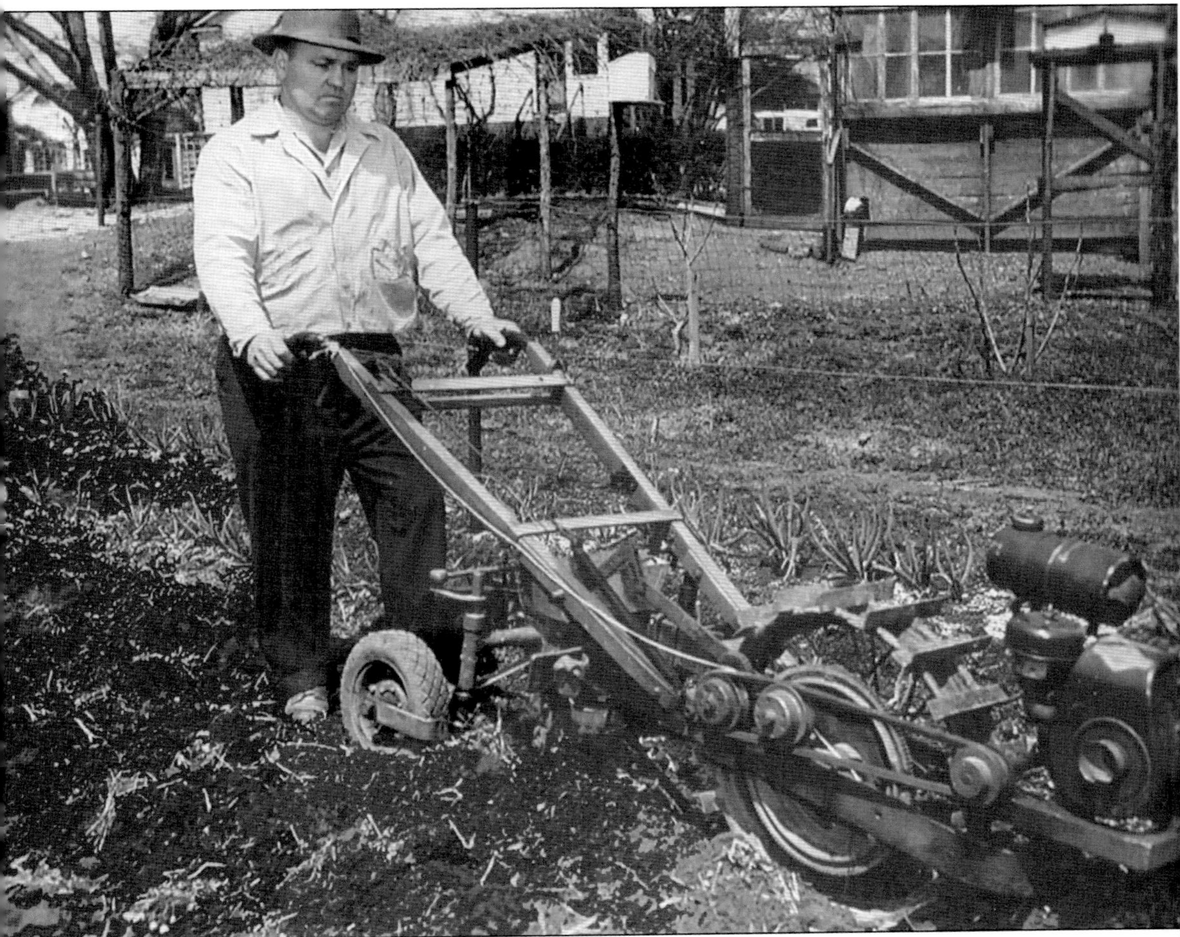

George Cooley is trying out the motorized plow he built after the close of World War II. Because lawn and farm equipment was not yet available, he took a spoke wheel, welded iron cleats, added a Briggs engine, and geared it down with a bicycle sprocket. He was proud of the plow and said "it would dig through anything." (Courtesy of Bill Cooley.)

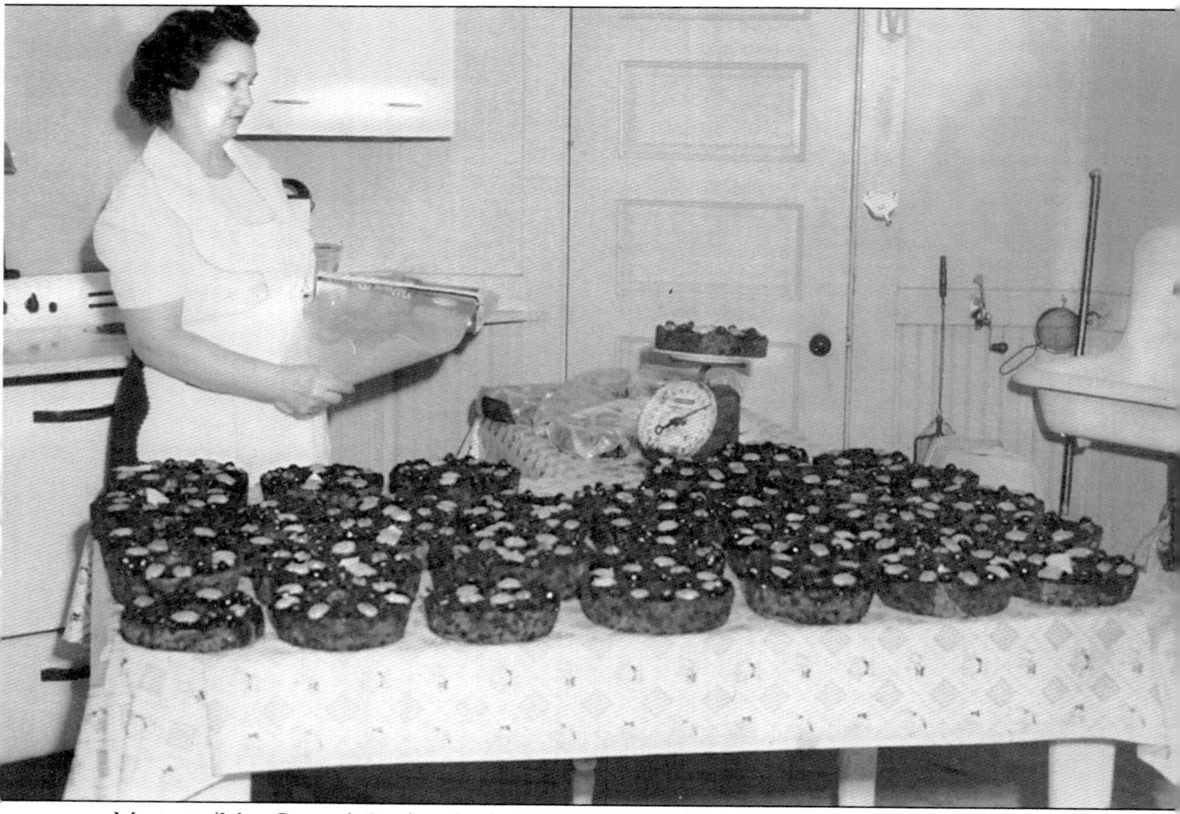

Marjorie (Mrs. George) Cooley also had a talent not to be surpassed. During the holidays, Marjorie would bake her delicious fruitcakes using a pressure cooker in 1-, 2-, and 3-pound sizes and sell them. After World War II was over and sugar available, she baked 300 pounds of fruitcakes and sold them for $1 per pound. (Courtesy of Bill Cooley.)

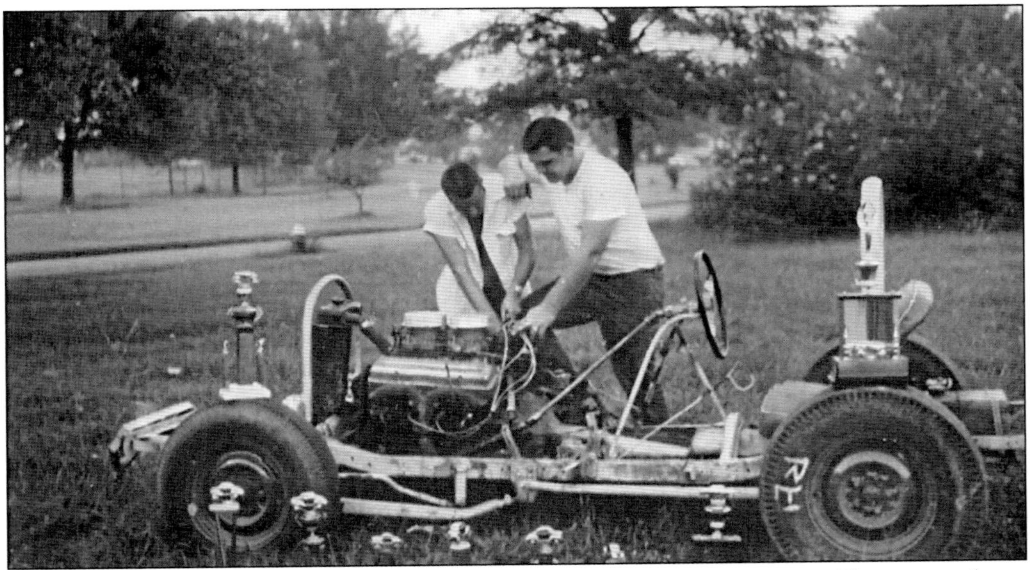

George Cooley was not the only member of the family who was innovative. This image shows Joe Charles Cooley, George's son, (left) and an unidentified friend with his racing dragster, a Chevy V-8 engine in a Crosley auto frame. Some of Joe's trophies can be seen around the car. (Courtesy of Bill Cooley.)

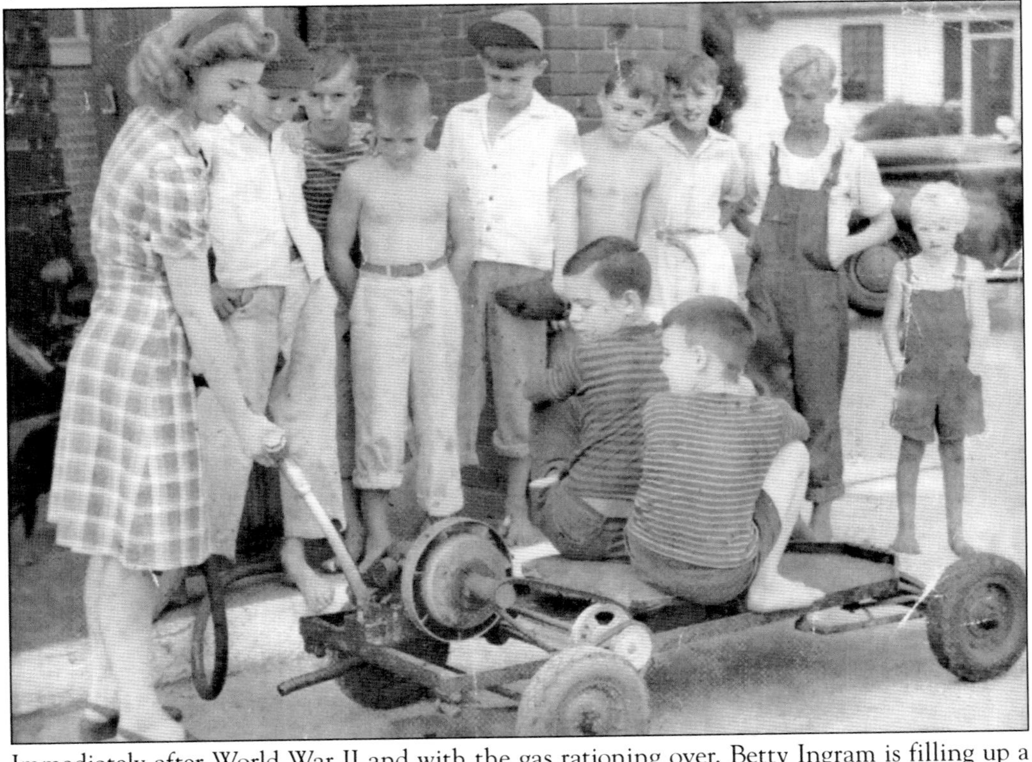

Immediately after World War II and with the gas rationing over, Betty Ingram is filling up a go-cart that George Cooley built for his sons, Bill (seated, left) and Joe Charles (seated, right). A group of unidentified friends looks on. (Courtesy of Bill Cooley.)

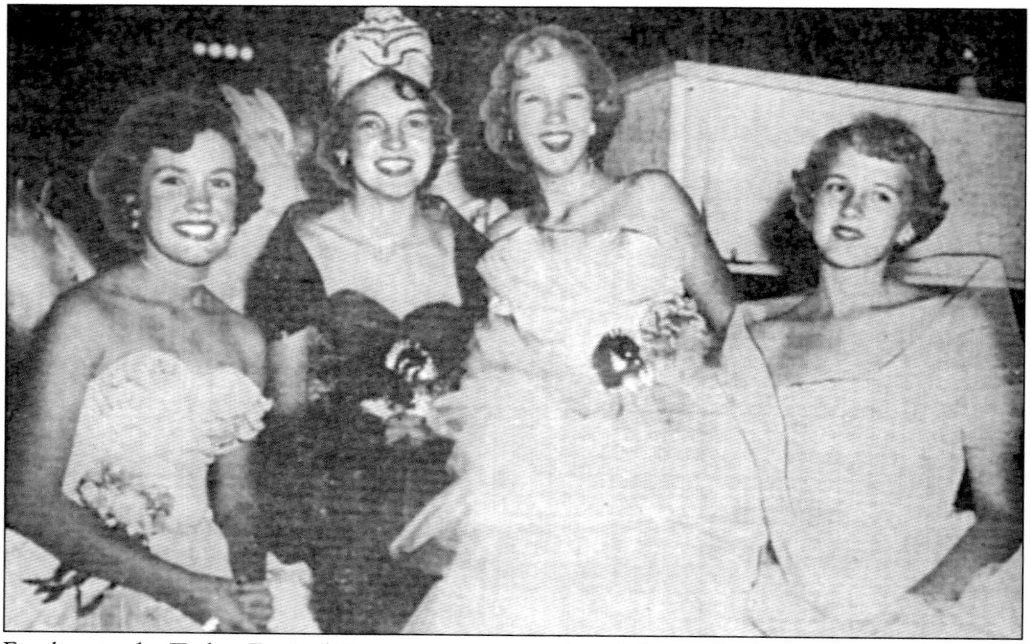

Finalists in the Turkey Festival Queen contest were, from left to right, Mary Ann Kelley, Queen Pat Hellon, Betty Mann and Frances Cork, who tied for third place. Pat Hellon, the winner, is the granddaughter of Rev. and Mrs. W. C. Chappell, and Betty Mann is the daughter of Roy and Elizabeth Mann of Bemiston. Frances's mother, Vera Sue Cork, taught at the R. L. Young Elementary School. (Courtesy of the *Parkway News*.)

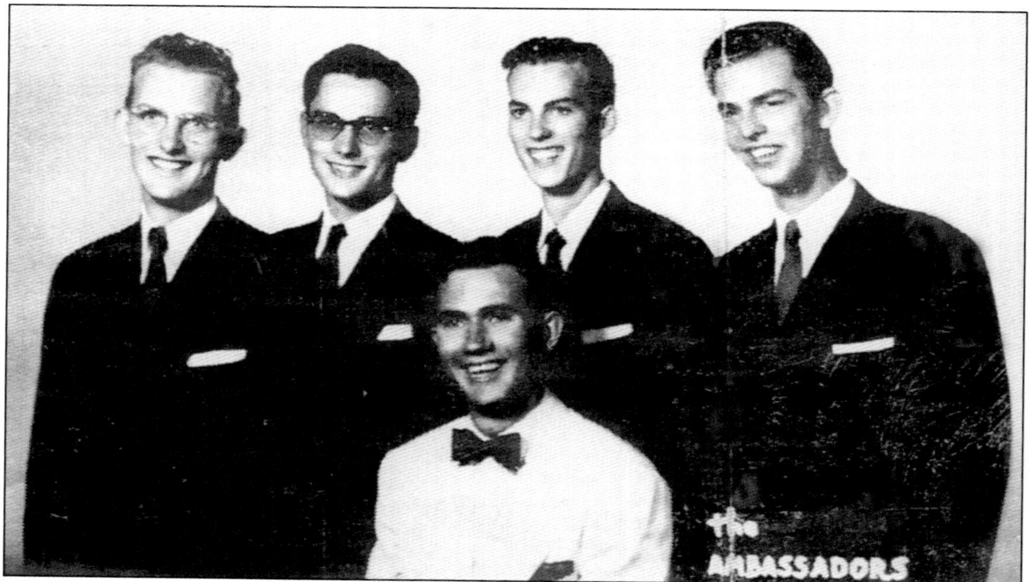

These are the Ambassadors of Lee College in Cleveland, Tennessee. The manager and pianist of this group is Max Morris (front), a native of Bemiston. His parents were Elbert and Dessie Morris. Others in the photograph are, from left to right, J. E. Davis, James Swilley, Stanley Smith, and Gerald Adams. The Ambassadors are a gospel singing group and made many appearances in the Talladega, Alabama, area. (Courtesy of the *Parkway News*.)

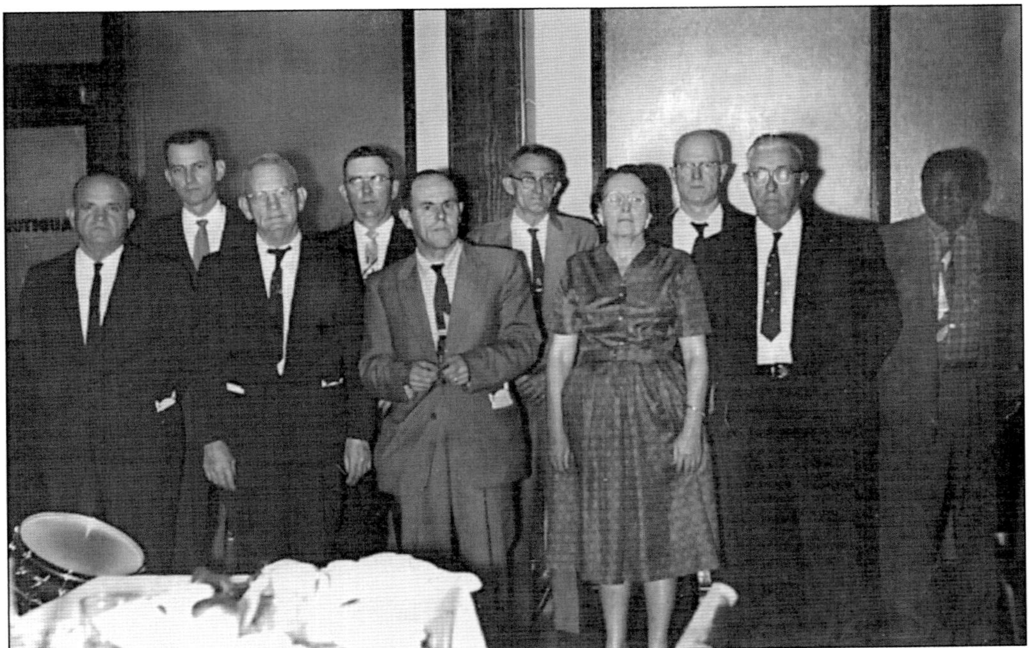

These employees received a 20-year gold pin for their 20 years of service to the Bemis Brothers Bag Company. From left to right are Sam Roberts, unidentified, Marshall Shaw, unidentified, Grady Williams, John Baker, Robbie (Mrs. Malcolm) Jones, Malcolm Jones, W. A. White, and unidentified. (Courtesy J. W. Baker.)

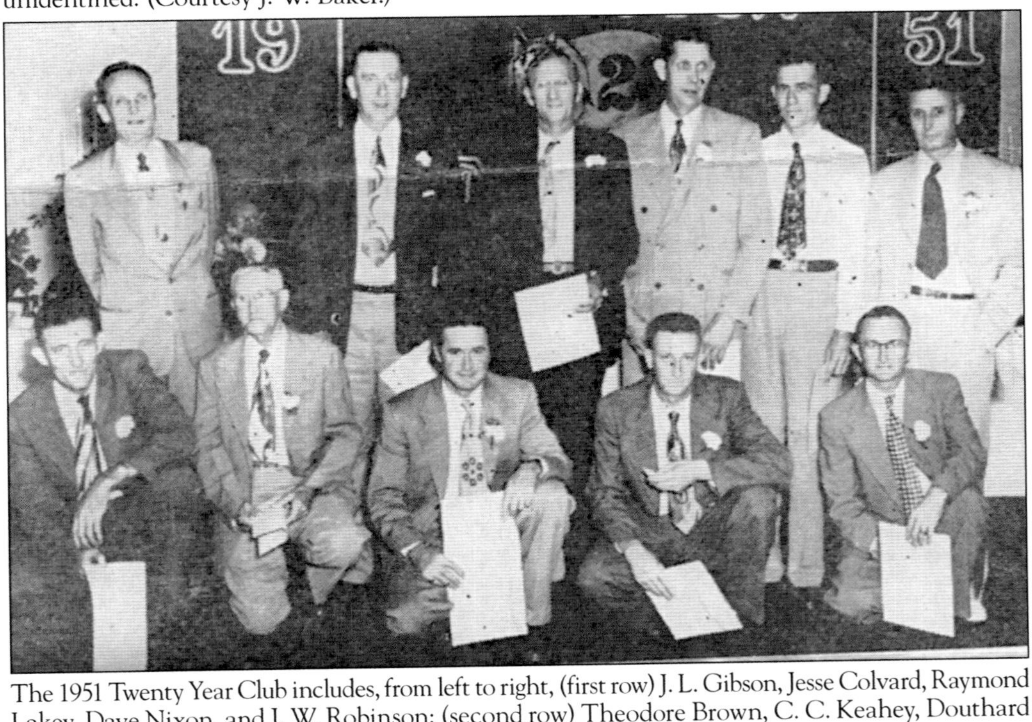

The 1951 Twenty Year Club includes, from left to right, (first row) J. L. Gibson, Jesse Colvard, Raymond Lakey, Dave Nixon, and J. W. Robinson; (second row) Theodore Brown, C. C. Keahey, Douthard Noah, John Staples, Roy Williams, and N. C. Wood. (Courtesy of the *Parkway News*.)

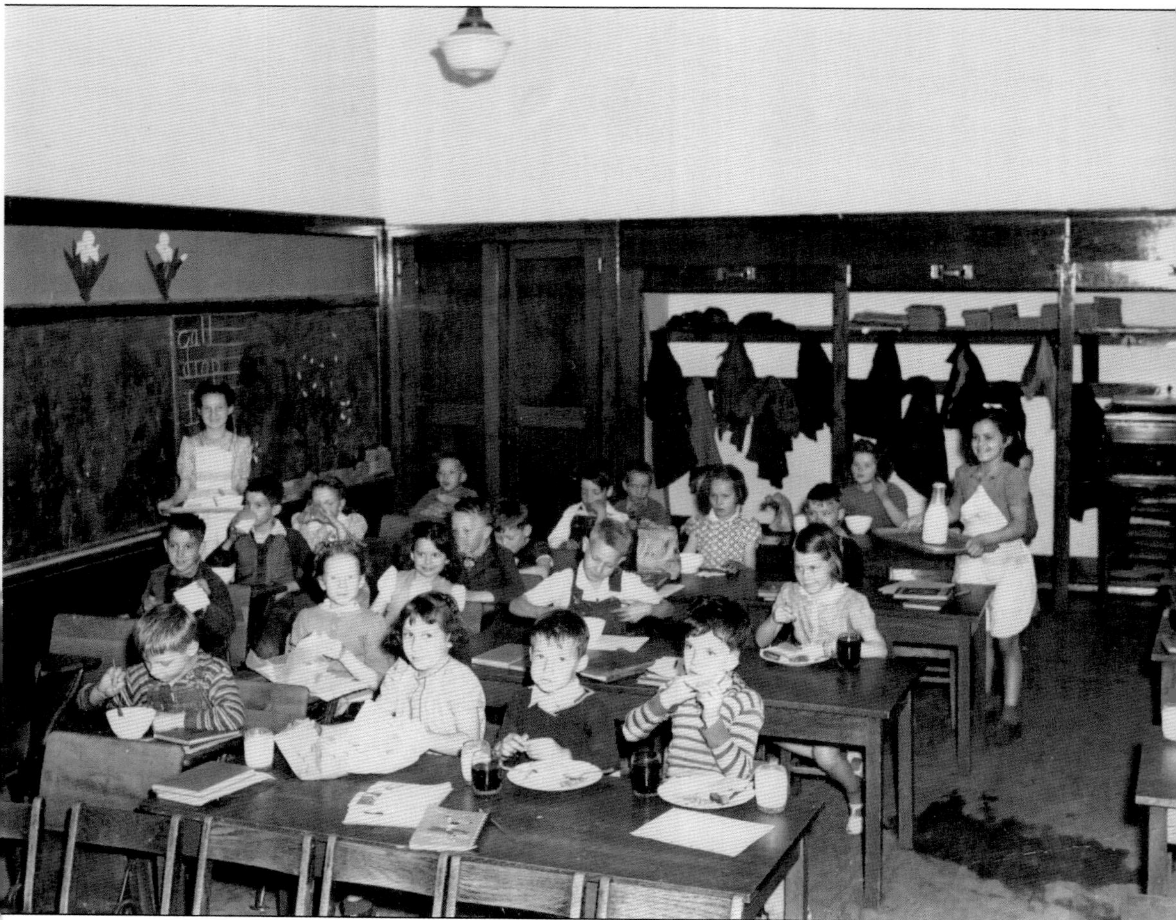

This *c.* 1938 first-grade class is eating lunch in the classroom. The school had a cart that came around to every classroom to provide meals to the students. The lunch room had not yet been built. The only students that could be identified are (in no particular order) Jean Vickers, Betty Shropshire, and Syliva Gaines. (Courtesy of Yvonne Grice.)

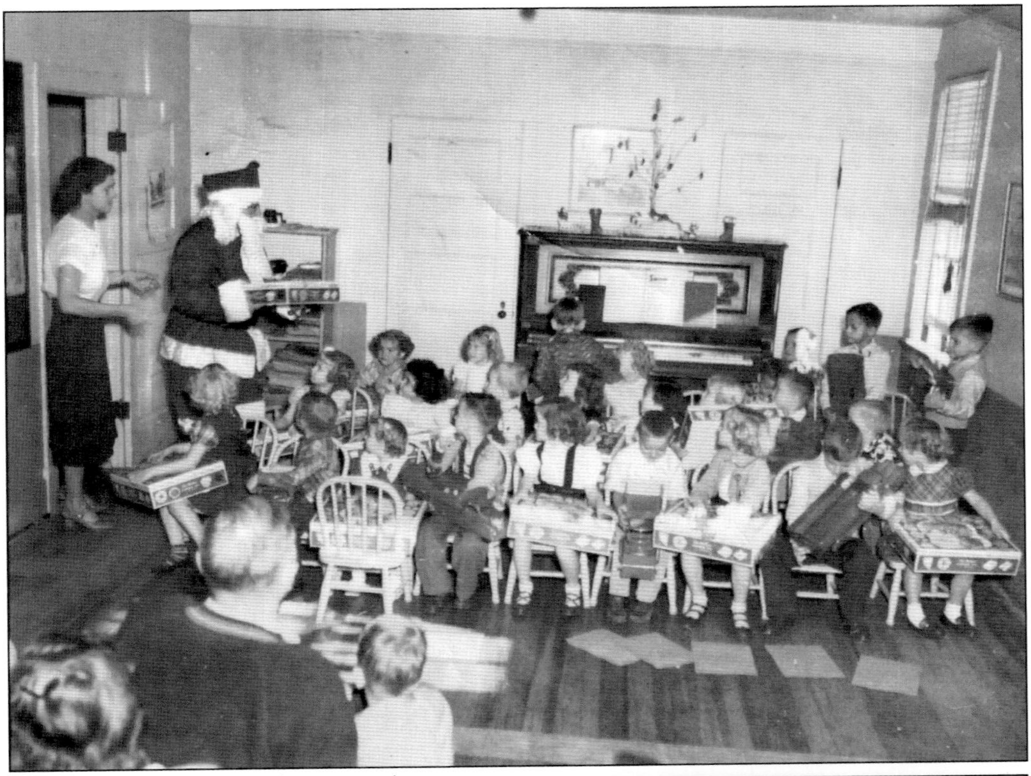

Santa is visiting this kindergarten class in 1952. It seems that every year Santa came by with fruit and toys for each child. The teacher on the left is Louise Spencer. (Courtesy of Mildred Brownlow.)

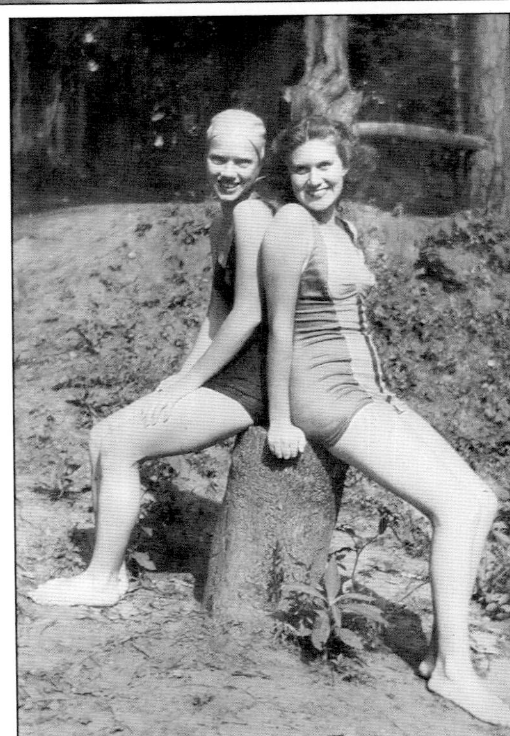

Jewel Dean Hazel (right) and Geneva Moxley are enjoying a day at the beach on Talladega Creek. (Courtesy of Bill Cooley.)

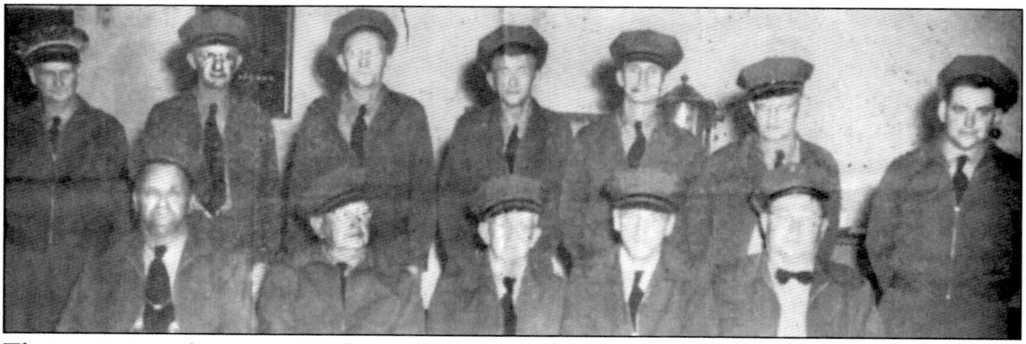

These men are shown at a barbeque dinner for the watchmen. They all worked in various departments in the Bemiston mill but also served on the watchmen force. They are, from left to right, (first row) R. A. King, H. A. Holcomb, Robert D. "Uncle Bob" Davis, G. P. Ellison, and K. D. Thompson; (second row) Morgan W. Parsons, J. R. Griffis, Douthard Noah, Joe Noah, Dalton Harwell, W. J. Miller, and Joe Seymour. The watchmen provided security and also kept an extra eye out for the children of parents who worked at the mill. (Courtesy of the *Parkway News*.)

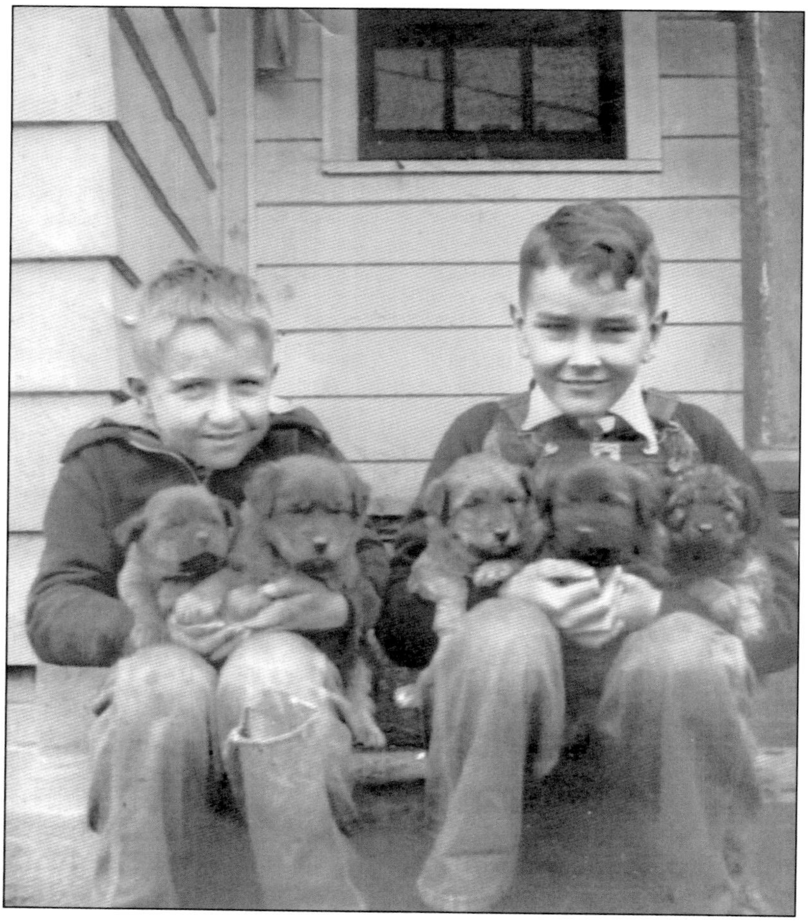

Joe Neal Sprayberry (right), who grew up to play baseball for the Bemiston Cats and later signed with the Pittsburgh Pirates, and E. W. Phillips advertise puppies for sale. (Courtesy of E. W. Phillips.)

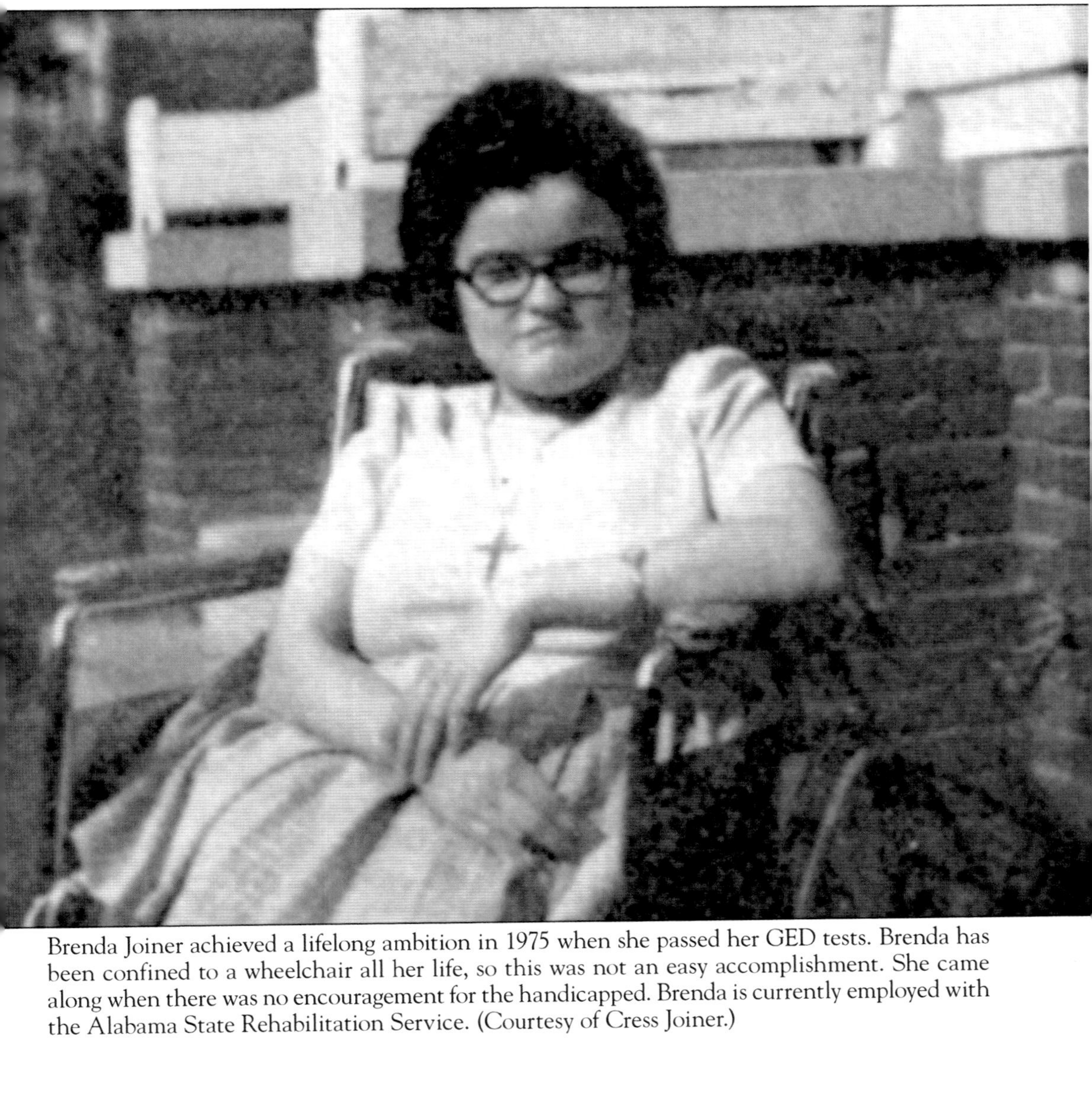

Brenda Joiner achieved a lifelong ambition in 1975 when she passed her GED tests. Brenda has been confined to a wheelchair all her life, so this was not an easy accomplishment. She came along when there was no encouragement for the handicapped. Brenda is currently employed with the Alabama State Rehabilitation Service. (Courtesy of Cress Joiner.)

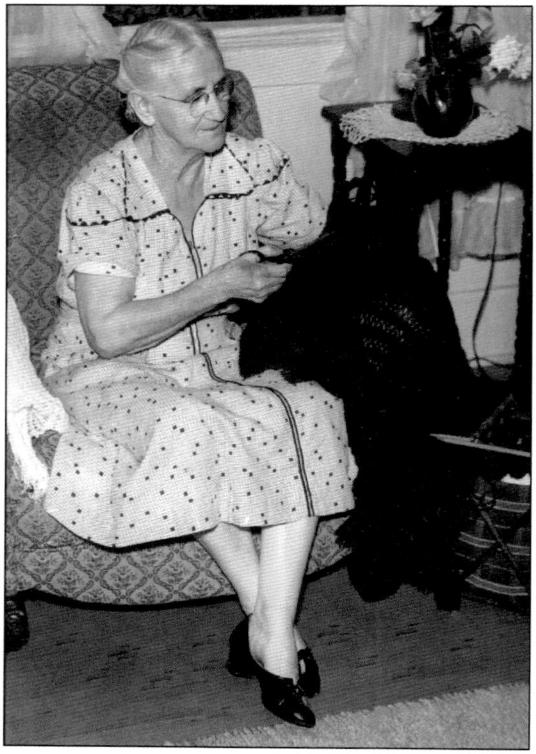

Meet Viola Smith Chappell, who was an exceptional lady in the neighborhood. She was a widow with five children. Most were old enough to work, and she stayed home and took care of the home fires and most of the children who lived around her because their parents worked. She was always available when anyone had a problem. Chappell could "conjure" the thrush and heal it, remove warts, and cool a bad burn. She was a tribute to her generation. (Courtesy of Dottie Braswell.)

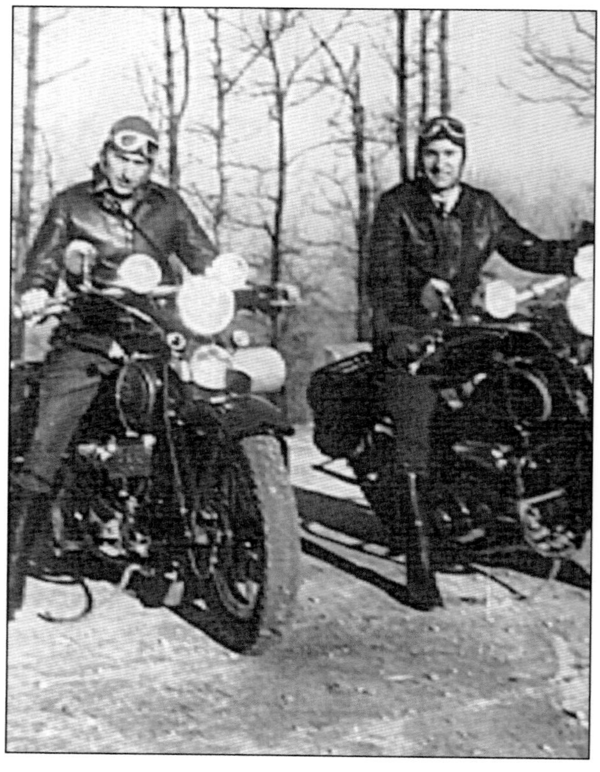

Shown here are John Farris (left) and Clinton Spencer getting ready for a ride. Farris was chief of security for the village and later became police chief for the City of Talladega. Spencer was the farm manager and enjoyed riding motorcycles with Farris. (Courtesy of Mildred Brownlow.)

Three

Sports

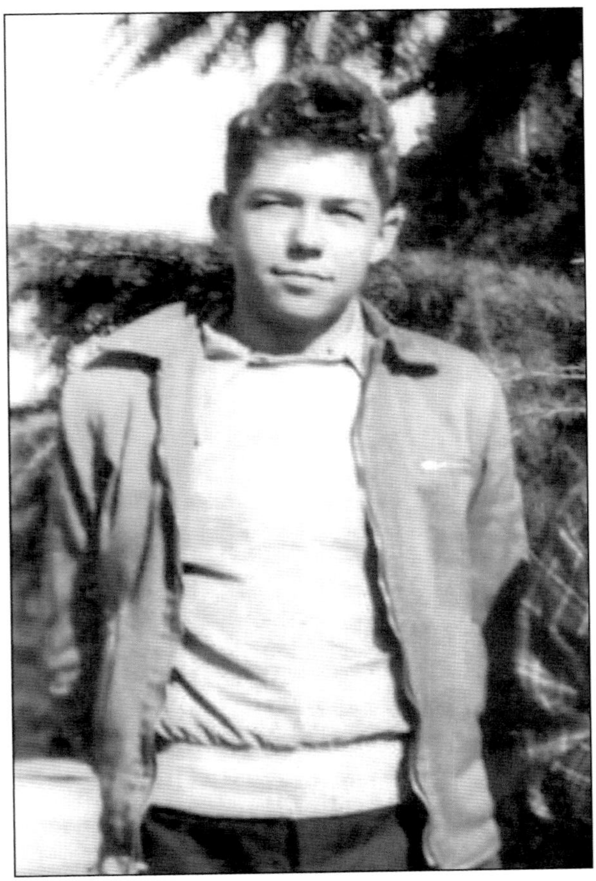

The Bemis Brothers Bag Company had a reputation for keeping the young people interested and participating in sports for character building. It was very important that every child had an opportunity to be a part of a team, and Ducky Cottle took full advantage of the opportunities afforded him. Harold "Ducky" Cottle excelled on the baseball field regularly. His superb pitching brought him recognition in Bemiston as well as Talladega and surrounding areas. For a young pitcher, he had exceptional control. In 24 innings, he walked only two men. Ralph Gandy, the Talladega High School coach, said at least three Major League Baseball scouts were looking at Ducky. After a two-year tour in the army, he signed with the Birmingham Barons in 1953. He was the son of I. C. and Louella Cottle of Bemiston, and was married to the former Joandell Speaks of Talladega, Alabama. (Courtesy of the *Parkway News*.)

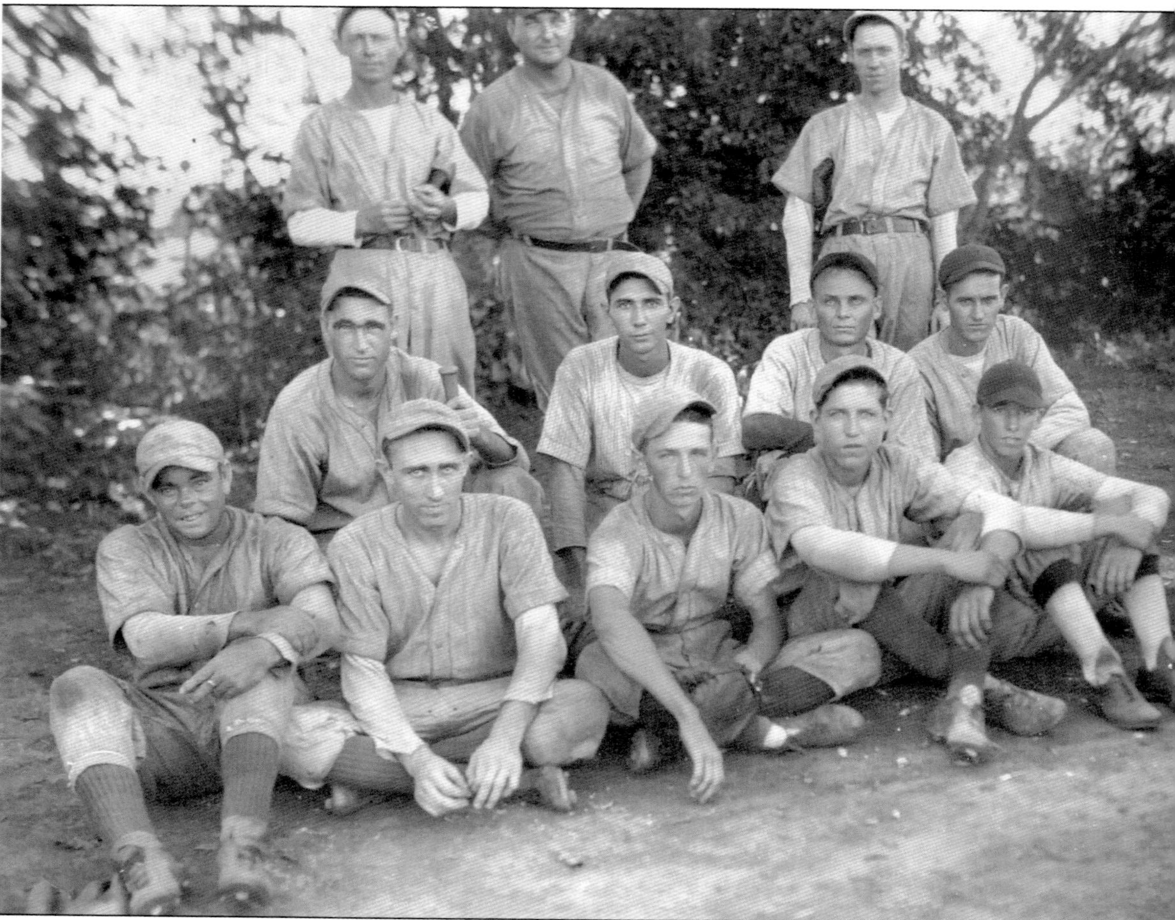

This is probably the first baseball team in Bemiston, pictured around 1930. The ones that could be positively identified are, from left to right, (first row, second from left) Claude Fite; (second row) Otis "Muley" Bates, Elbert Morris, Theodore Brown, and Thurman Cochran. The rest could not be identified. (Courtesy of E. W. Phillips.)

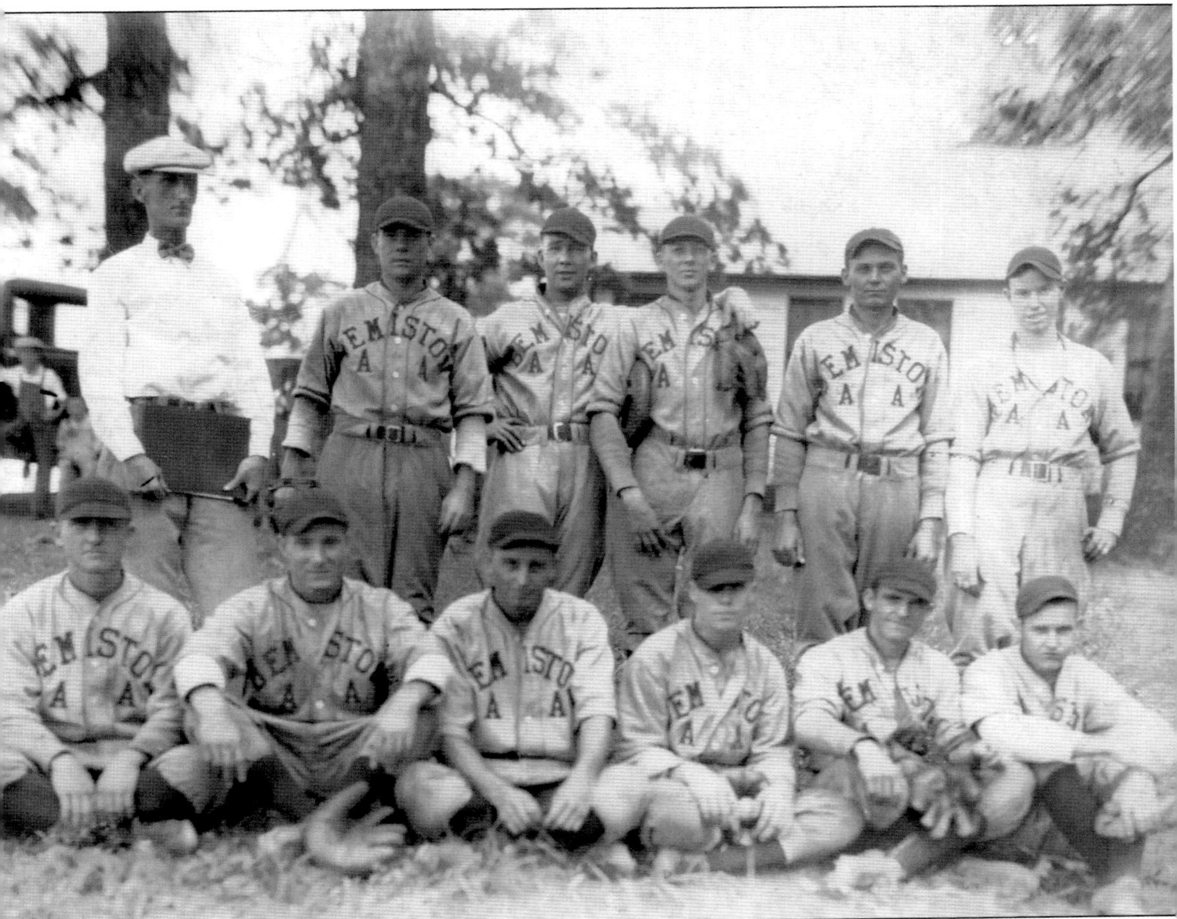

On this *c.* 1931 baseball team are, from left to right, (first row) unidentified, Red Lakey, Cush Wood, unidentified, Sam Roberts, and Thurman Cochran; (second row) E. W. Phillips (manager), three unidentified, Theodore Brown, and Ed Daniels. (Courtesy of E. W. Phillips.)

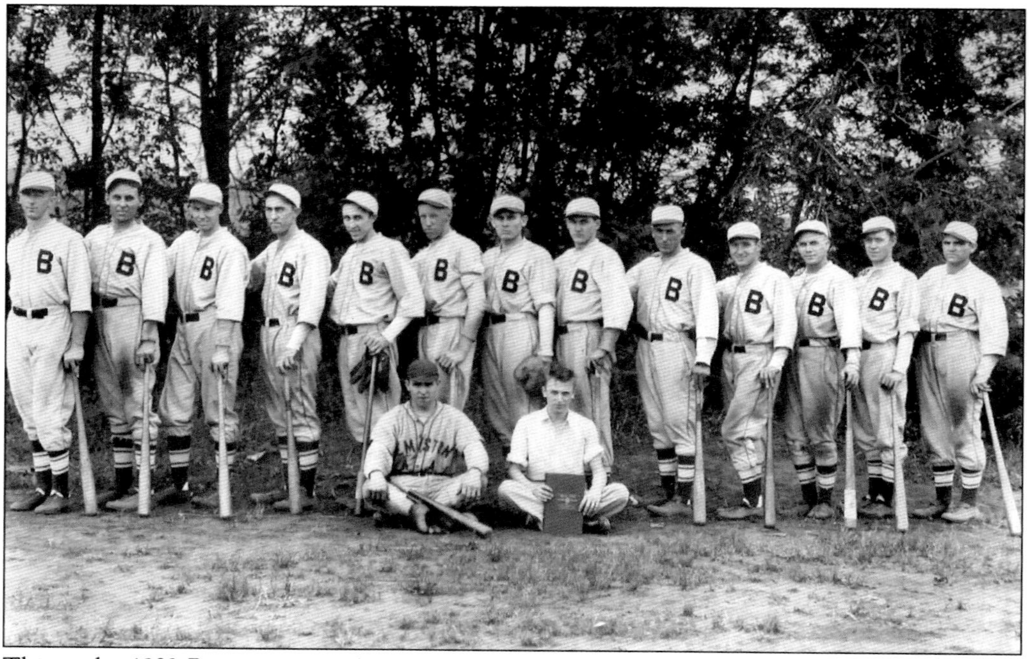

This is the 1932 Bemiston Cats baseball team. The only identified player is Sam Roberts (far right). (Courtesy of J. W. Baker.)

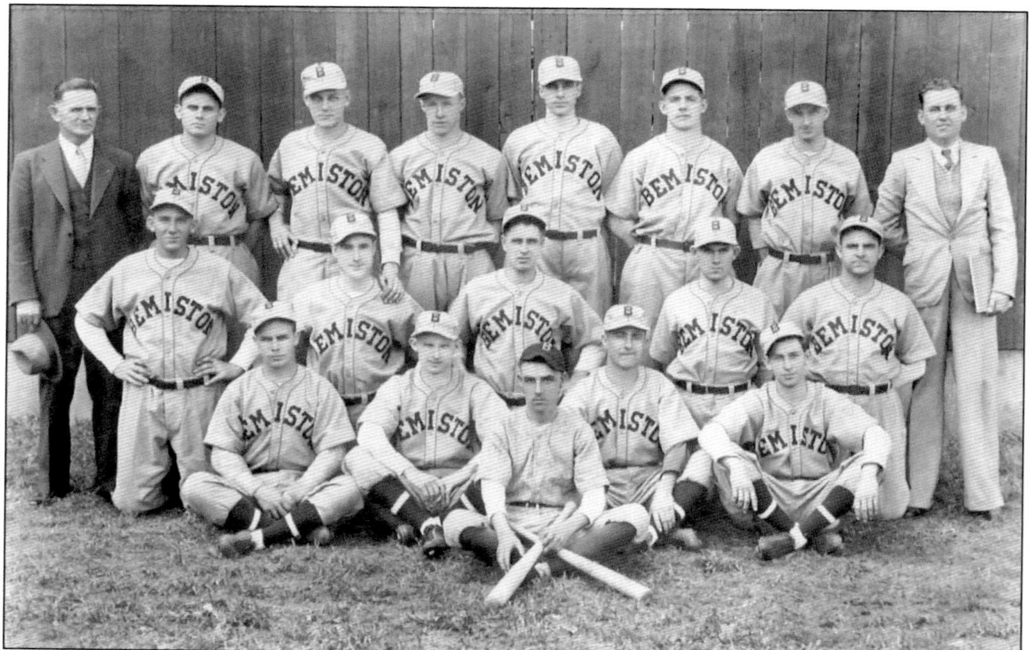

Pictured is the 1935 Bemiston Cats baseball team. From left to right are (first row) John Alvin Baker, batboy; (second row) Frank Horn, Leroy Chappell, Jake Clements, and Bernard Forbus; (third row) Vic Lawson, Red Lakey, Joe Shapiro, Spot Green, and Sam Roberts; (fourth row) coach Charlie Davis, Preston "Piggy" Brown, Donald Ramey, Henry Bergfeld, Rodney King, Ernest Hayes, Jack McClend, and Andrew "Popsickle" Brown. (Courtesy of J. W. Baker.)

The 1942 baseball team is pictured here. From left to right are (first row) Joe Wayne Ingram, batboy; (second row) Comer Brown, Hugh Harrington, Tap Wallis, and Joe Shapiro; (third row) two unidentified, L. B. Rutledge, Hoyt Nunn, and unidentified; (fourth row) unidentified, Jack Rutledge, Saxon Vickers, Leroy Chappell, and coach John Moore. (Courtesy of J. W. Baker.)

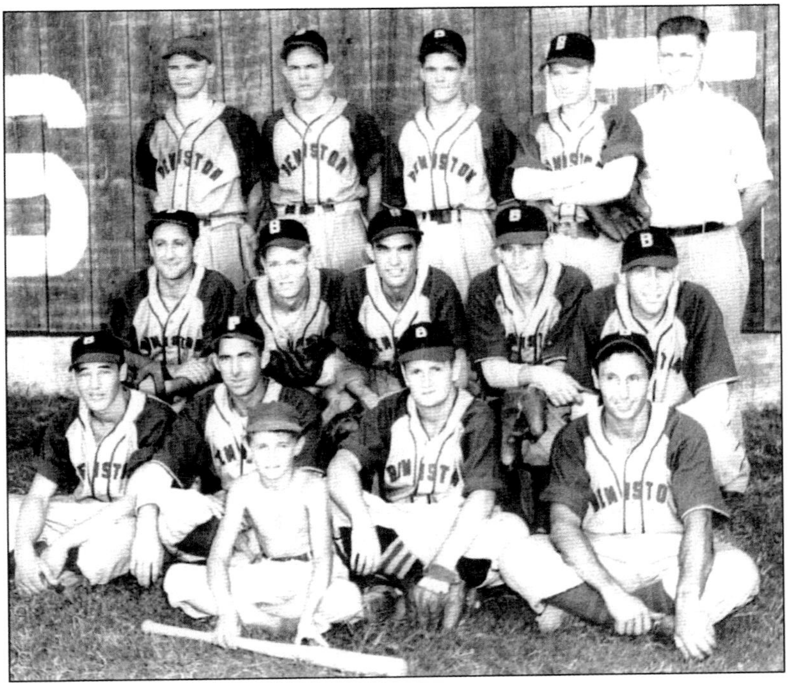

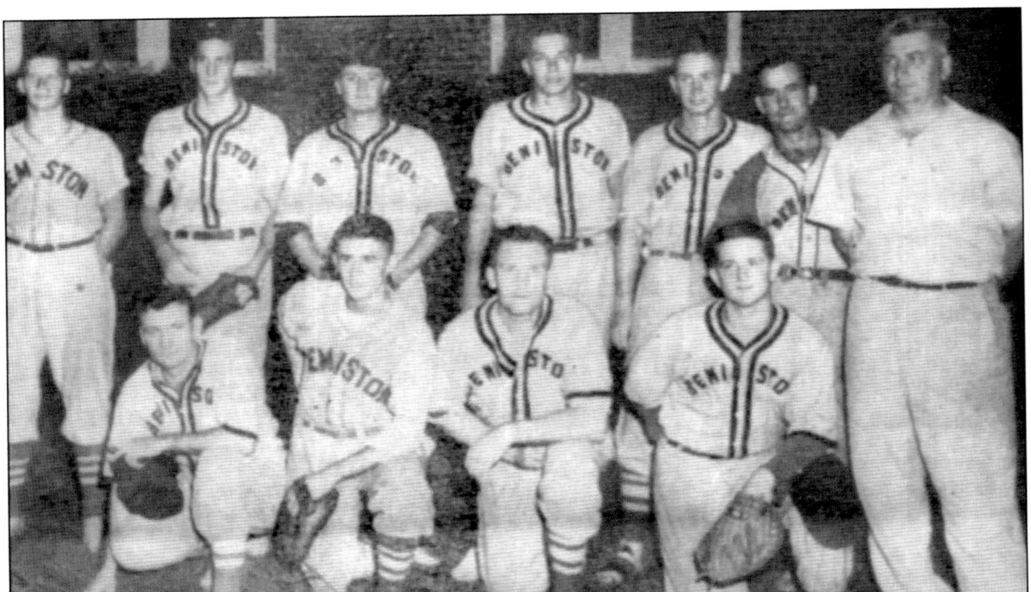

The 1949 baseball team is pictured here. From left to right are (first row) James Ford, Joe Wayne Ingram, Fred Moore, Joe Neal Sprayberry, and coach John L. Moore; (second row) Reginald Rogers, Bradley Askew, Leon White, Harold Cottle, Dan Bussey, and Earl Harrington. (Courtesy of the *Parkway News*.)

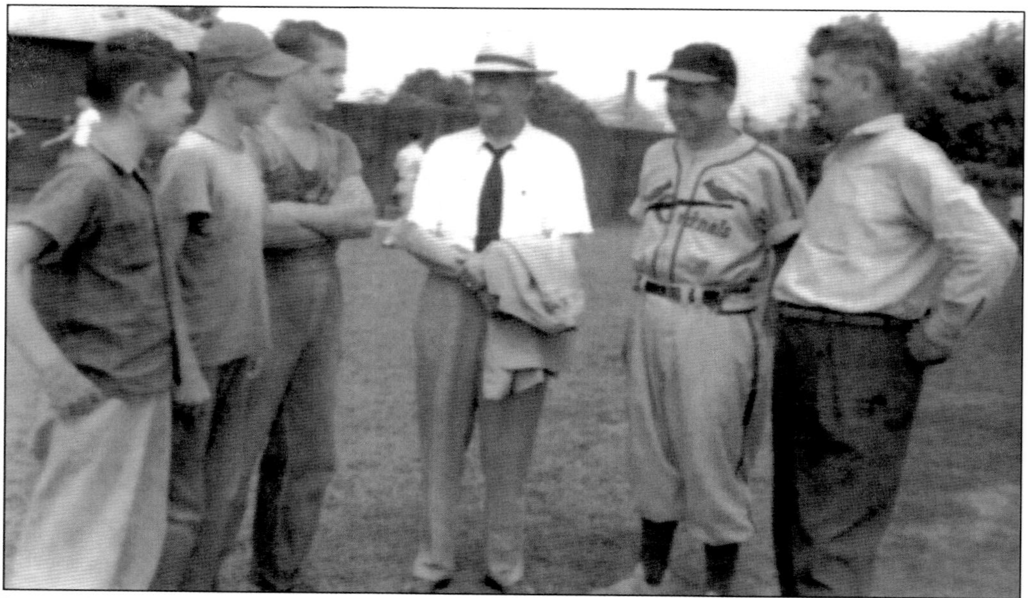

Joe Neal Sprayberry also had a promising future in baseball. He first started playing baseball while in R. L. Young Elementary School, then as catcher on the Bemiston Midget team, and later with the American Legion Junior team and Talladega High School team. He helped win three county and district championships. In 1948–1949 season, he played with the Bemiston Cats, who finished fourth in the state semipro tournaments both years. He signed with the Pittsburgh Pirates in 1950. A single photograph of Joe Neal was unavailable, but this picture shows, from left to right, Burford Robinson, Joe Wayne Ingram, Joe Neal Spragberry, Ben Bruner, an unidentified Cardinal scout, and John Moore, the Bemiston coach. (Courtesy of the *Parkway News*.)

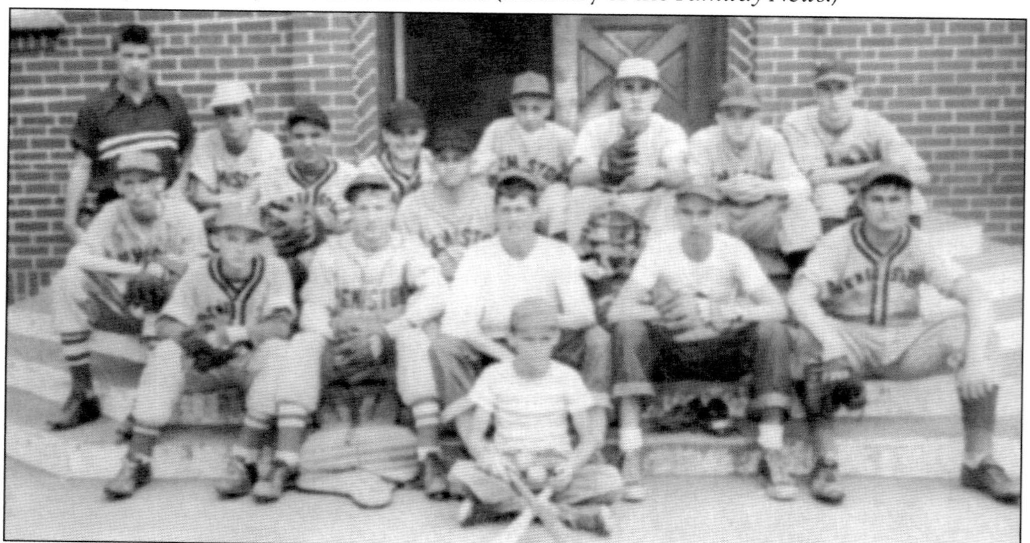

The 1952 baseball team is pictured above. From left to right are (first row) Dorman Hughston, batboy; (second row) Elgin Robinson, Leonard Brand, Gerald White, Kenneth Daniels, and Roy Baker; (third row) Dough Hill, Carl "Cooter" Folsom, and Bert Garner; (fourth row) Joe Wayne Ingram (manager), Clyde Williams, three unidentified, Donald Roberts, and Bradley Askew. (Courtesy of Doug Hill.)

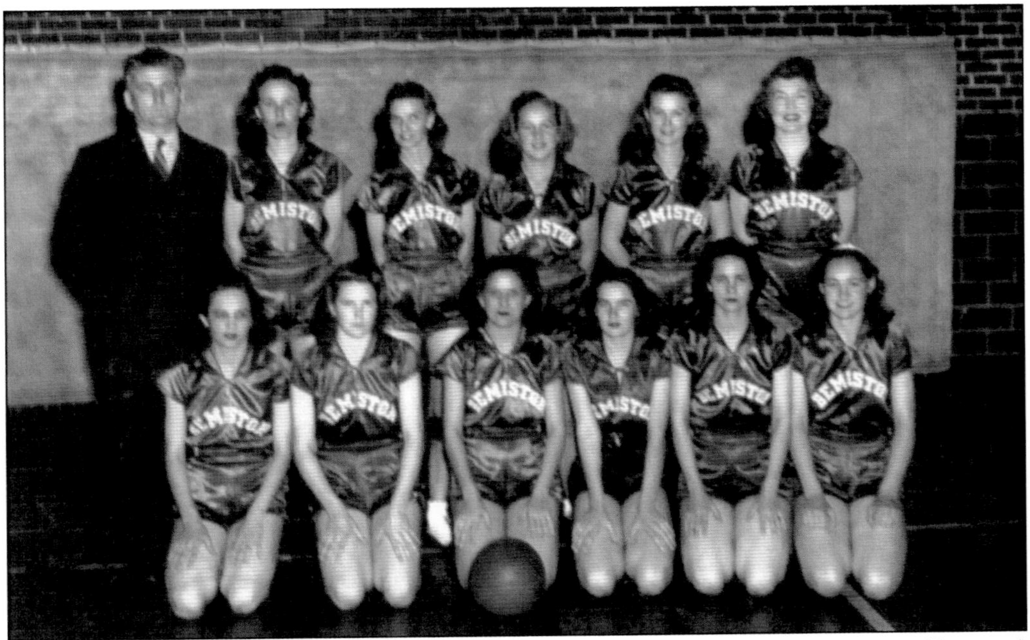

The 1942 Bemiston Kittens basketball team is pictured above. From left to right are (first row) Katherine Holmes, Lina Evans, Willene Senn, Barbara Duncan, Adele Jacks, and Mildred Spencer; (second row) coach John Moore, Daphene Baker, Inez Lakey, Johnnie Cook, Betty Ingram, and Peggy Smith. (Courtesy of Mildred Brownlow.)

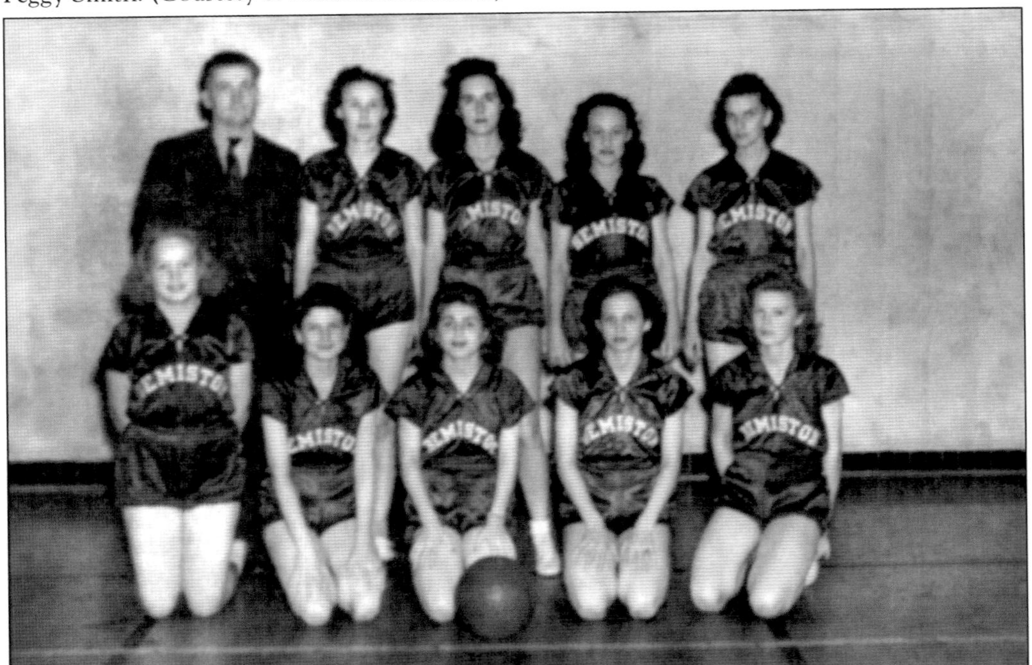

The 1944 Bemiston Kittens basketball team are, from left to right, (first row) Johnnie Cook, Ruth Brownlow, Wren Owens, Katherine Holmes, and Betty Ingram; (second row) coach John Moore, Daphene Baker, unidentified, Jean Jackson, and Inez Lakey. (Courtesy of Mildred Brownlow.)

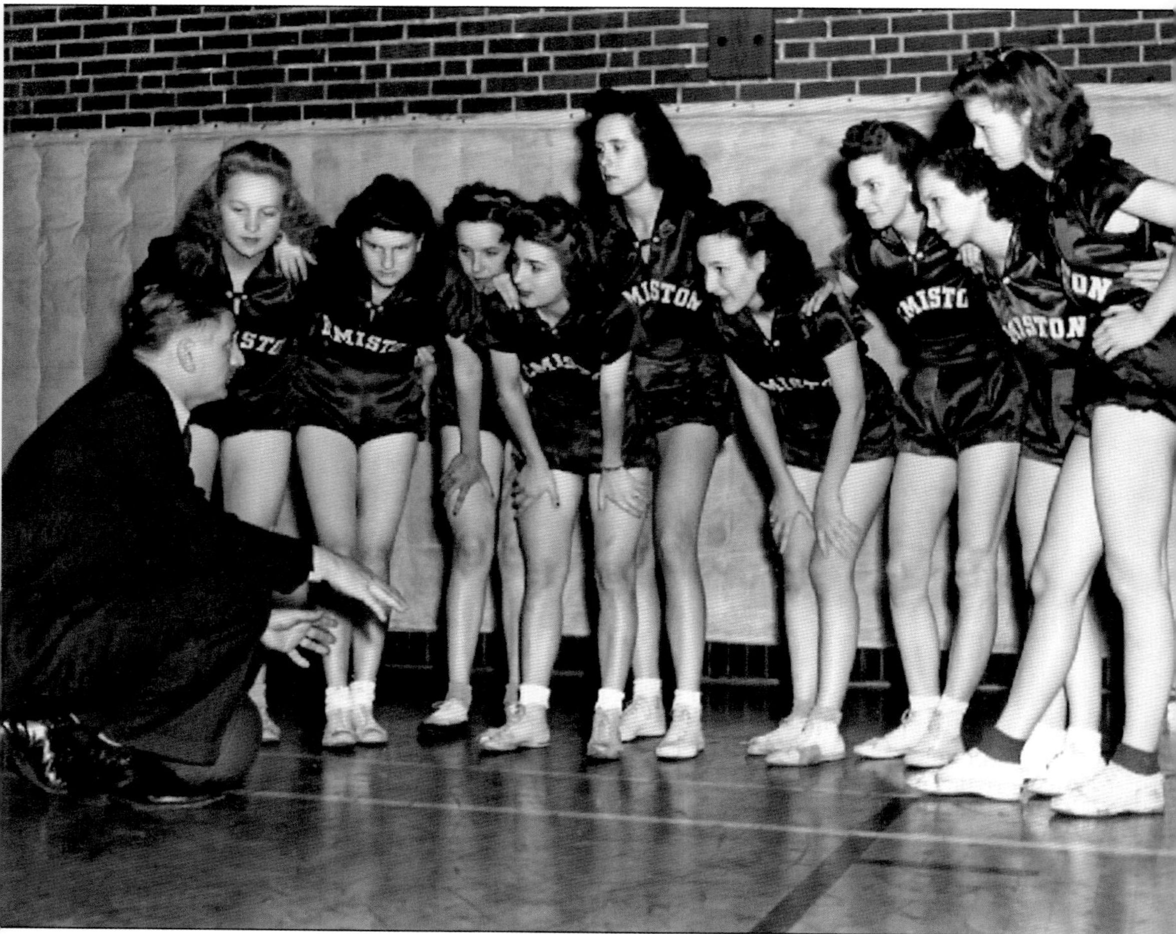

Coach John Moore gives last-minute instructions to the 1945 Bemiston Kittens basketball team before a game. From left to right are John Moore, Johnnie Cook, Ruth Brownlow, Daphene Baker, Wren Owens, unidentified, Jean Jackson, Inez Lakey, Katherine Holmes, and Betty Ingram. (Courtesy of Bobbye Trammell.)

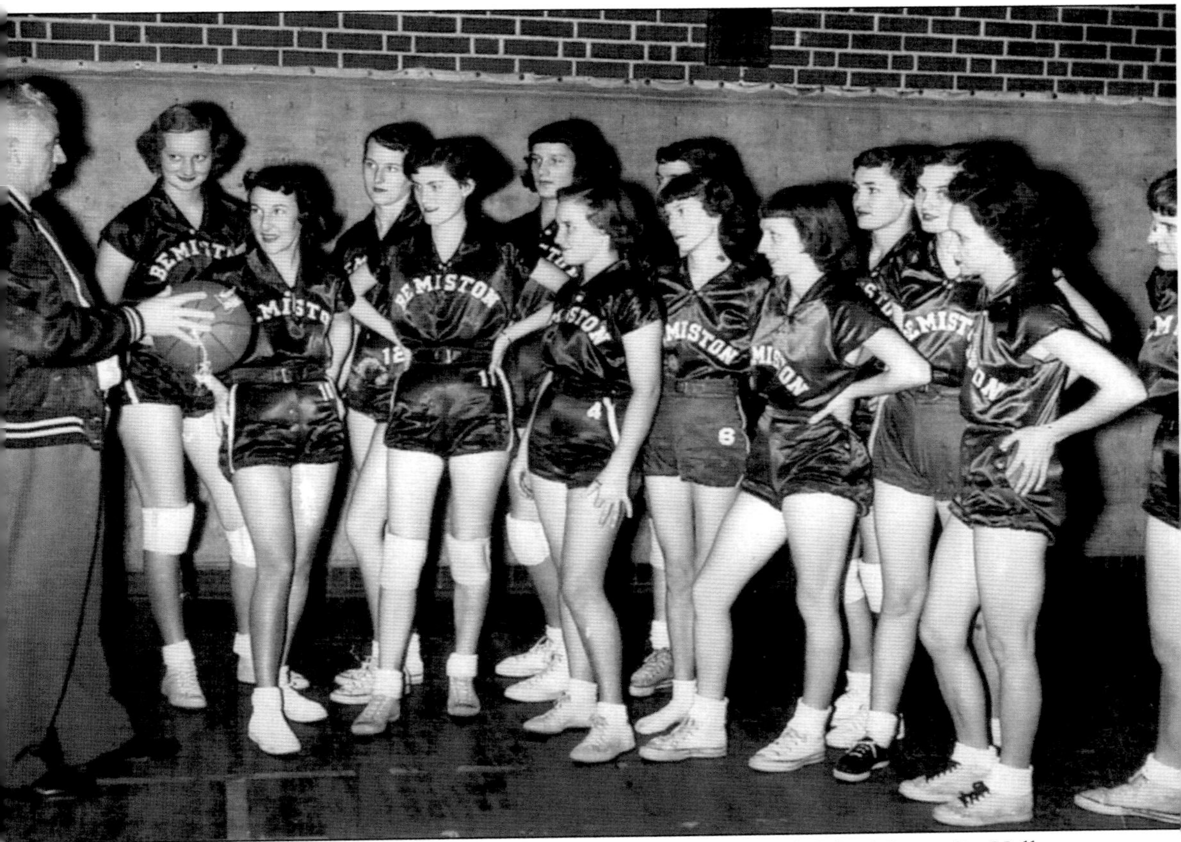

The 1950 Bemiston Kittens basketball team was, from left to right, coach John Moore, Pat Hellon, Jean Jackson, Louise Fulton, Frances Hughston, Shirley Turner, Ophelia Gambrell, Barbara Moore, Mary Elizabeth Hicks, Linda Chappell, Mildred Spencer, Gail Watkins, Katherine Holmes, and Sue Duncan. (Courtesy of Bill Cooley.)

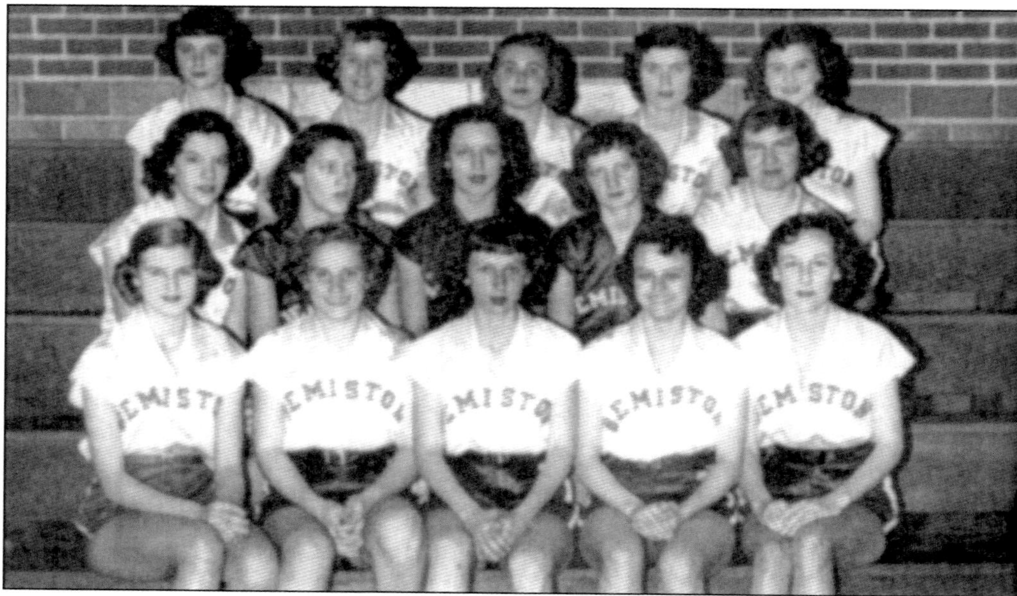

The 1952 Bemiston Kittens basketball team was, from left to right, (first row) Virginia Patterson, Ophelia Gambrell, Linda Chappell, Yvonne Grice, and Jean Jackson; (second row) Mary Duncan, Elizabeth Patterson, Jean Price, unidentified, and Sue Duncan; (third row) Barbara Moore, Louise Fulton, ? Reeves, Frances Hughston, and Mary Ann Brownlow. (Courtesy of *Bemistory* magazine.)

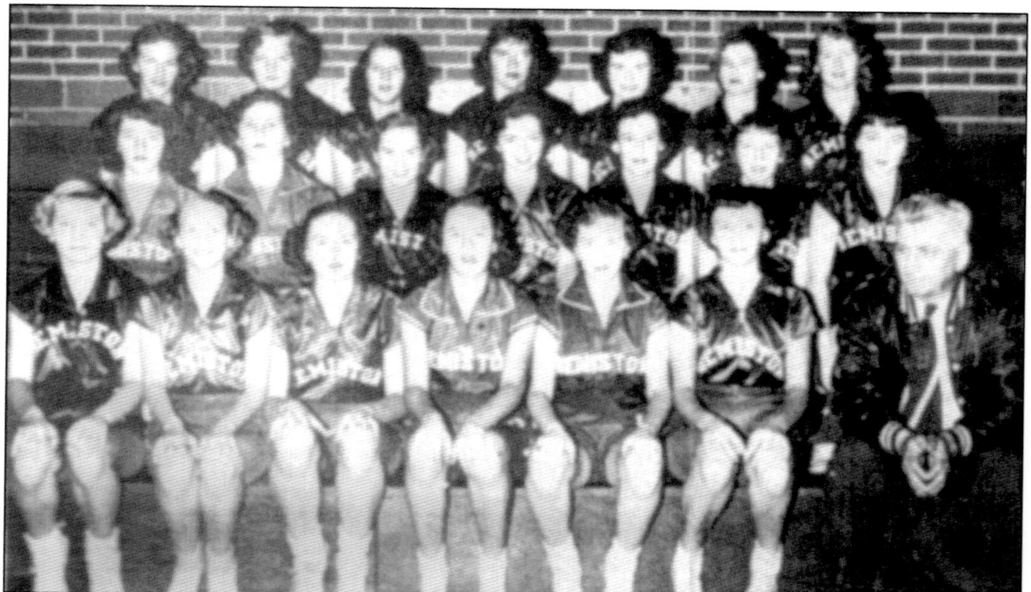

The 1953 Bemiston Kittens basketball team was, from left to right, (first row) Dorothy Forrest, Faye Turner, Theresa Bowen, Glenda Peters, Billie Joyce Seymore, Ruby Malone, and coach John Moore; (second row) Myra Osbourn, Mary Catherine Folsom, Ophelia Gambrell, Betty Cook, Jean Jackson, Linda Gail Chappell, and Barbara Moore; (third row) Martha Williams, Jean Price, Elizabeth Patterson, Sue Duncan, Frances Hughston, Geraldean Hughston, and Louise Fulton. (Courtesy of the *Parkway News*.)

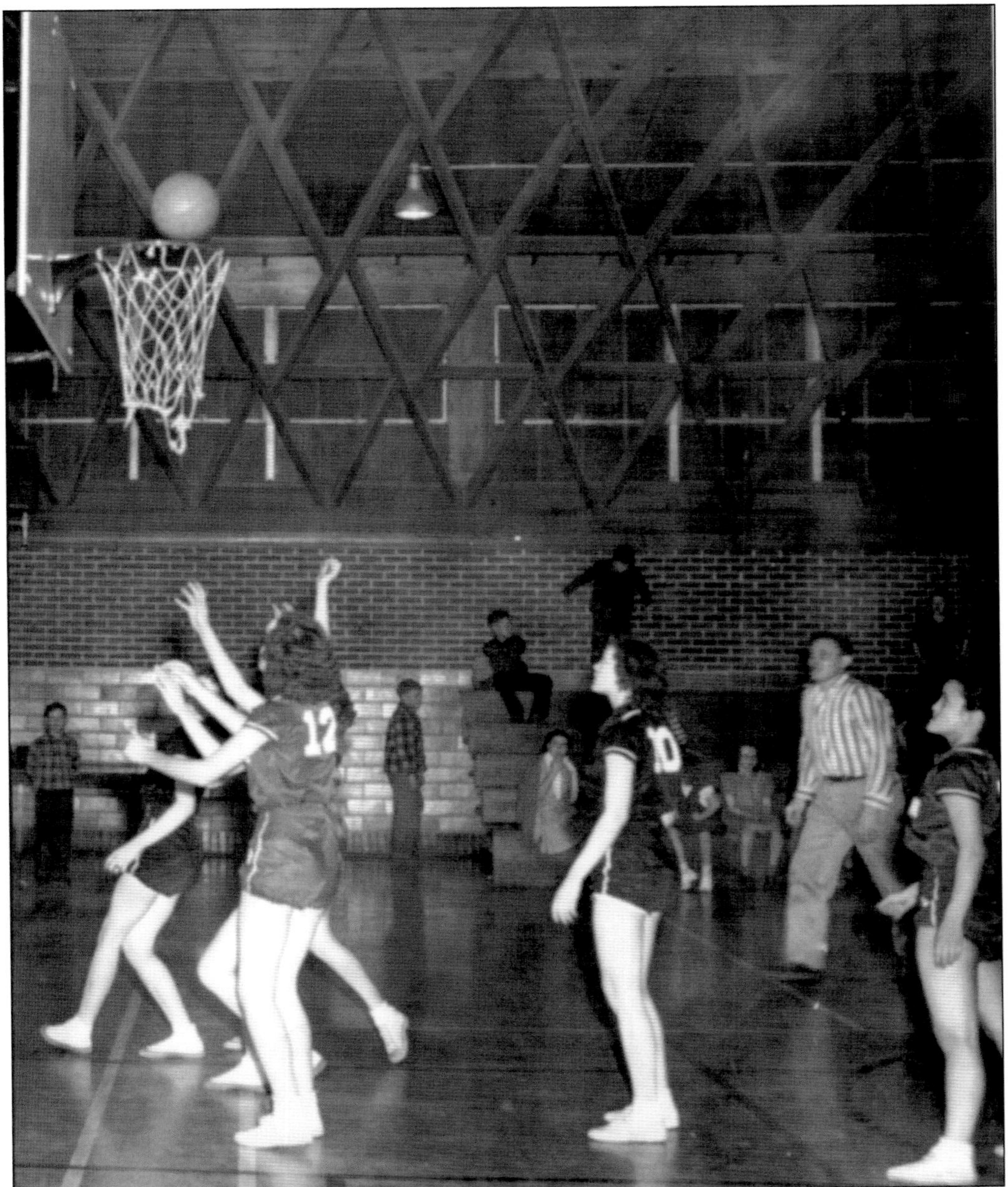

This image shows the Bemiston Kittens in action. The only people identifiable are the referee, Preston "Piggy" Brown, and Jean Vickers (lower right). (Courtesy of Yvonne Grice.)

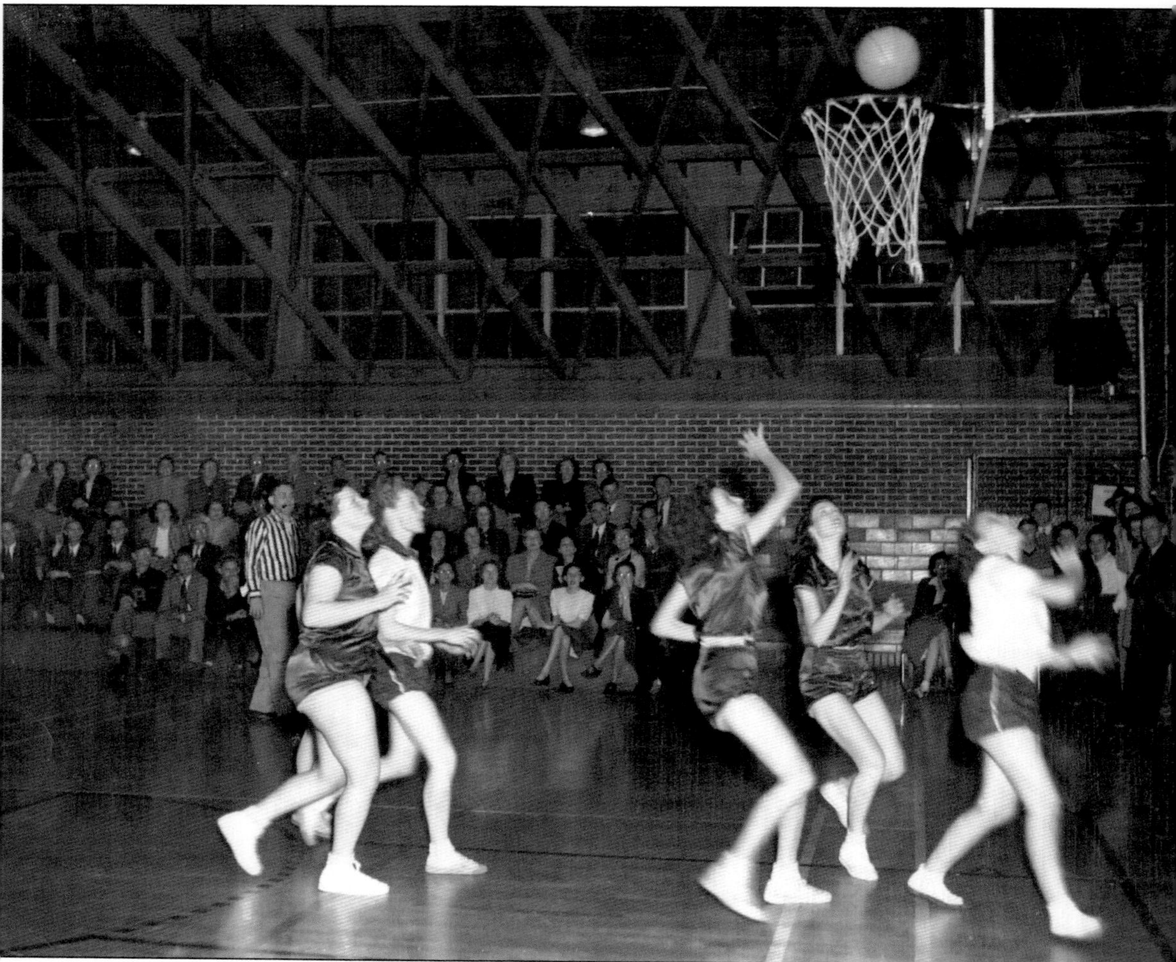

This is an action shot of the Bemiston Kittens, evidently ringing the basket. (Courtesy of Yvonne Grice.)

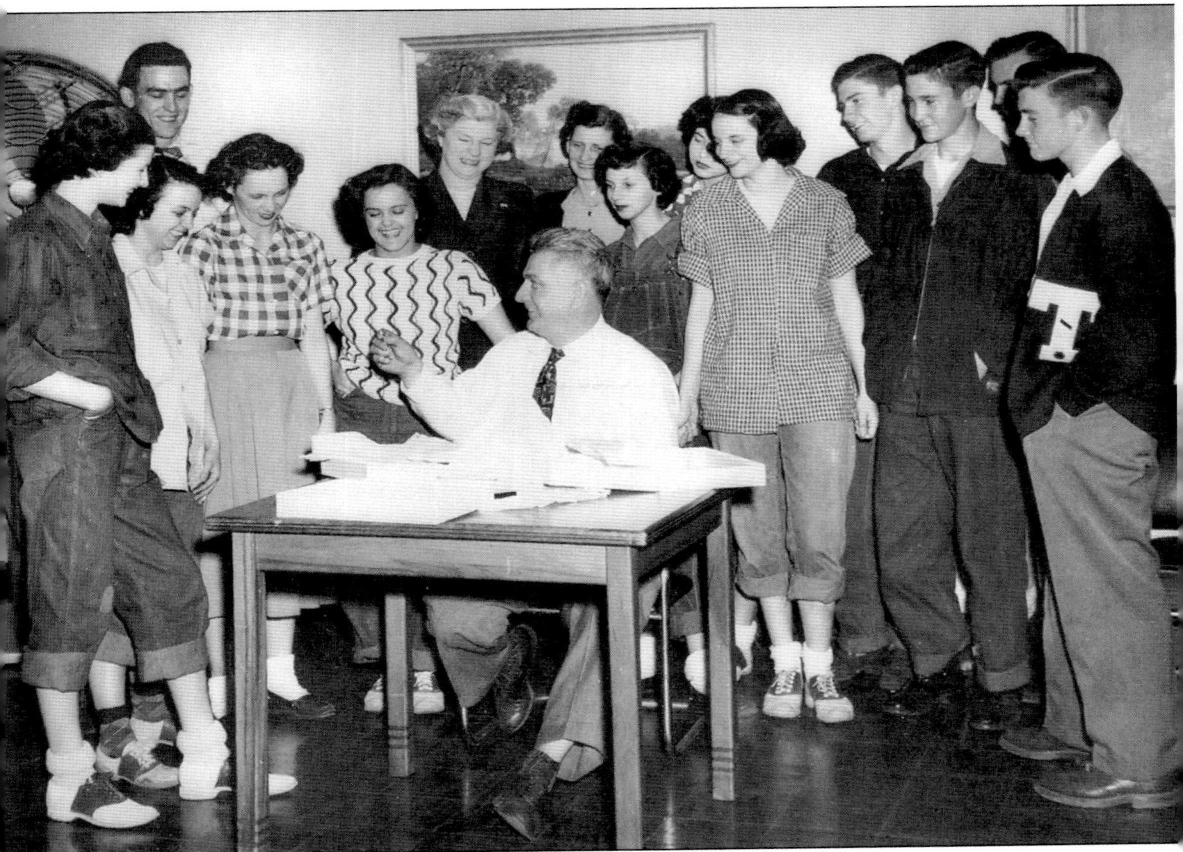

John L. Moore, recreational director and coach of both the girls' and boys' basketball teams, is shown as his players are honoring him with a gift of appreciation. Shown in the picture, in no particular order, are Betty Estes, Yvonne Grice, Sam Grice, Katherine Holmes, Jean Culberson, Edith Moore, Evie Estes, Mary Elizabeth Hicks, Jean Wright, Barbara Moore, John Paul Moore, Jack Spencer, Denson Haynes, and Donald Roberts. (Courtesy of Bill Cooley.)

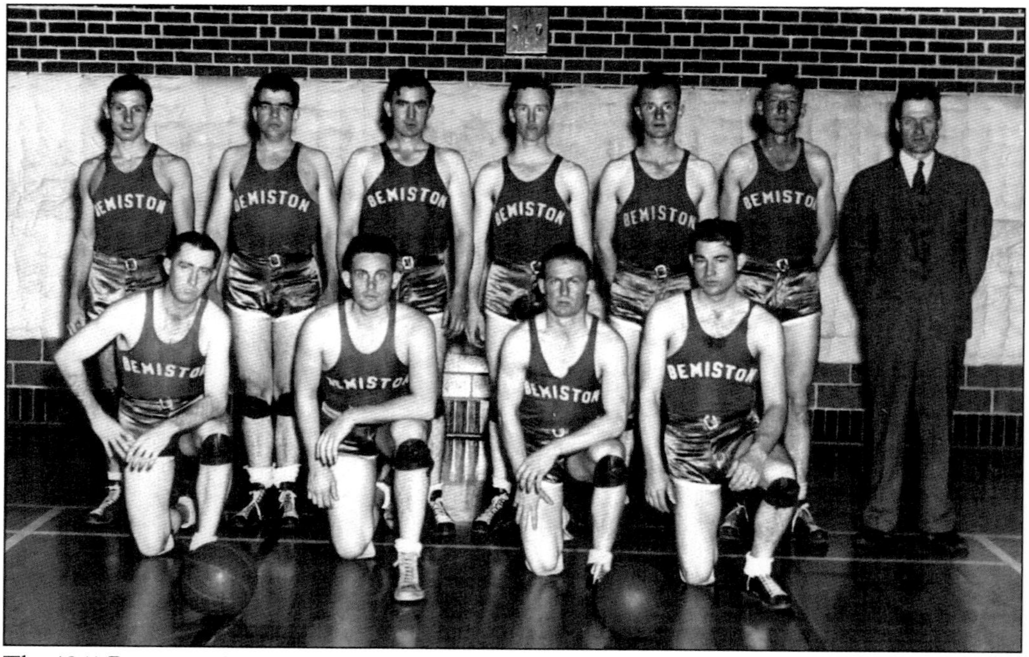

The 1941 Bemiston Cats team included, from left to right, (first row) Frank Ed Williams, Preston "Piggy" Brown, unidentified, and Bert Spencer; (second row) Joe Shapiro, ? Caldwell, four unidentified, and coach Art Decatur. (Courtesy of Mildred Brownlow.)

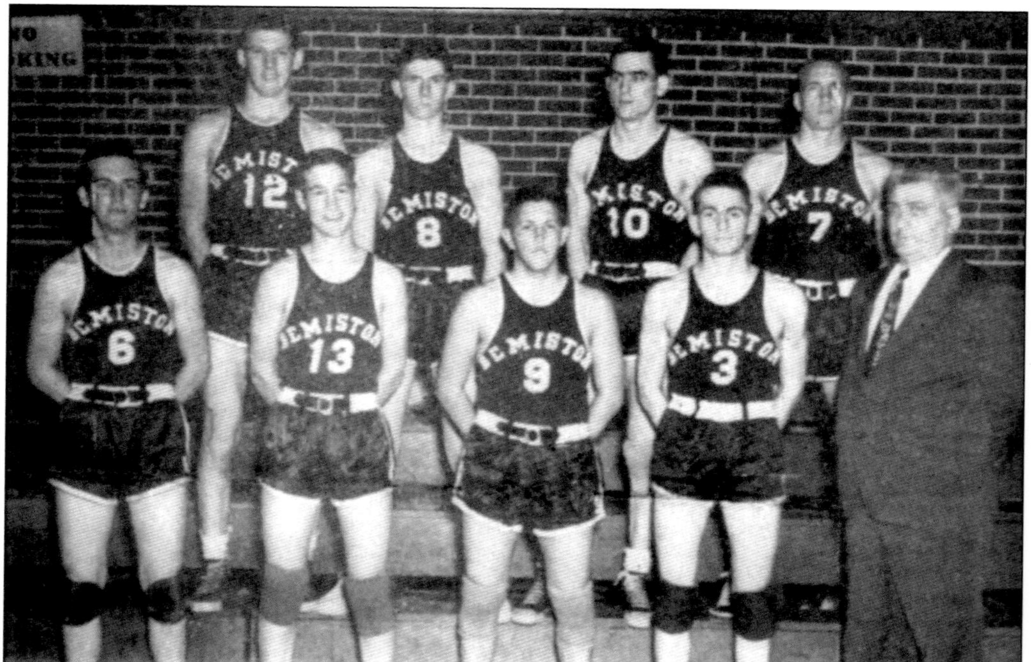

The 1951 Bemiston Cats basketball team included, from left to right, (first row) Lavoyd Vernon, Jack Spencer, Bert Garner, Claud Tinney, and coach John L. Moore; (second row) Jimmy Durham, John Paul Moore, Sam Grice, and John McBride. (Courtesy of Sam Grice.)

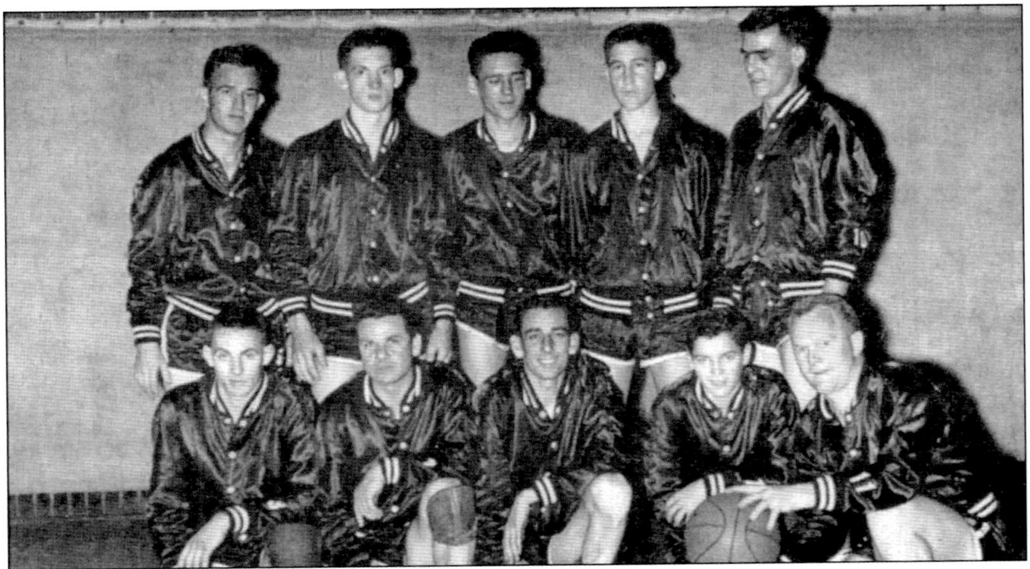

The 1952 Bemiston Cats basketball team included, from left to right, (first row) Claud Tinney, ? Kinslow, Don Culberson, Jan Patterson, and ? Gilbert; (second row) H. E. Hyche, ? Pope, ? Price, Jack Spencer, and Sam Grice. (Courtesy of the *Bemis Echoes*.)

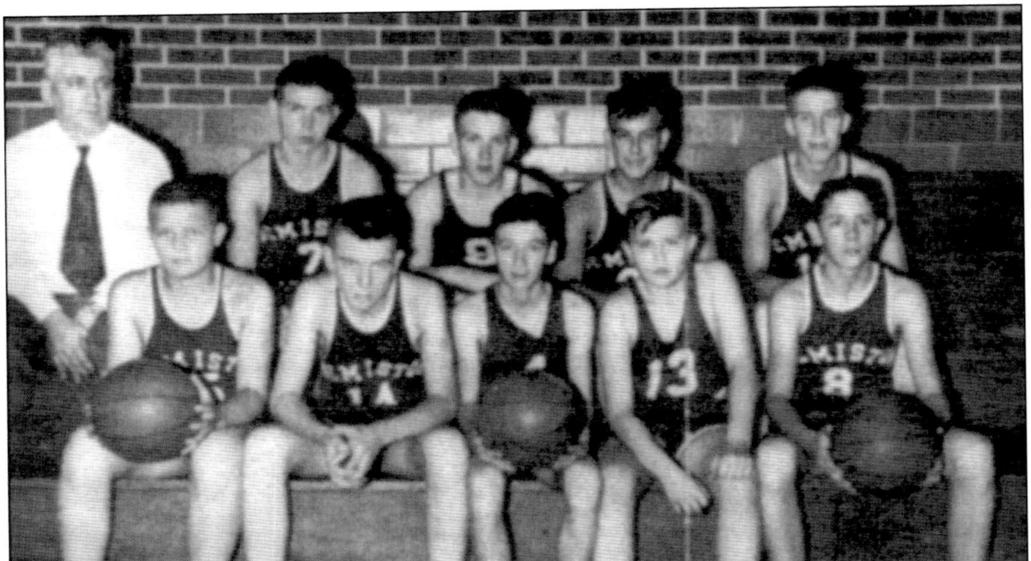

Playing for the 1954 Junior Bemiston Cats were, from left to right, (first row) "Bo" Williams, Charles Foreman, Ernie Mitchell, Walter Clark, and Bob Garner; (second row) coach John L. Moore, Jerry Canada, Wayne Bowen, Mickey Vickers, and Wayne Trammell. These boys played nine games that season and won eight. (Courtesy of the *Parkway News*.)

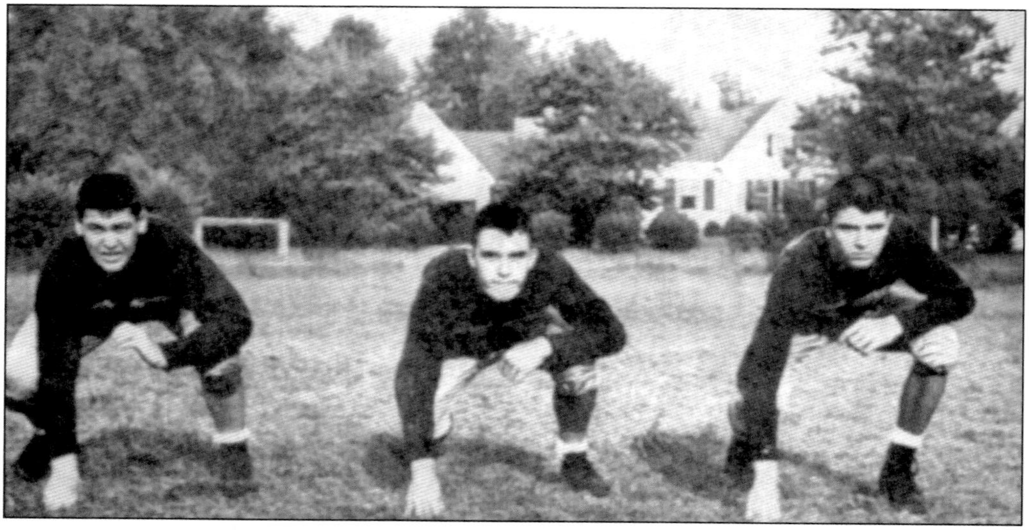

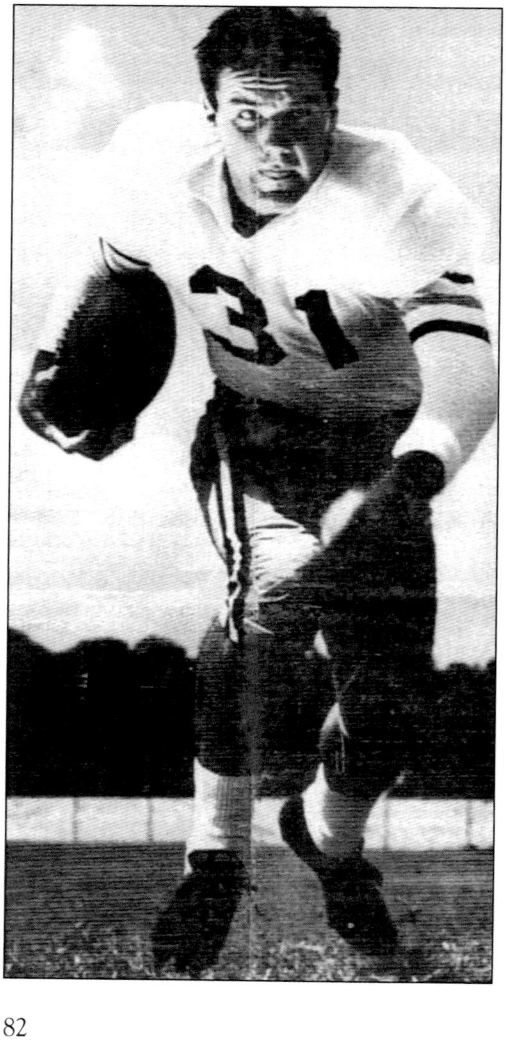

These three fellows were football players with Talladega High School. Bemiston did not have a football team, but the boys were ready when the season started because of their previous athletic training under John Moore. They are, from left to right, Joe Charles Cooley, Joe Thurman, and Lamon Bowen. Another Bemiston boy, James William Carpenter, was also on the team but could not be in the picture because of an injury. (Courtesy of Bill Cooley.)

Shown here is Glenn Turner, son of Henry and Myrtle Turner, who played football for Georgia Tech. Glenn was credited by the *Parkway News* as the man who really won the 1952 Sugar Bowl over Mississippi with a 24-7 victory. (Courtesy of the *Parkway News*.)

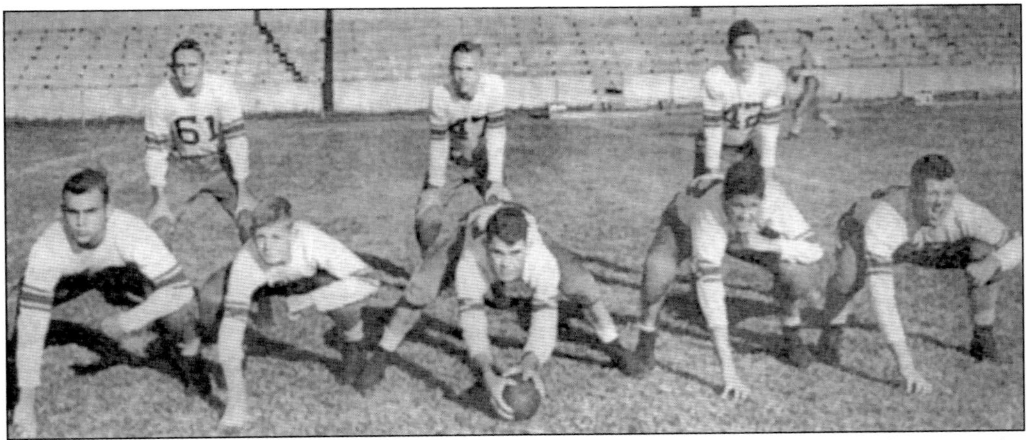

These are some Talladega High players from Bemiston in 1949. They had played a game the previous week against the Sylacauga Aggies. They are, from left to right, (first row) Billy Cooley, Joe Mel Smith, Buford Robinson, Billy Bert Garner, and Bobby Jones; (second row) Robert Wyatt, Jerry Spratt, and Reginald Rogers. (Courtesy of the *Parkway News*.)

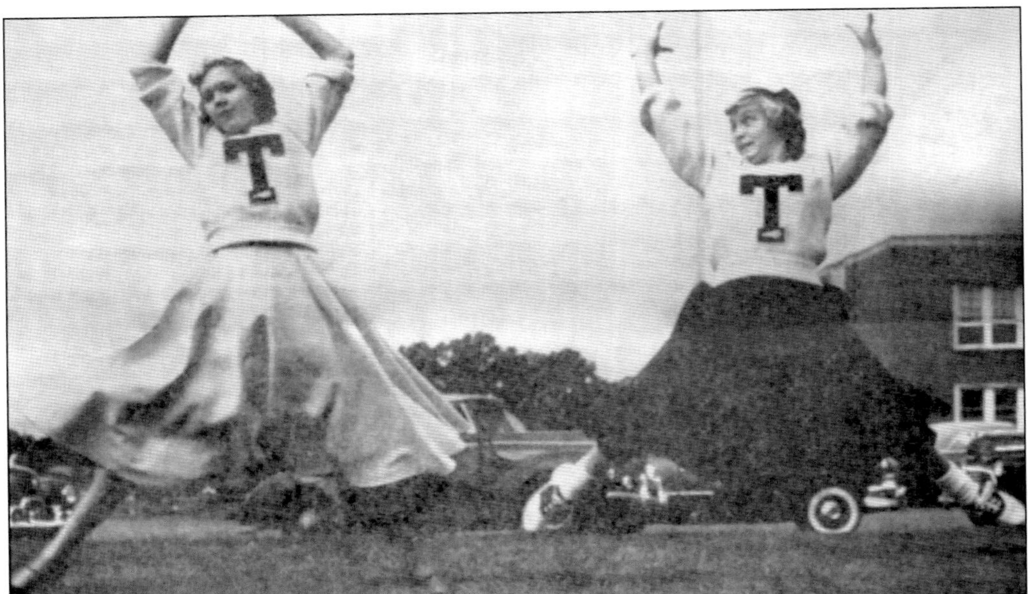

These girls are showing their team spirit. Shown are Betty Mann (right), head cheerleader at Talladega High School, and Dorothy Forrest. Both girls are from Bemiston. (Courtesy of the *Parkway News*.)

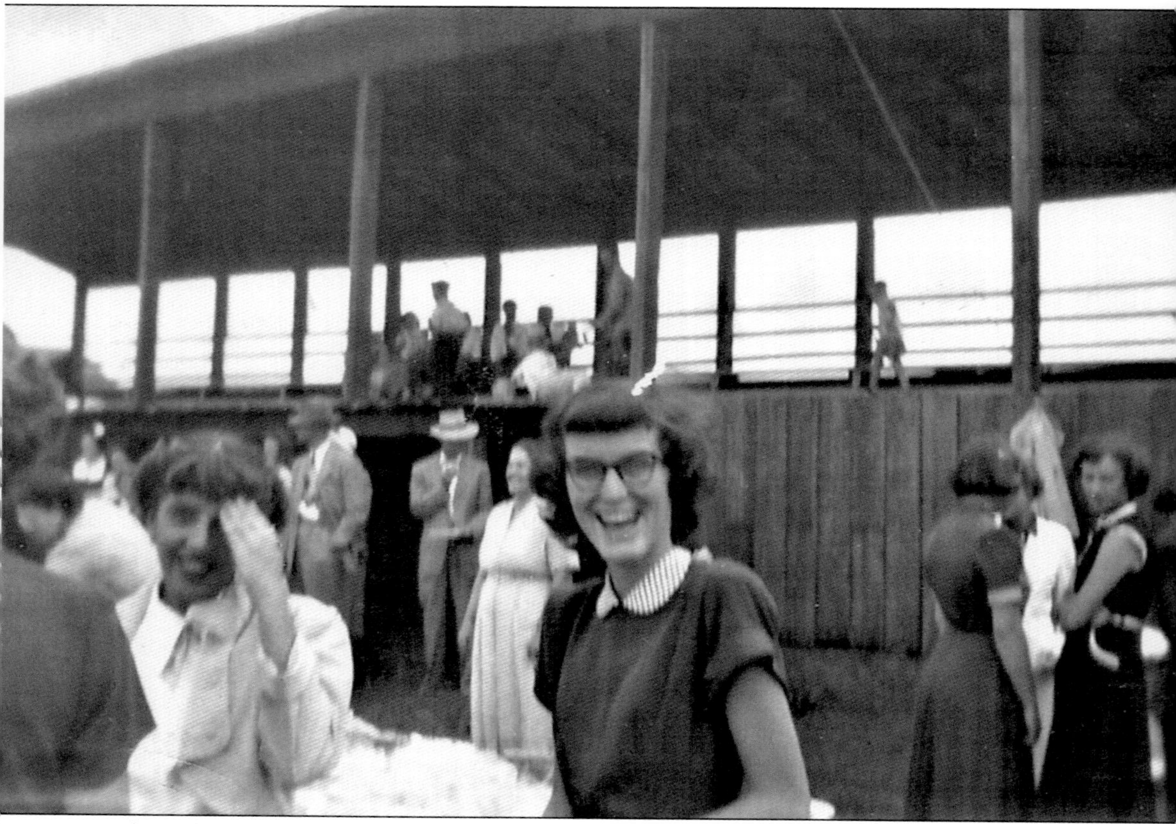

The Roberts Stadium (a baseball stadium) was sometimes used for social functions. This group is shown at a church picnic. Shown facing the camera are Gail Shaw (right) and Frances Hughston. (Courtesy of Frances Hughston.)

Four

The War Years

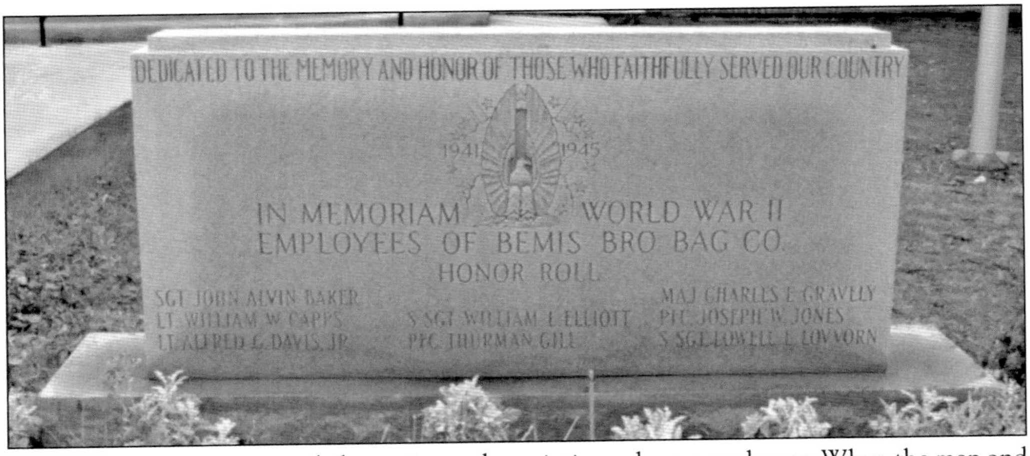

The war years were emotional, depressing, sad, patriotic, and yes, even happy. When the men and women came home, there were happy reunions for the families, but for many families, there was sadness because 11 local fighting men died making all this possible; these families will be broken forever. This caption was in the *Birmingham News-Age Herald*, on Sunday, February 27, 1949: "Bemis Bro. Bag Co. at Talladega, Alabama, has an honor roll for all employees who entered the service and a marble monument for those who died, both are exceptionally kept." This recognition is something of which the Bemiston community should be proud. (Courtesy of J. W. Baker.)

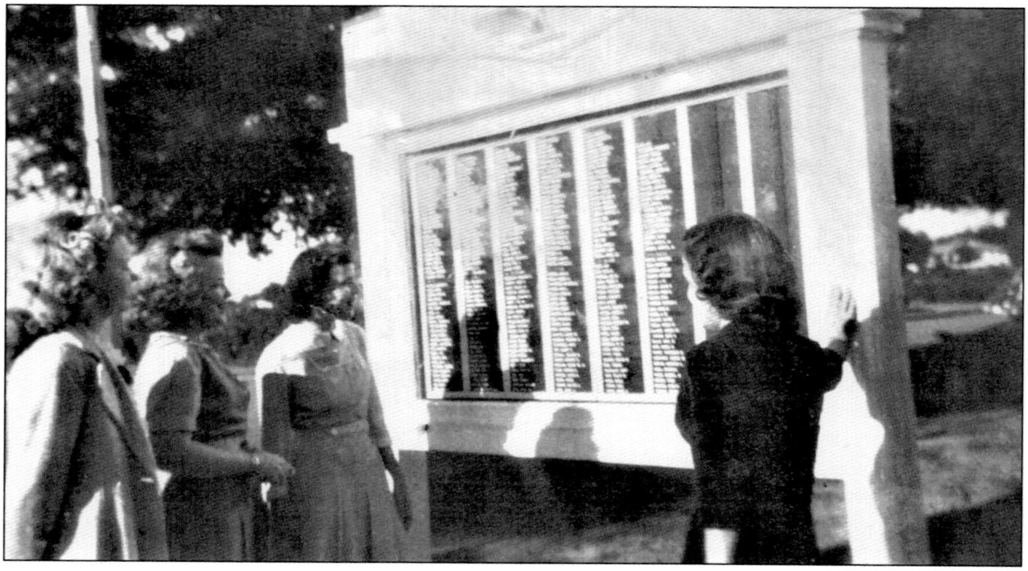

Dot Wallace, Sara Wallace, Bobbye Jo Baker, and Jean Vickers are reading the honor roll of the men and women who were in service. This roll was kept up on a daily basis. There were 300 service people on this roll. (Courtesy of J. W. Baker.)

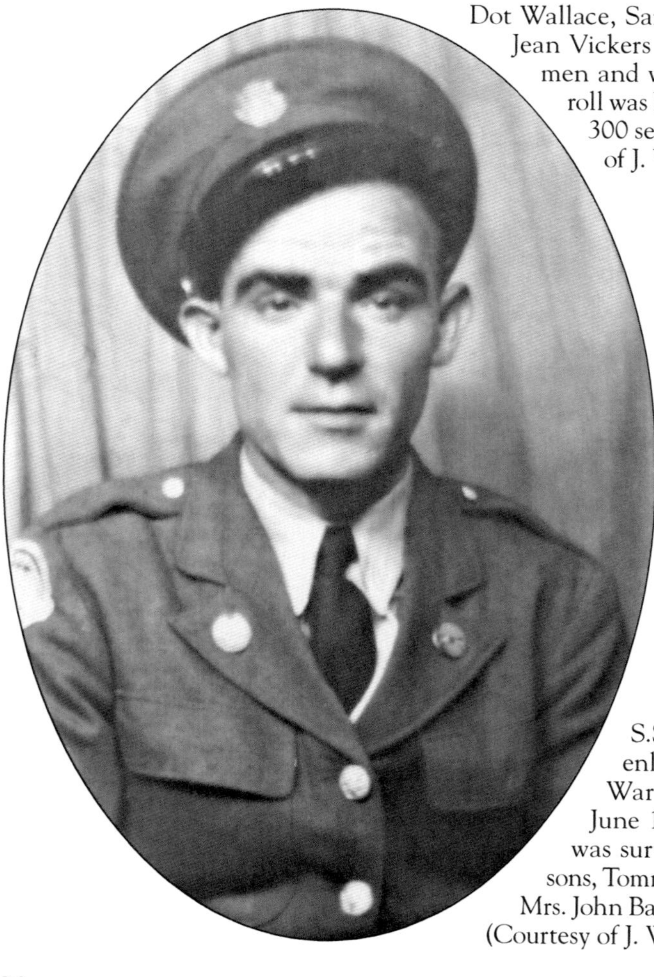

S.Sgt. John Alvin Baker, U.S. Army, enlisted in 1940. He served in World War II and was killed in action on June 1, 1945, on Mindanao Island. He was survived by his wife, Margaret; two sons, Tommy and Donald; his parents, Mr. and Mrs. John Baker; three sisters; and two brothers. (Courtesy of J. W. Baker.)

First Lt. William W. "Billy" Capps, U.S. Army Air Force, served in World War II and was killed in an aircraft crash in February 1943. He was survived by his parents, Mr. and Mrs. W. C. Capps, and two sisters, Margie and Catherine. (Courtesy of J. W. Baker.)

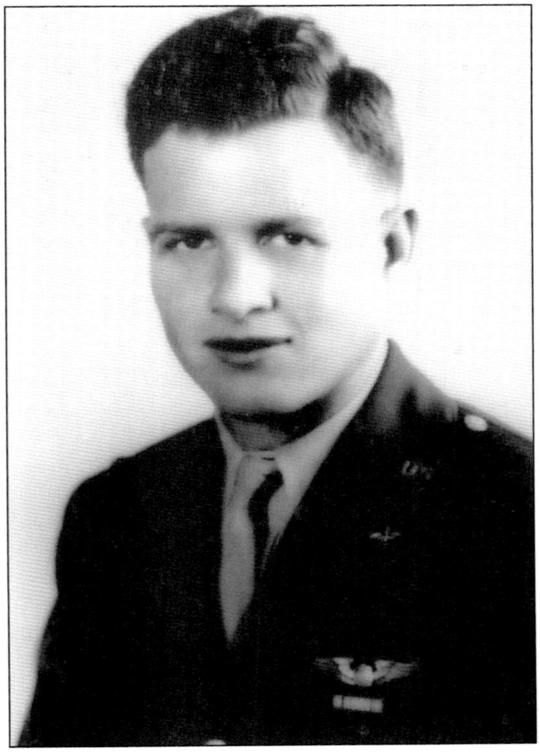

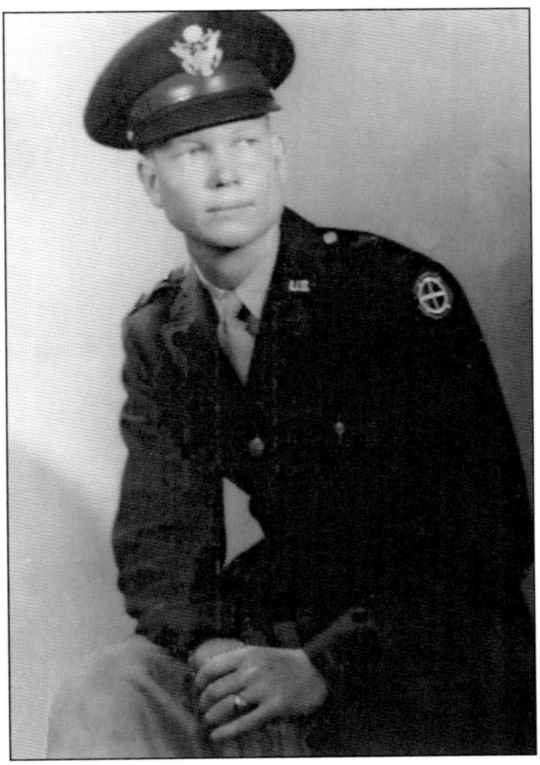

First Lt. Alfred G. Davis, U.S. Army, served in World War II and died in a German prison on November 22, 1944. He was survived by his father, Gus Davis. (Courtesy of J. W. Baker.)

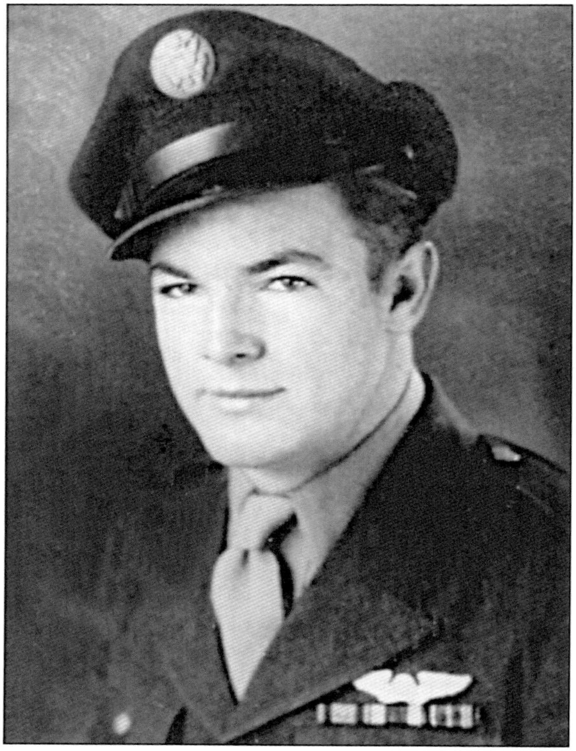

T.Sgt. William Langdon Elliott, U.S. Army Air Force, served in World War II and was killed in action on December 11, 1944. He was survived by his parents, Mr. and Mrs. W. C. Elliott, and one sister, Virginia. (Courtesy of J. W. Baker.)

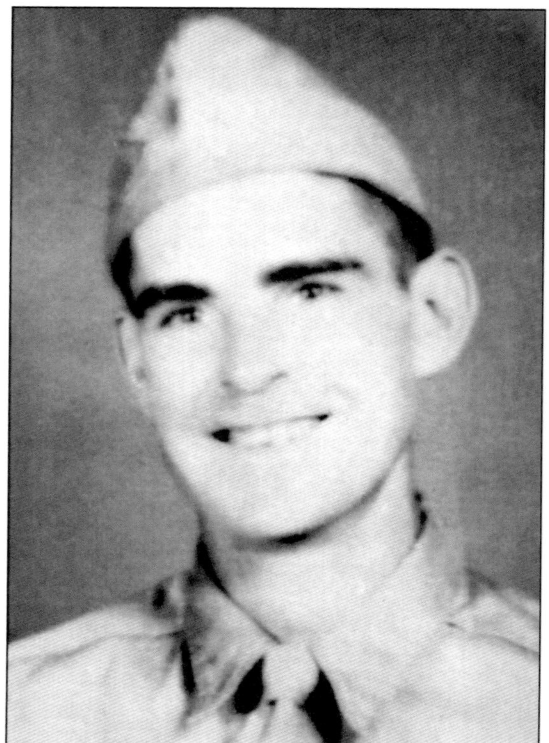

PFC Thurman Gill, U.S. Army, served in World War II and was killed in action. He was survived by his wife and one daughter. (Courtesy of J. W. Baker.)

Maj. Charles E. Gravely, U.S. Army, served in World War II and was killed in action in Europe on September 3, 1944. (Courtesy of J. W. Baker.)

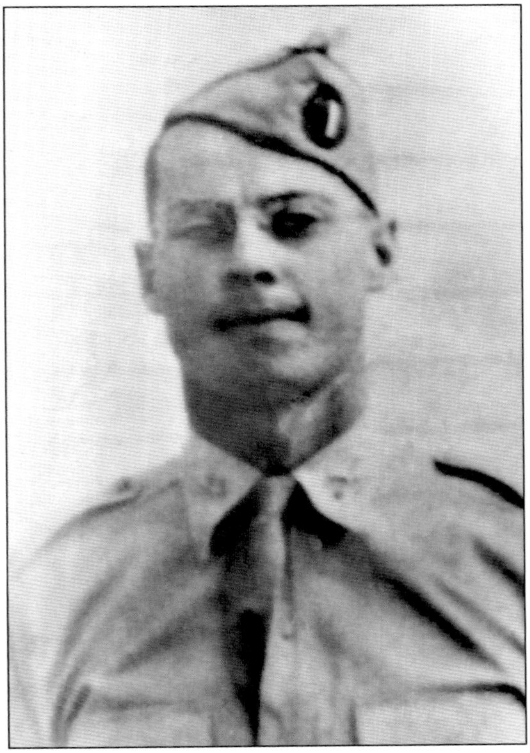

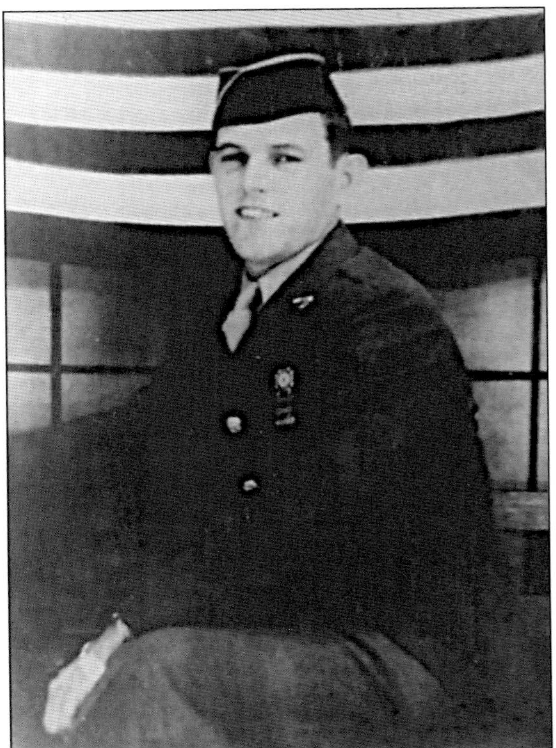

PFC Joseph W. Jones, U.S. Army, served in World War II and was killed in action in Europe. (Courtesy of J. W. Baker.).

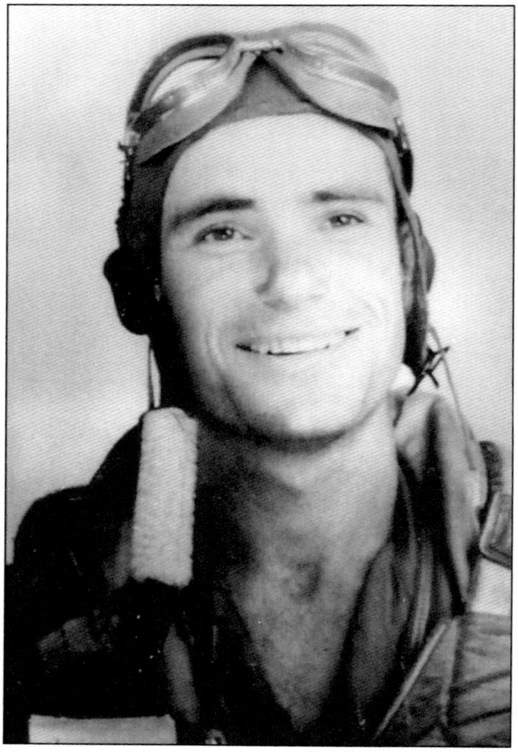

S.Sgt. Lowell E. Lovvorn, U.S. Army Air Force, served in World War II and was killed in action on January 28, 1945. He was survived by one sister, Lillian. (Courtesy of J. W. Baker.)

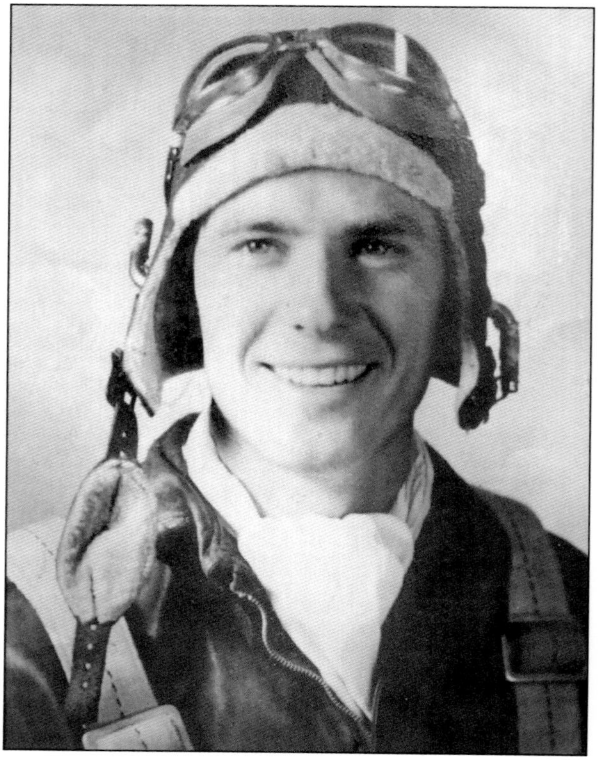

First Lt. James R. Peters, U.S. Army Air Force, served in World War II and was killed in an aircraft crash on September 17, 1940. He was survived by his parents, Mr. and Mrs. Worth Peters, one brother, and one sister. (Courtesy of J. W. Baker.)

Sgt. Vachel L. "Big Buddy" Shaw, U.S. Army, served in World War II and was killed in action on April 4, 1945. He was survived by his parents, Mr. and Mrs. Gideon Shaw, four brothers, and four sisters. (Courtesy of J. W. Baker.)

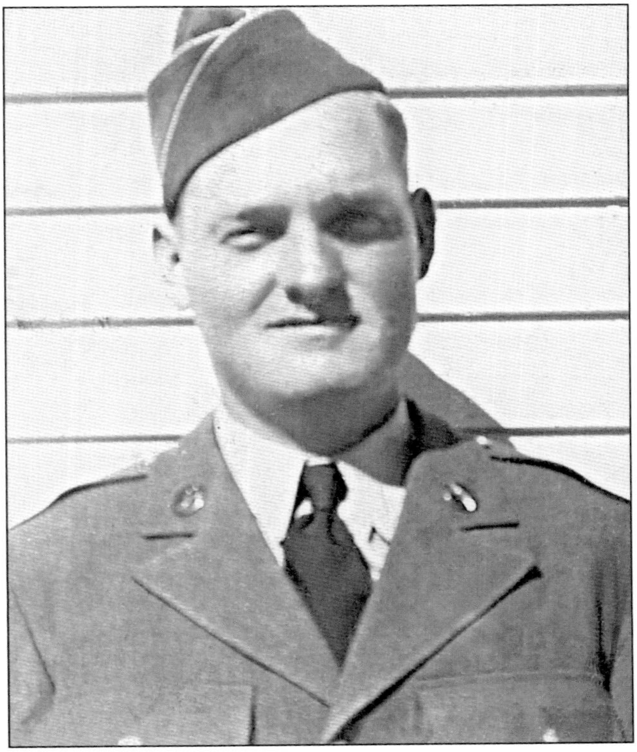

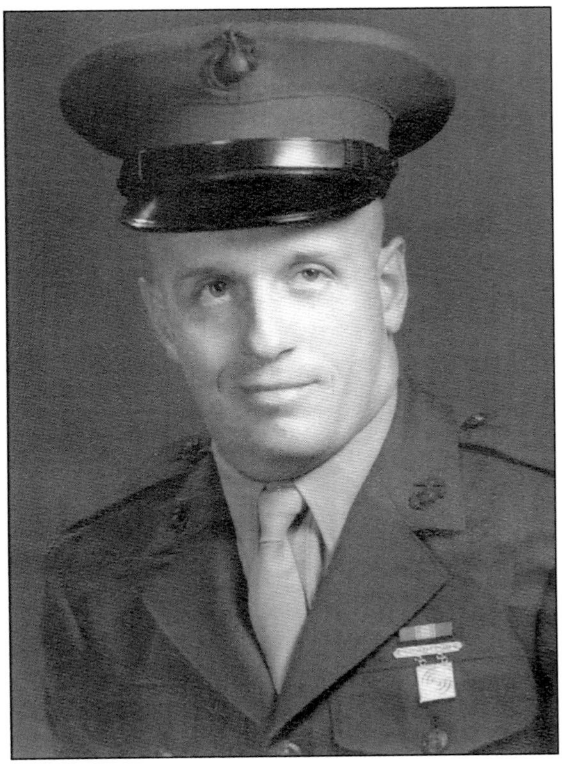

Jr. Cpl. William Marshall "Little Buddy" Shaw, U.S. Marine Corps, served in the Vietnam War. He was killed in action on May 12, 1967. He was survived by his parents, Mr. and Mrs. Marshall Shaw, and one sister. (Courtesy of J. W. Baker.)

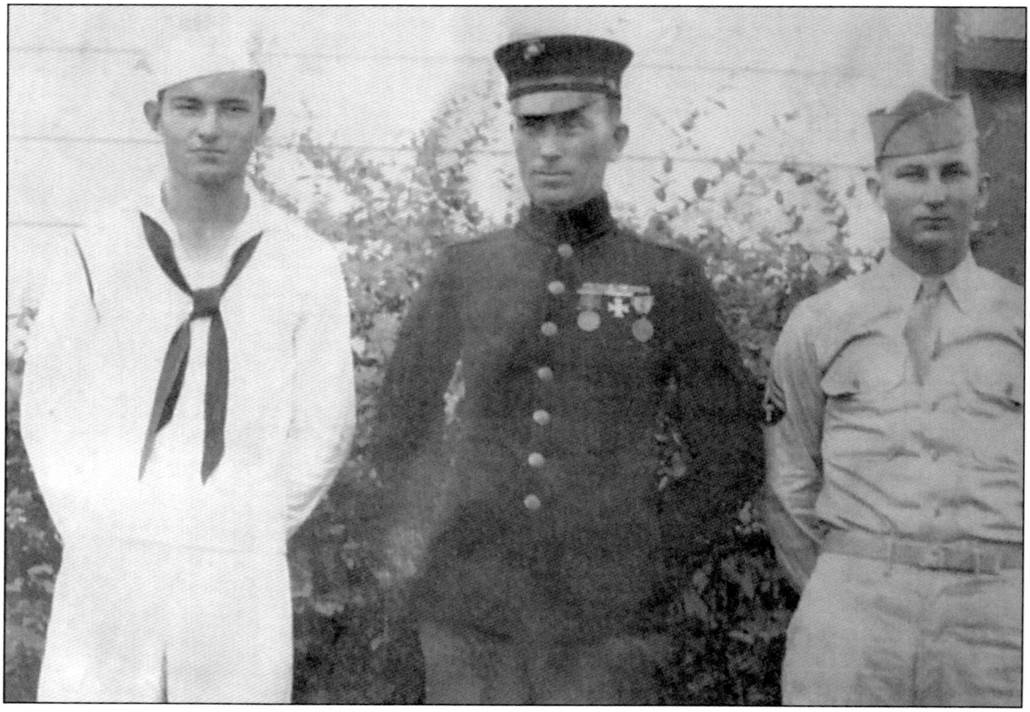

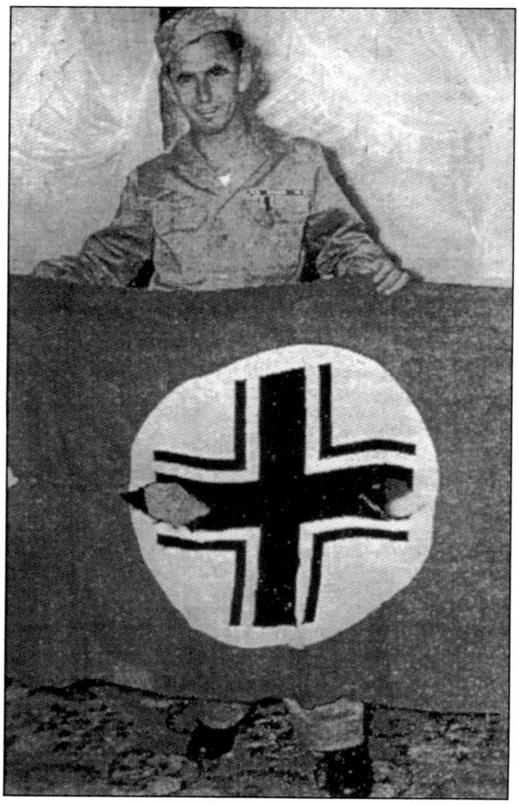

These three men—(from left to right) Stewart Ellison, U.S. Navy, World War II; Easom Ellison, World War I; and Harold Ellison, U.S. Army, World War II—served their country with pride. (Courtesy of J. W. Baker.)

Bascom Clyde Williams is shown holding a tattered Nazi flag. He fought throughout France, Germany, and Austria. He was discharged on October 11, 1945. (Courtesy of the *Parkway News*.)

Lonnie Richard Brown (far left), son of Theodore and Stella Brown, is shown on duty in Amdong, Korea, with some unidentified brothers-in-arms. (Courtesy of the *Parkway News*.)

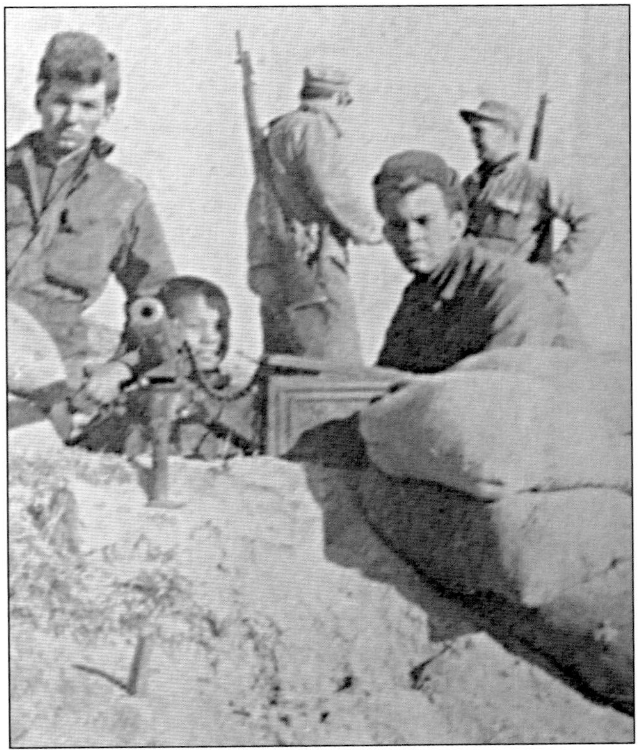

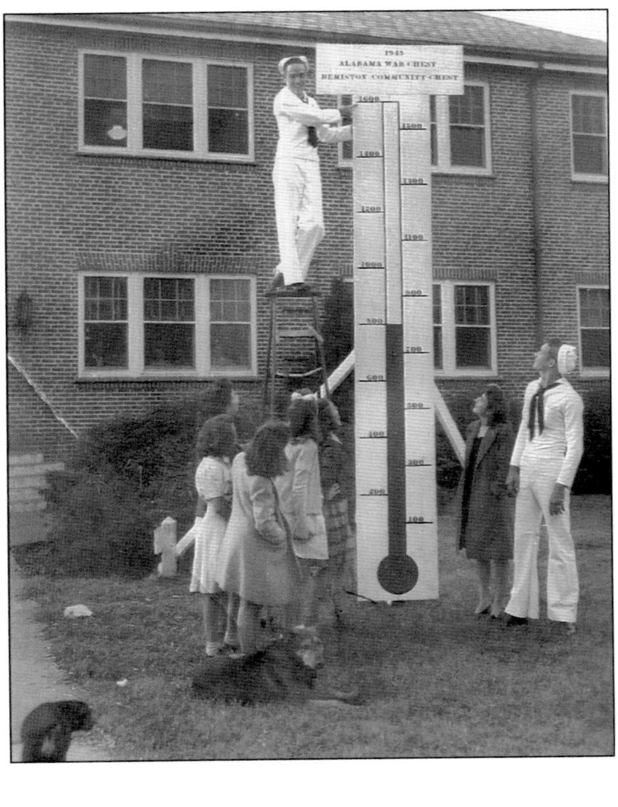

Odell "Butch" Baker is showing the Bemiston Alabama War Chest quotas to Gaston and Wren Owens (right) and some other onlookers while he and Gaston were on leave from the navy. (Courtesy of Bobbye Trammell.)

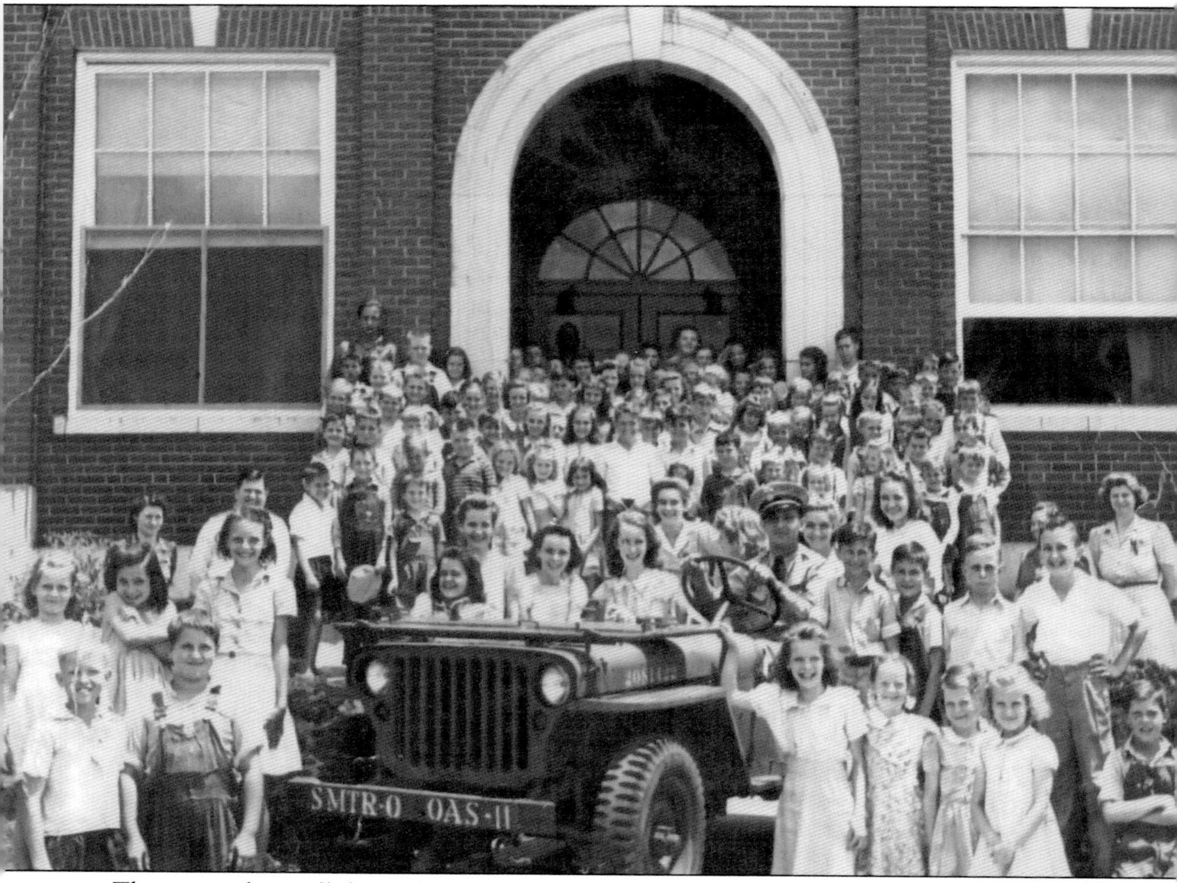

This image shows all the students and teachers of Raymond L. Young Elementary School in May 1943. The students collected scrap metal and newspaper to purchase this Jeep for the war effort. Shown with the Jeep along with Lt. R. E. "Buster" Hogan are, in no particular order, Jean Vickers, Geraldine Colvard, Bobbye Jo Baker, Mary Catherine Parks, Barbara Duncan, June Lewis, Imogene Brown, and Mildred Spencer. (Courtesy of Bobbye Trammell.)

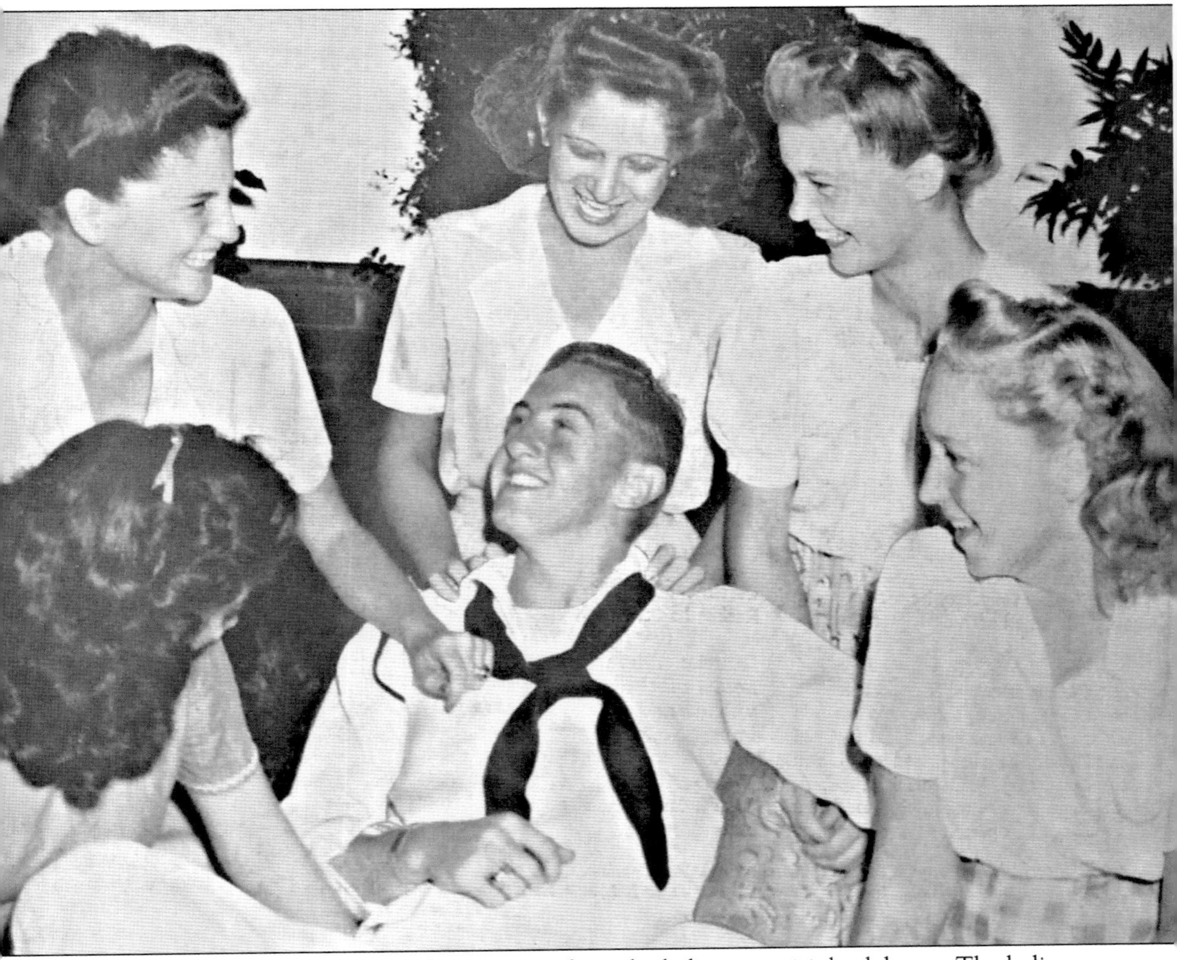

Kendell "Buddy" Drake is enjoying the attention from the ladies on a visit back home. The ladies are, from left to right, Doris Ann Drake, Ruth Brownlow, Willene Senn, Betty Ingram, and Johnnie Cook. (Courtesy of *Bemistory* magazine.)

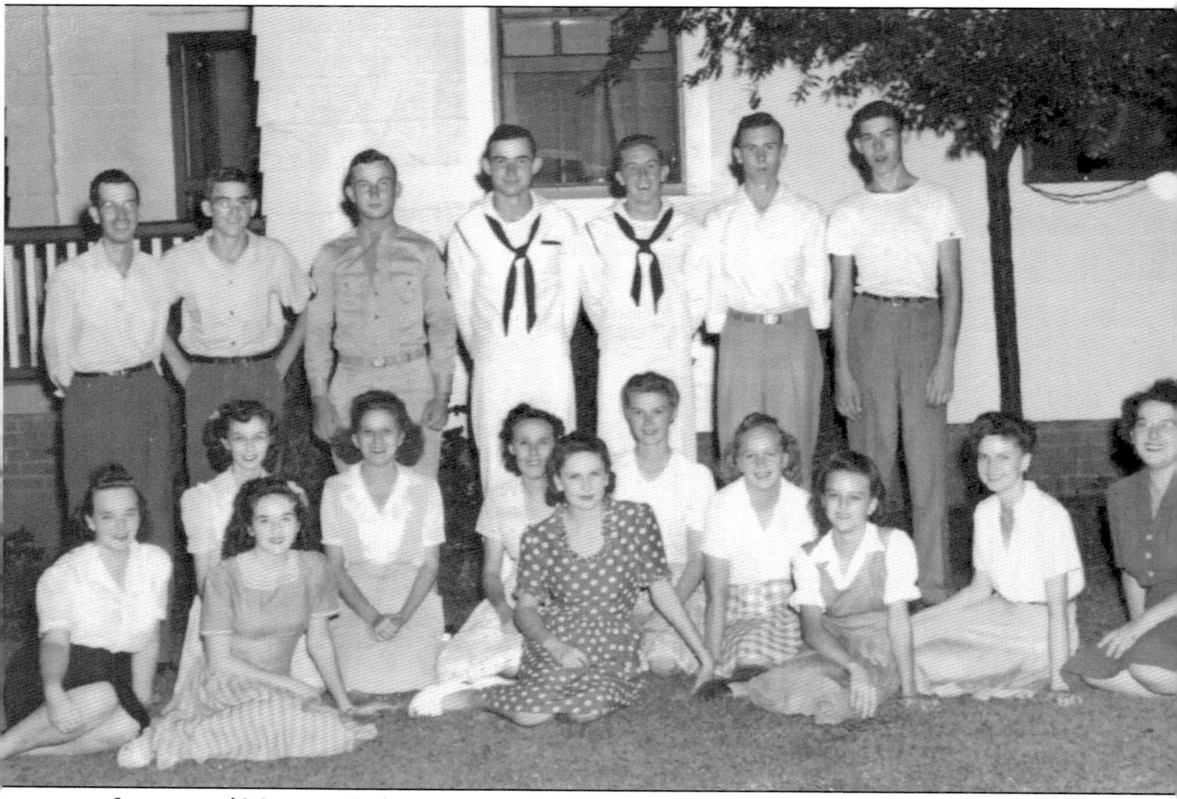

Layton and Maureen Bailey entertained servicemen Harold Ellison, Stewart Ellison, and Buddy Drake (in uniforms) during a leave home. Shown from left to right are (first row) unidentified, Doris Ann Drake, Mary O'Neal, Johnnie Cook, Yvonne Vickers, Ruth Brownlow, and Maureen Bailey; (second row) Nellie Jean Whitaker, Willene Senn, Daphene Baker, and Betty Ingram; (third row) Layton Bailey, Sam Grice, Harold Ellison, Stewart Ellison, Buddy Drake, unidentified, and Tommy Duncan. (Courtesy of J. W. Baker.)

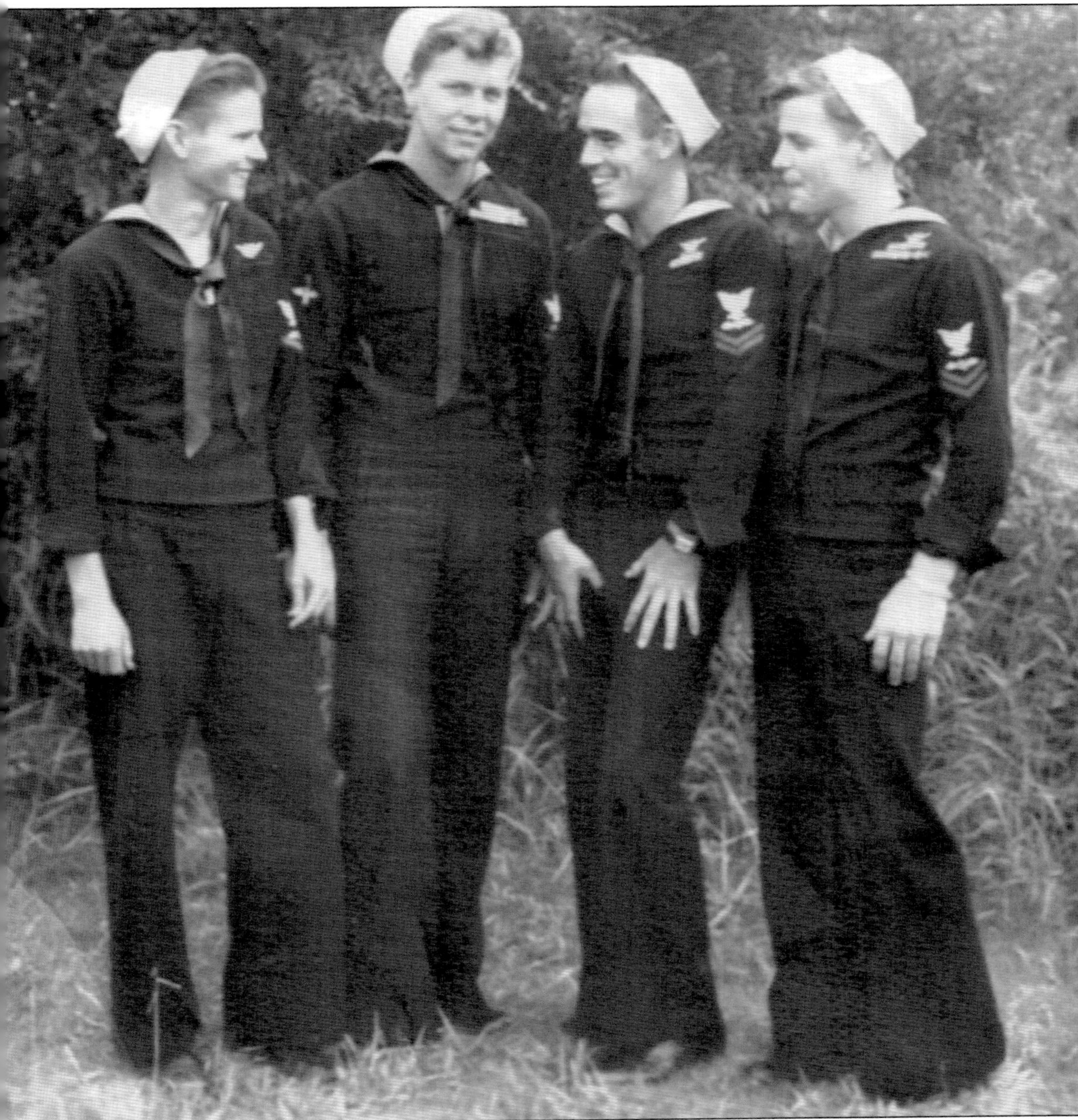

Odell "Butch" Baker brought some navy buddies home to visit during leave. From left to right are Duncan Easterling, George Thorsen, Butch Baker, and Frank Odum. They were stationed in Jacksonville, Florida. (Courtesy of Bobbye Trammell.)

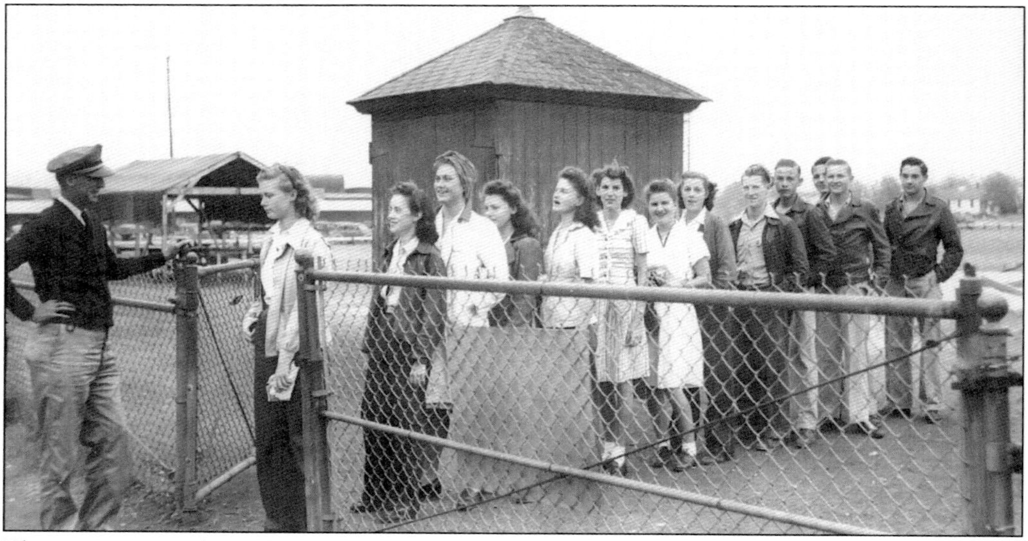

These young people are lined up to go to work in the plant after school. They were allowed to work from 4:00 p.m. until 8:00 p.m., if they were over 16 years old, to help with the war effort. They are security guard Howard Tyson, Betty Ingram, Mary Alice Williams, Ruby King, Rayford Caldwell, Ruth Brownlow, Doris Bone, Margarette Benefield, unidentified, William Patterson Jr., Hubert Williams Jr., Jimmie Brownlow, unidentified, and Buddy Cameron. (Courtesy of Yvonne Grice.)

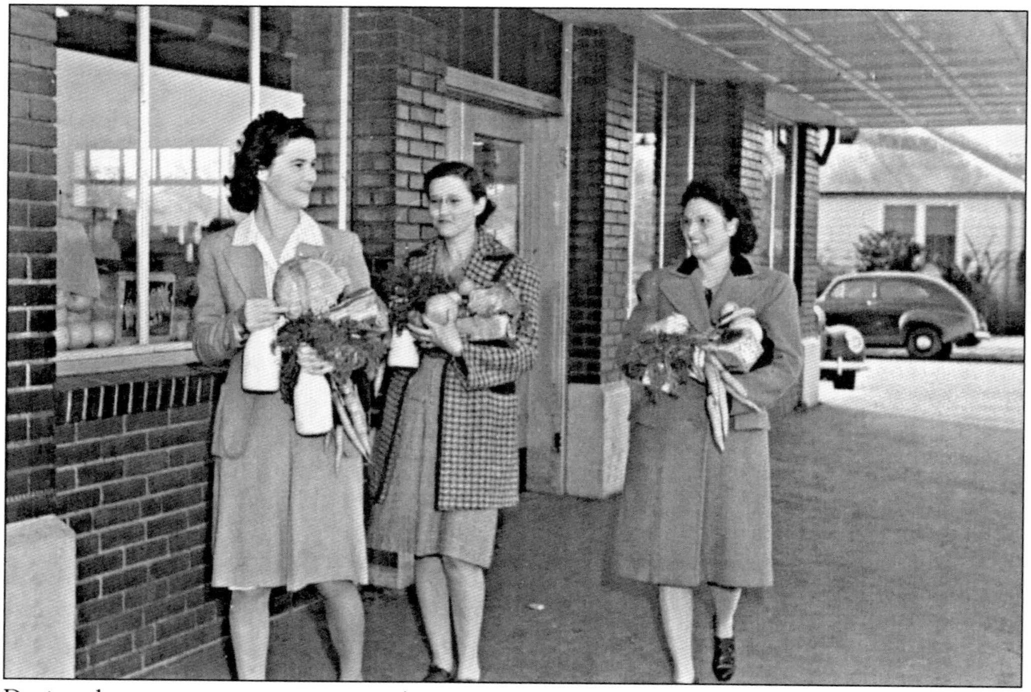

During the war, paper was scarce, and everyone made an effort to preserve it. From left to right, Louise Spencer, Ester Ellison, and Willie Brownlow are carrying their wares from the grocery store in their hands to help. (Courtesy of Mildred Brownlow.)

Janice (Mrs. Russell A.) Wells, wife of the general manager of the Bemis Brothers Bag Company, did her part during the war. She was chairman of the volunteer services. As chairman, she worked to maintain community organizations and agencies' relationships, and she acted as coordinator for all services and supplies. (Courtesy of the *Parkway News*.)

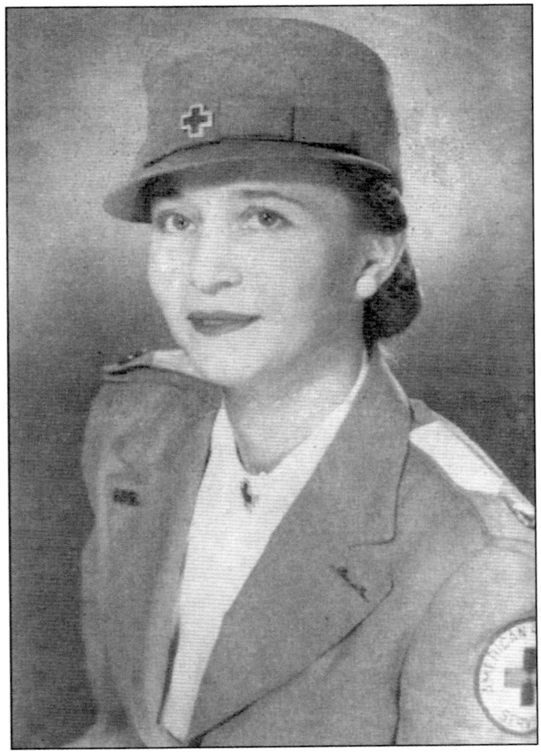

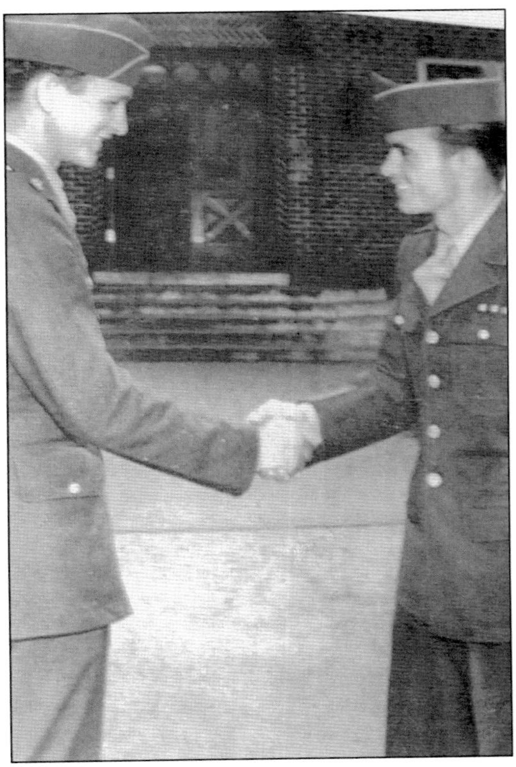

Bram O. Horne (right) and Cpl. James G. Vickers were among the first men to return home. They shake hands as they make plans to shed their uniforms and return to work in the plant. (Courtesy of the *Parkway News*.)

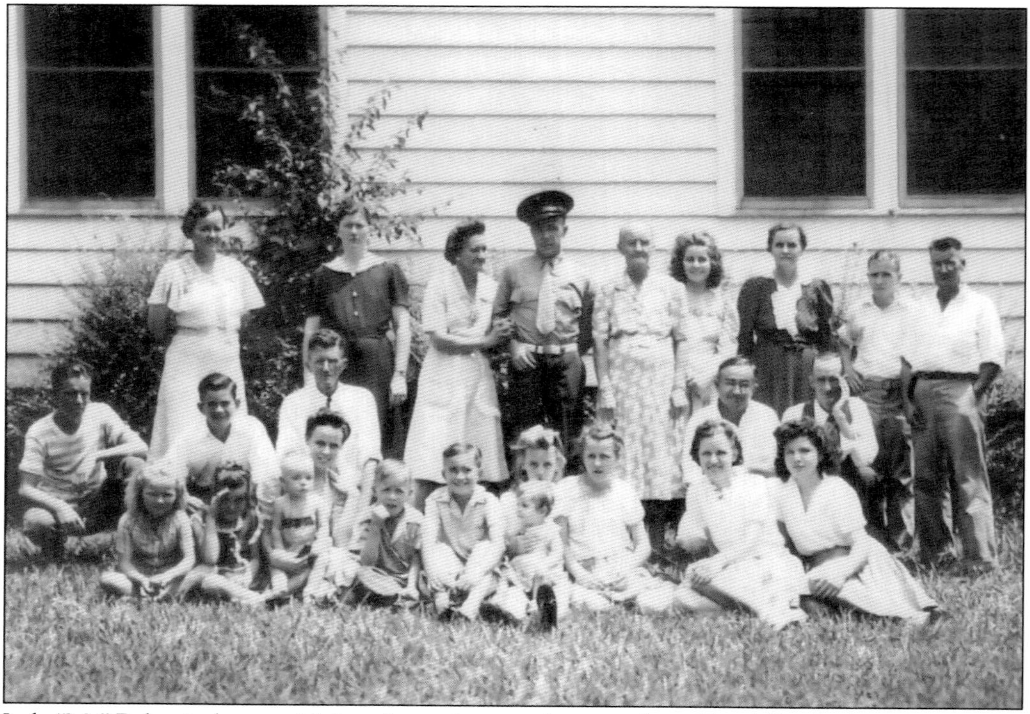

Lula "Ma" Baker is shown with her clan welcoming her grandson Clay Albright (standing, fourth from left) home after being wounded. He is shown with his mother, June Albright (to his left), and "Ma" (to his right). The rest are brothers, sisters, and other relatives. Ma Baker worked in the sewing department at the Bemis Brothers Bag Company. (Courtesy of J. W. Baker.)

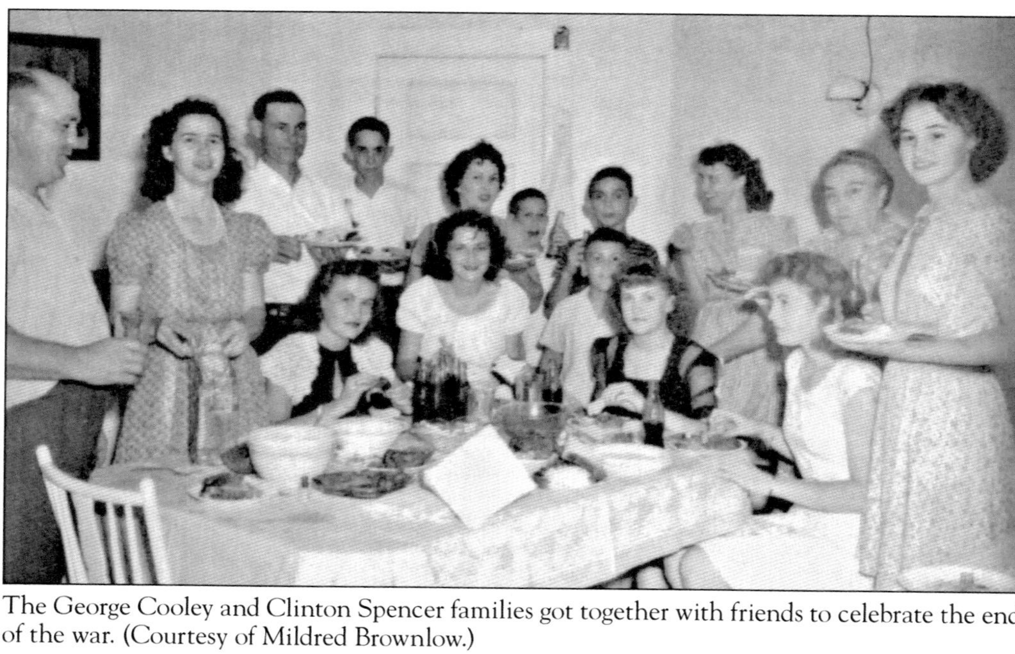

The George Cooley and Clinton Spencer families got together with friends to celebrate the end of the war. (Courtesy of Mildred Brownlow.)

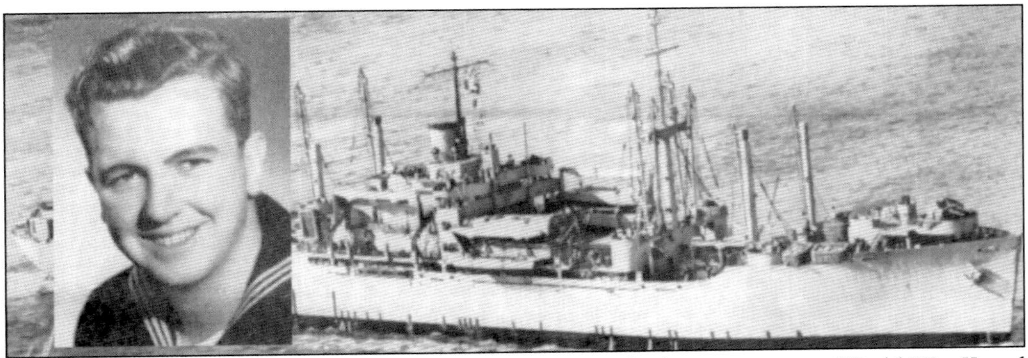

William F. William was stationed on the USS *Talladega*, which saw service in World War II and was recommissioned in 1951. He was the son of T. H. and Estelle Williams of Bemiston. His grandmother was Lula "Ma" Baker.

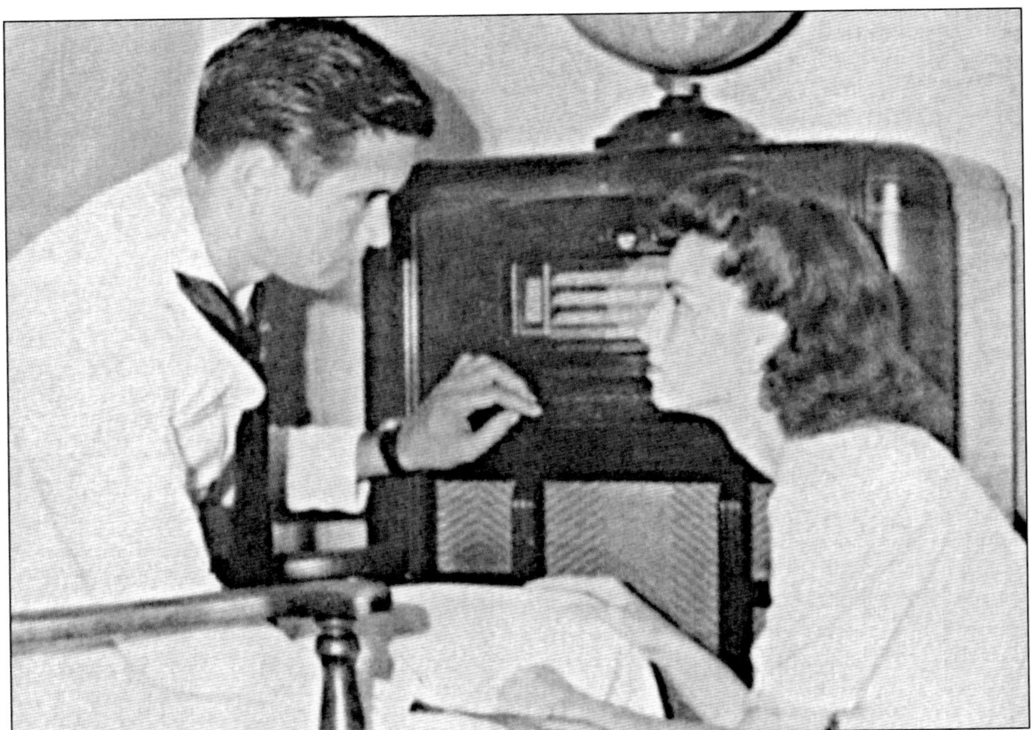

Raymond Lakey and his wife, Inez, listened to the news of the Normandy invasion on a radio at home in Bemiston. The day was June 6, 1944, and it was the first time Raymond had been on leave for 12 months.

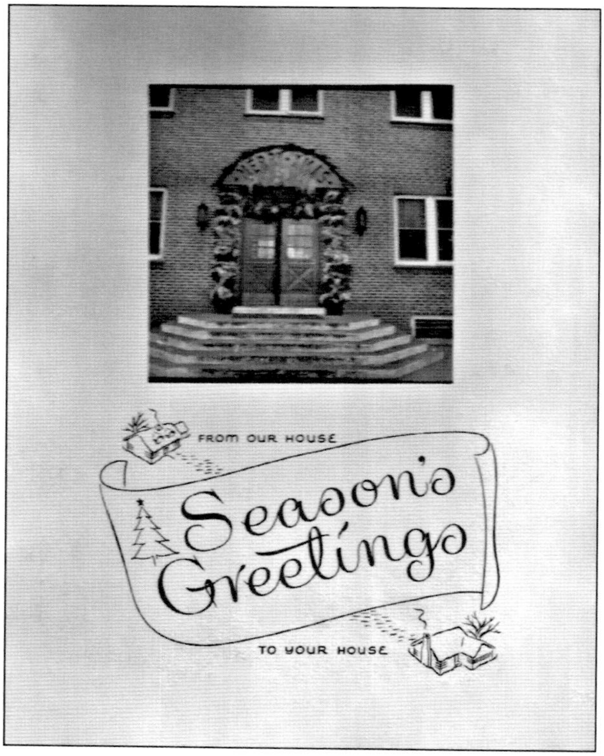

This is a Christmas card received on Christmas 1945. This may have been the only time the company sent a Christmas card to the residents of Bemiston. It could have possibly been to celebrate the end of World War II. (Courtesy of J. W. Baker.)

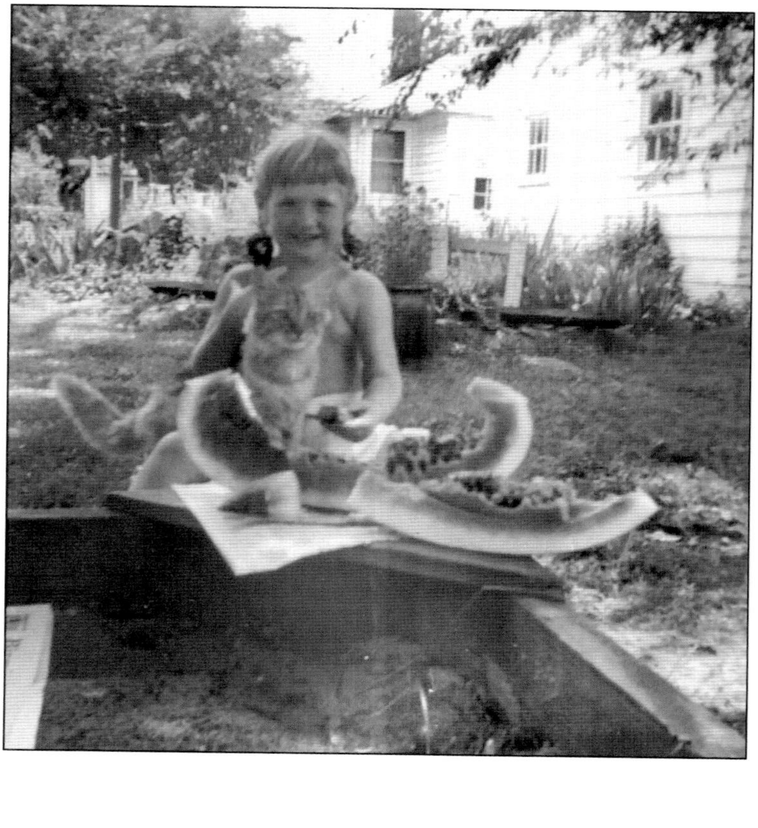

Kathy Brownlow is shown having a good time on a hot afternoon, enjoying a slice of watermelon and entertaining her cat. Brownlow is the daughter of Mildred Brownlow. (Courtesy of Mildred Brownlow.)

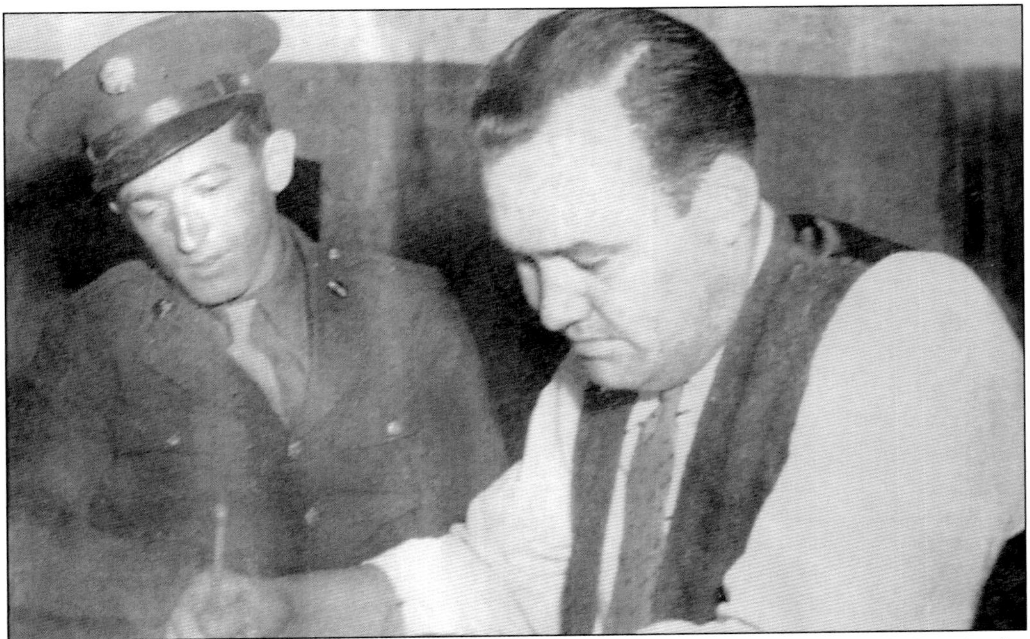

Valient Key is shown just after returning home after the war, checking with E. C. Lamb, the credit union supervisor, at Bemiston Credit Union on the available savings accounts. (Courtesy of *Bemistory* magazine.)

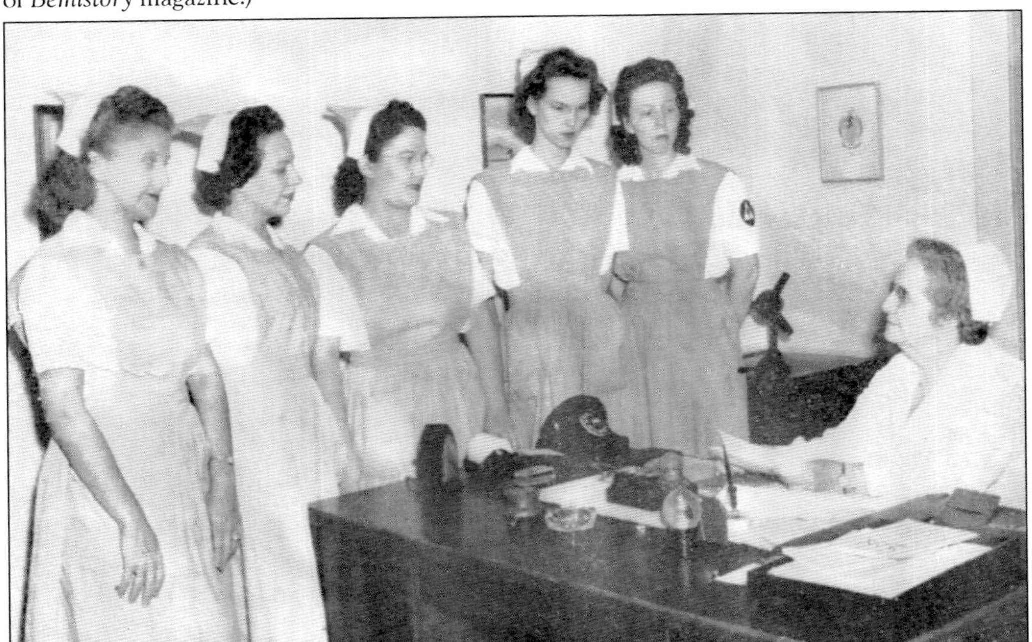

These five nurse's aides have given more than 400 combined hours of active duty at Citizens Hospital. Shown from left to right are Willene Senn with 135 hours, Sara Bruner with 65 hours, Maureen Bailey with 107 hours, Frances Smithwick with 47 hours, and Louise Patterson with 47 hours. Shown also is Claudia Sims (seated), the superintendent at Citizens Hospital. (Courtesy of Willene Hughston.)

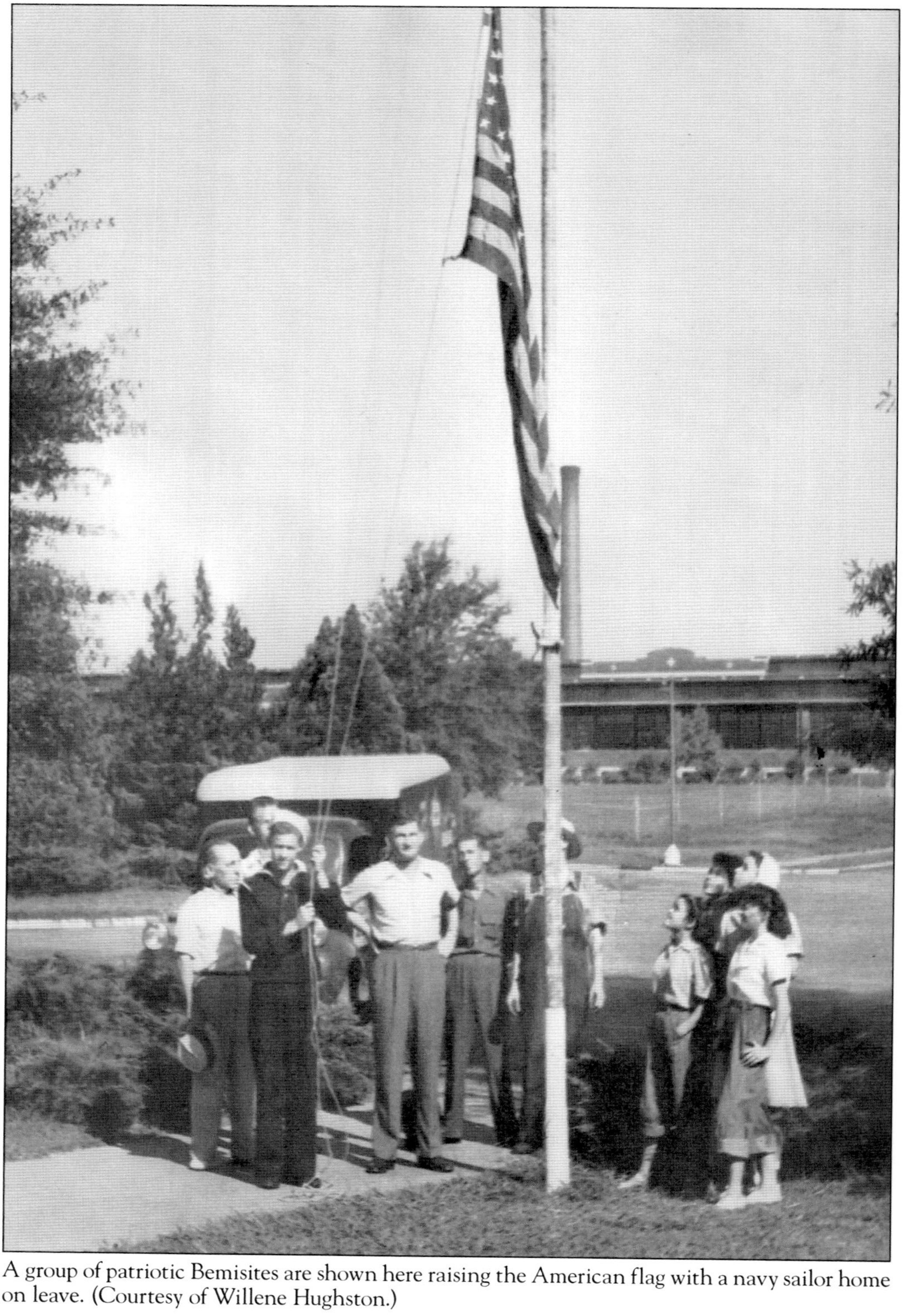

A group of patriotic Bemisites are shown here raising the American flag with a navy sailor home on leave. (Courtesy of Willene Hughston.)

Five

Landmarks

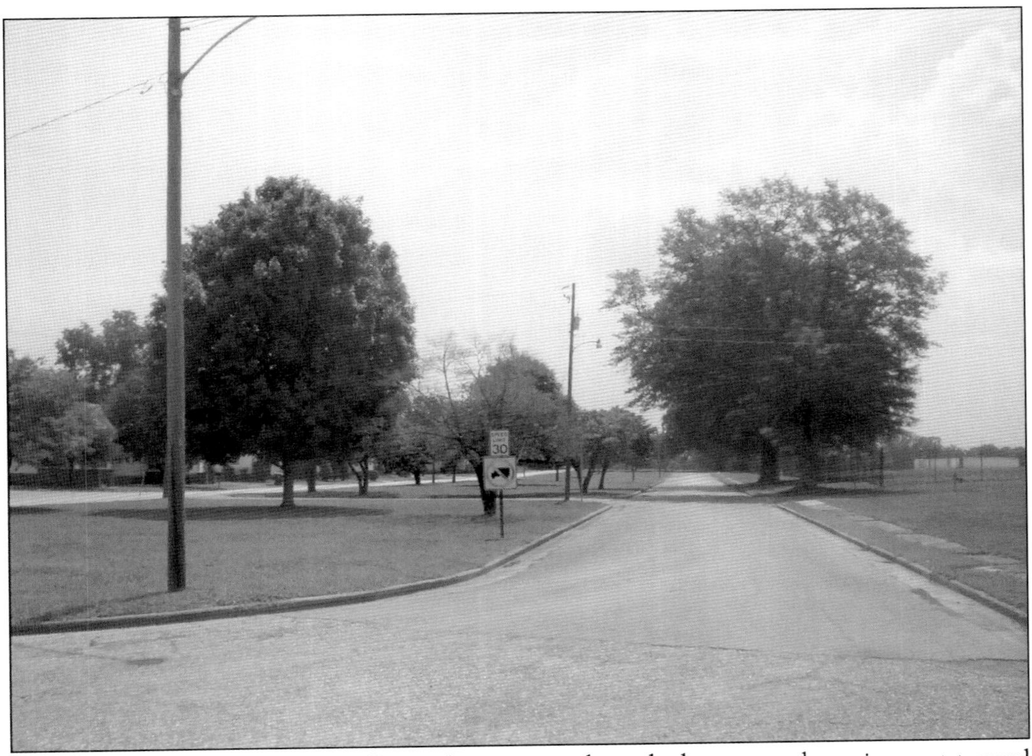

When entering the Bemiston Village, after coming through the gate and turning east toward the village, there is beautiful Parkway Drive, which is a double drive through the village from east to west. It goes the length of the entire village and exits to Highway 21 South on the eastern entrance. (Courtesy of Todd Wilson.)

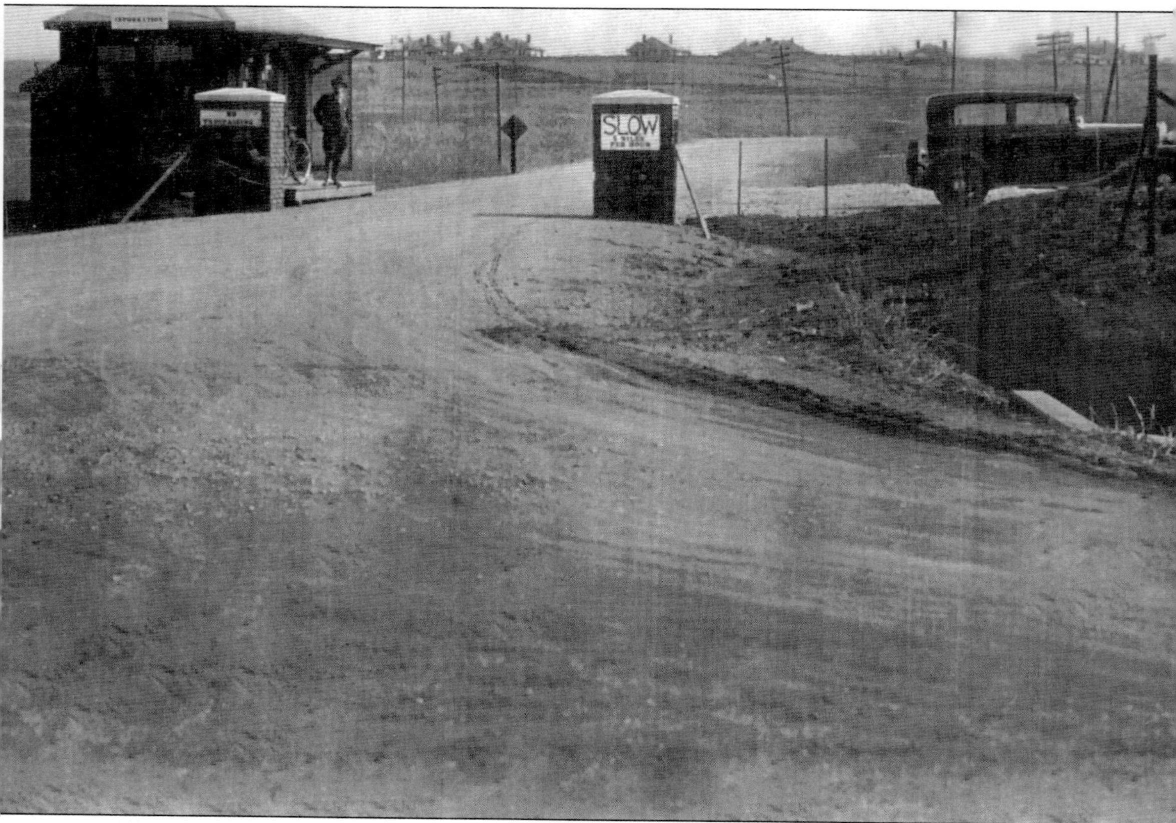

This was a "gated" community. When the plant and village were being built, security was very important in 1929–1930 because of the Great Depression, and there were so many people out of work. For this reason, a gate was established at the only entrance to the village at that time. Euell Lakey is shown at the guardhouse. The brick pillars on either side of the entrance are still standing. The guardhouse is gone. (Courtesy of J. W. Baker.)

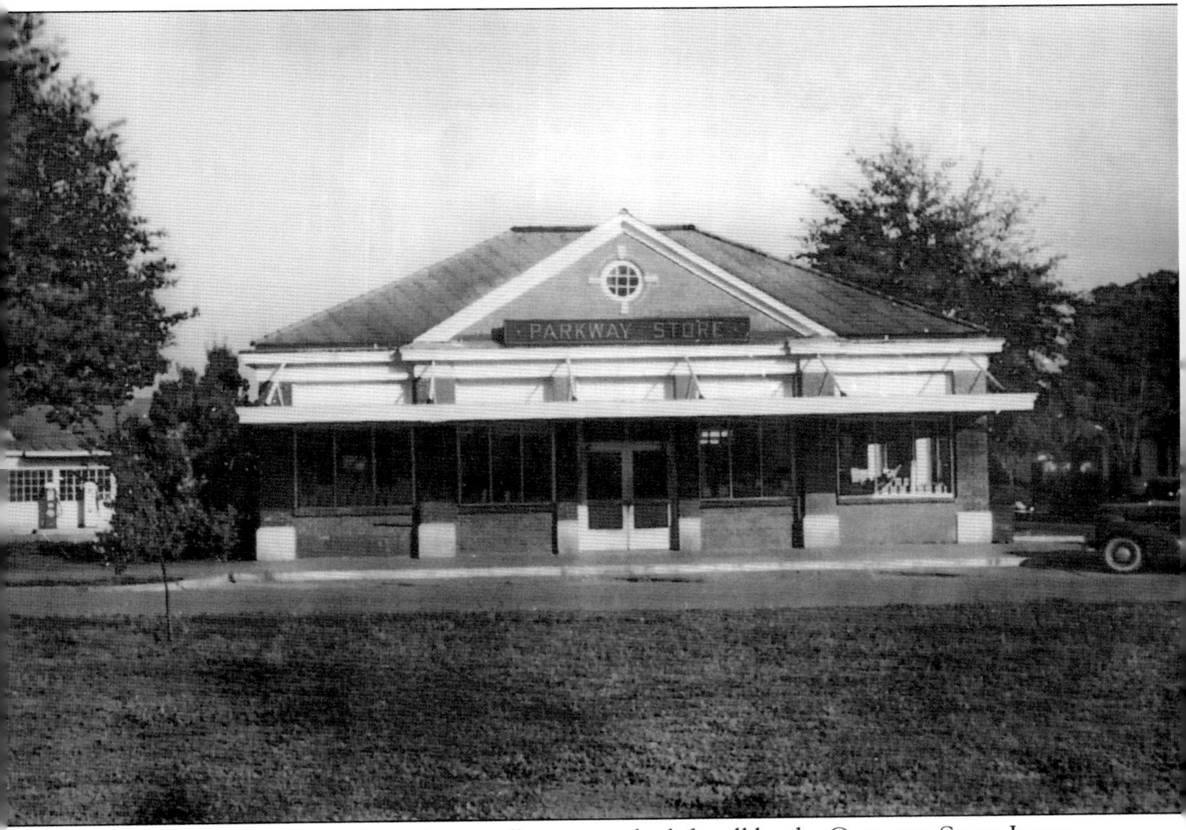

If one goes about five blocks from the guardhouse, on the left will be the Company Store. It was located in the center of family housing, a block from the Community Building and the main office at the plant. No one was ever denied food from this store. If an employee did not have money, they could either charge it or use a coupon (called a scrip book). The store also housed a barbershop, where all the men gathered for their storytelling. It was later moved into the Community Building, along with the beauty salon. (Courtesy of J. W. Baker.)

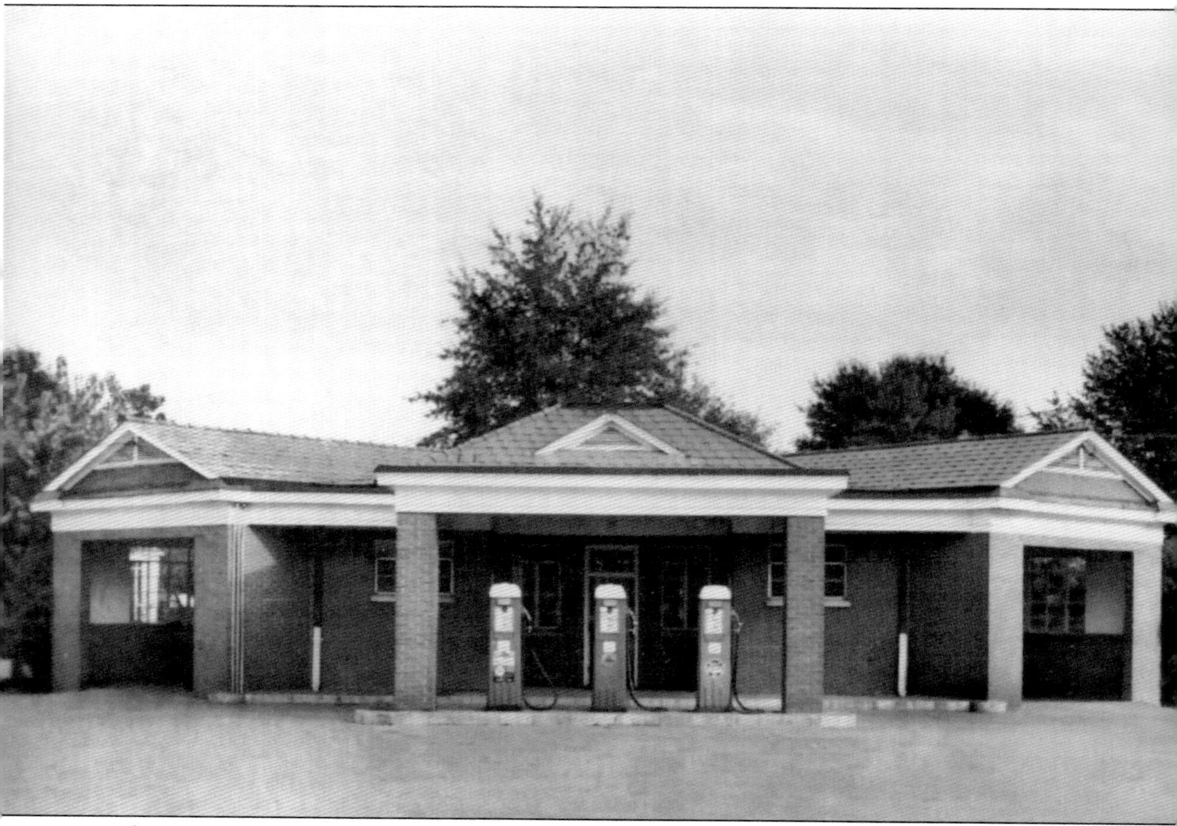

The service station and garage were directly behind the Company Store. Although there were not many automobiles in the village, it was always available to the community. It did not matter if it was airing up a bicycle tire or fixing a skate that had come apart. There were two mechanics on duty, and they also sold parts and tires. (Courtesy of J. W. Baker.)

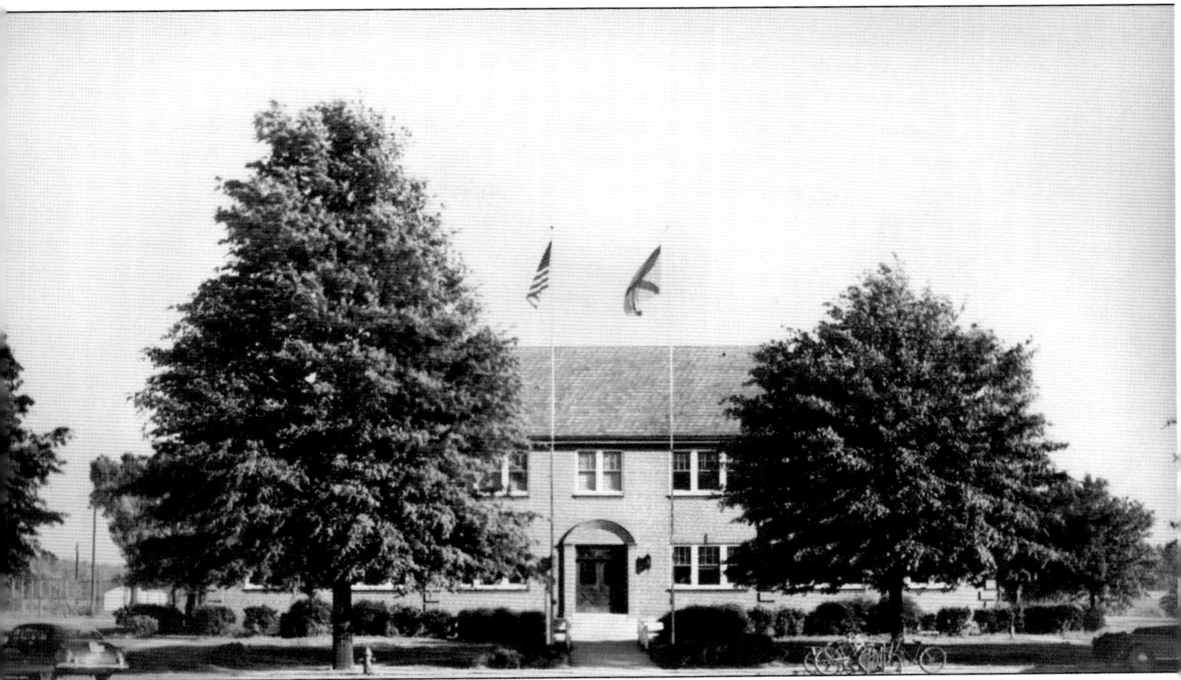

The Community Building is a block from the store and faces the main office building. The Community Building was renamed the John L. Moore Recreation Center in memory of the longtime recreational director and was instrumental in molding many young lives. It was the hub of the community and was full of old and young people. There was always someone to talk to or to play a game of cards or checkers. It finally came to be known as the "glory hole." It played host to all the clubs and Scout troops. It had a beauty shop, a barbershop, a library, a gym, a game room, a kitchen, a ladies lounge, a sewing room, and a snack bar in the auditorium, where movies and square dances were held. (Courtesy of Todd Wilson.)

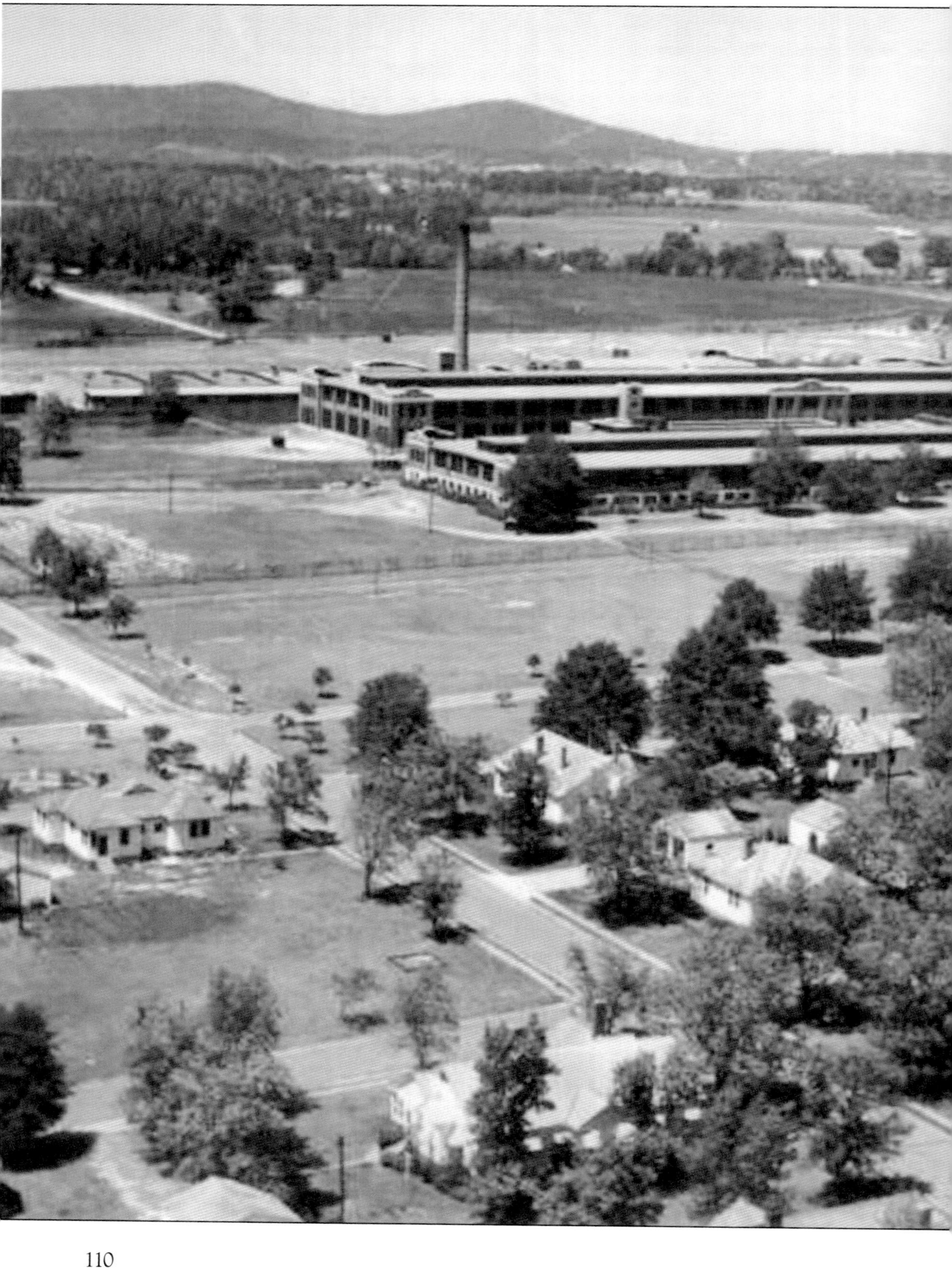

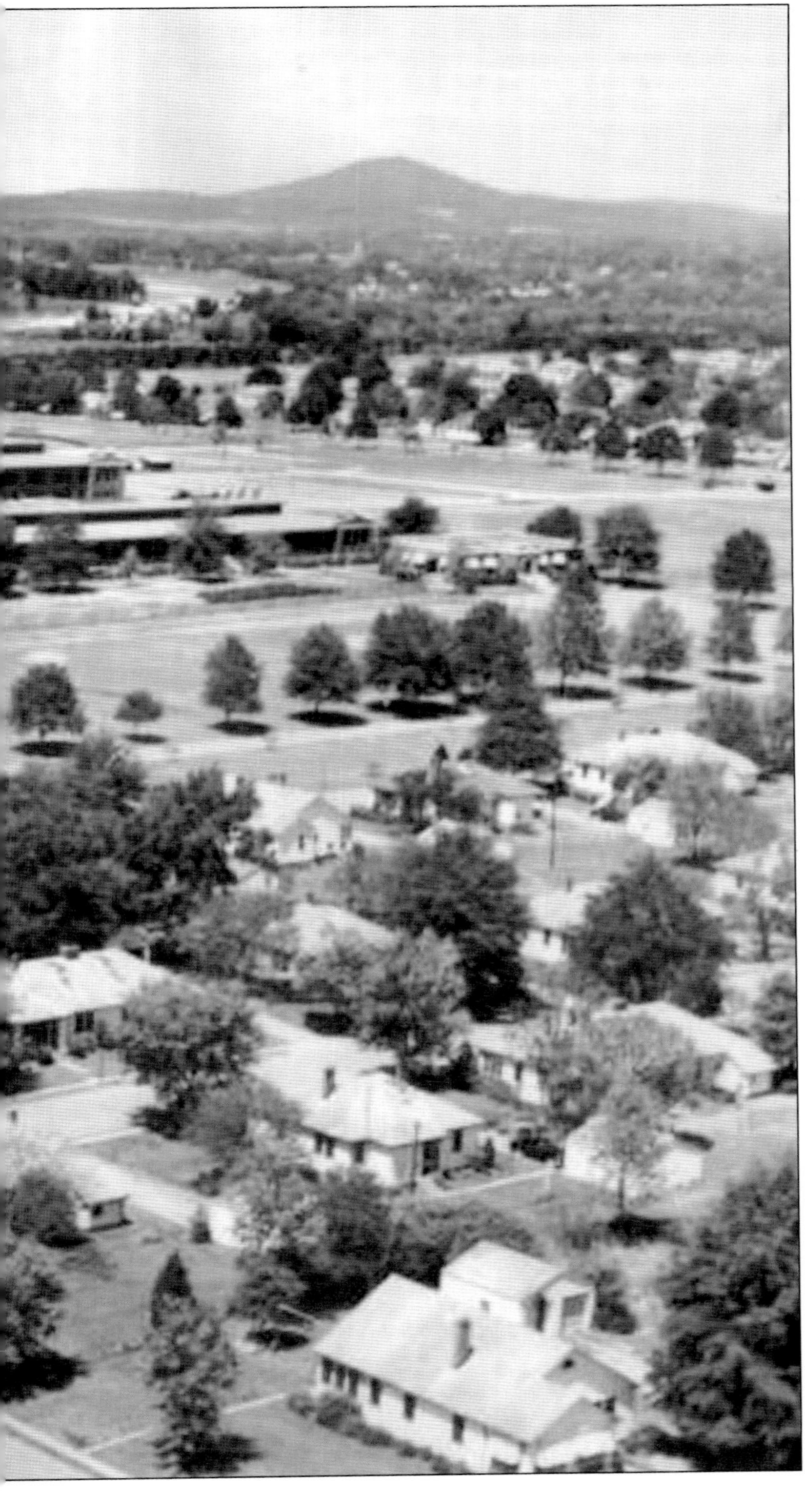

This is an aerial view of the plant and village. This shows a complete layout of the working and living areas of Bemiston. The plant was located within walking distance of the village to make it more convenient for the workers. It was arranged in a horseshoe shape, which gave the impression that the plant was the stage and the village the audience. (Courtesy of J. W. Baker.)

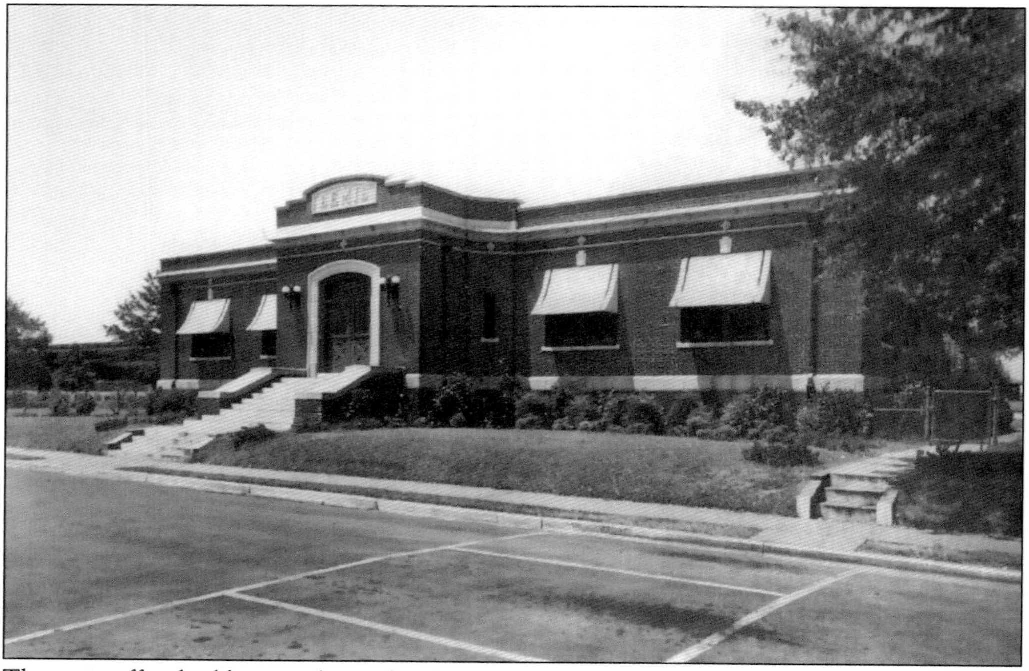

The main office building was located in front of the plant. This office held all records and offices for the executives of the company. (Courtesy of J. W. Baker.)

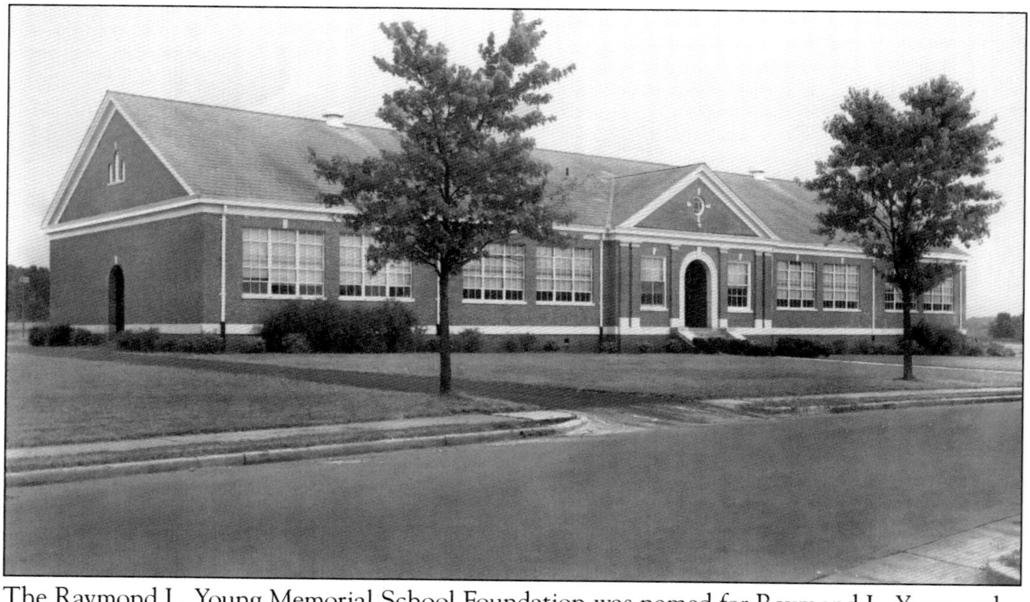

The Raymond L. Young Memorial School Foundation was named for Raymond L. Young, who was to be the first superintendent of the Bemiston village and plant. Unfortunately, Young died on the train on the way from St. Louis, Missouri, and never arrived in Bemiston. Russell A. Wells, who was to be Young's general manager, was on the train also and was appointed to fill the position. Raymond L. Young's and Russell A. Wells's portraits still hang in the school. It goes by the name R. L. Young Elementary School now. (Courtesy of J. W. Baker.)

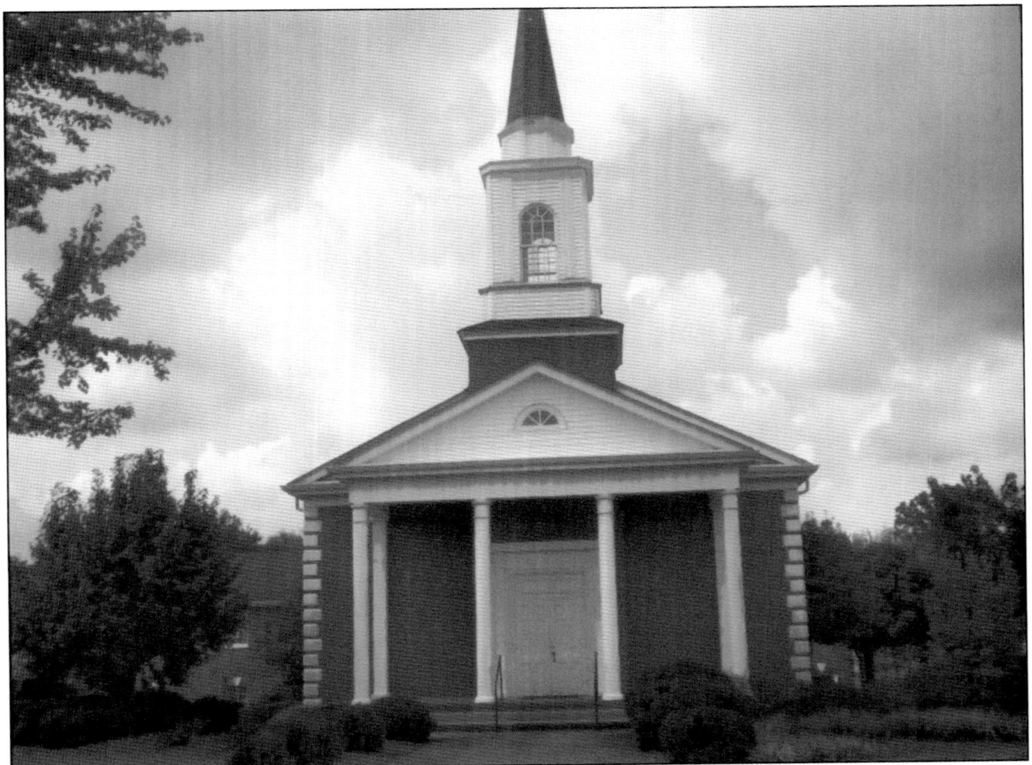

The Bemiston Baptist Church was on the west side of the school. It was built in 1951. Before it was constructed, the church services were held in the Community Building and later in a residential house. The Bemis Brothers Bag Company donated the property on which to build the church and matched any funds raised by the congregation for construction. (Courtesy of Todd Wilson.)

The Bemiston United Methodist Church is one block northeast of the school. It was built in 1953. Previously, services were held in the school building and later in a residential house. The Bemis Brothers Bag Company also deeded the building site to the church. (Courtesy of Todd Wilson.)

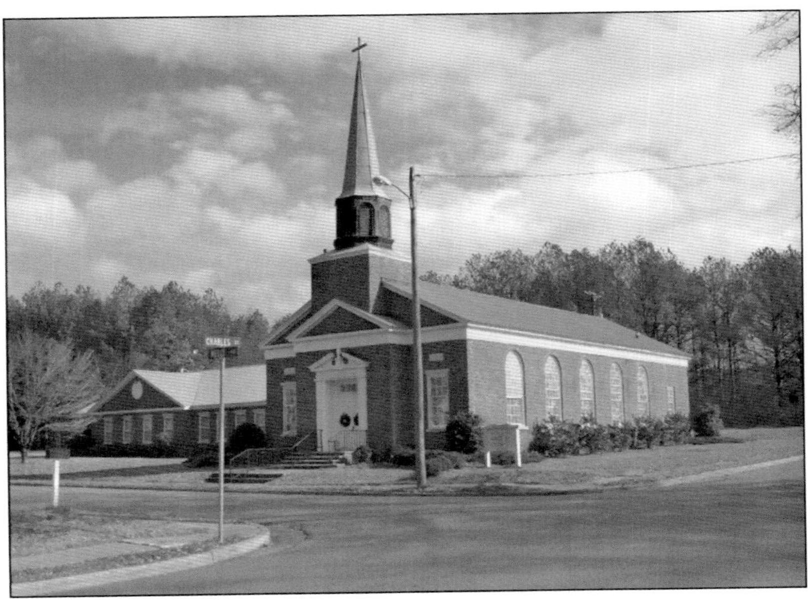

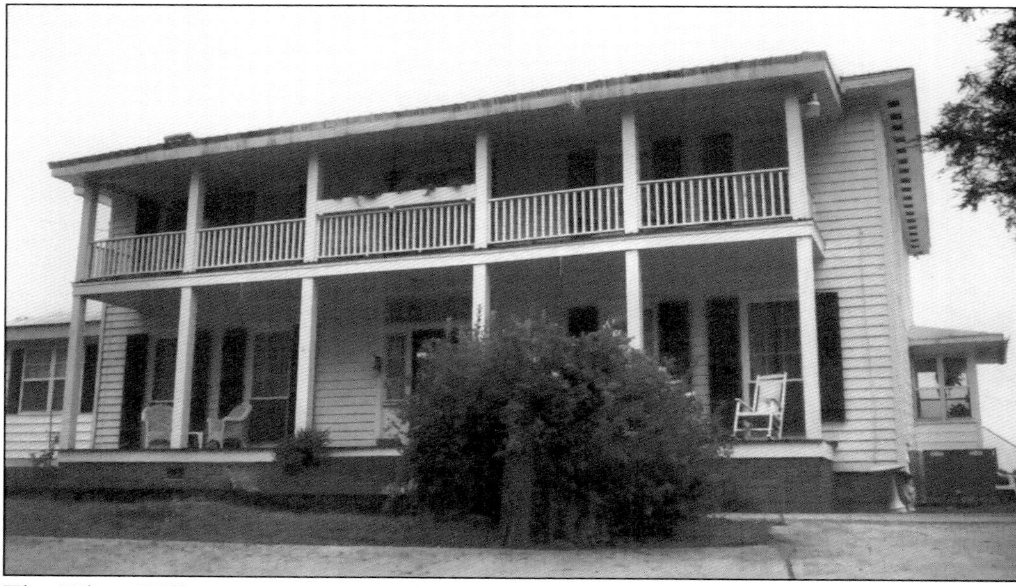

The White-Williams House was built by Alexander White, congressman of the Talladega District in 1832. He later went to Texas to make his home. In 1928, the Bemis Brothers Bag Company bought the property and used it as a farmhouse for laborers. It was later renovated for the plant engineer, Norman Wood. Terry and Peggy King lived in it until it was purchased by Howard and Hazel Williams in 1977, and it is still occupied by the Williams family. (Courtesy of Howard Williams.)

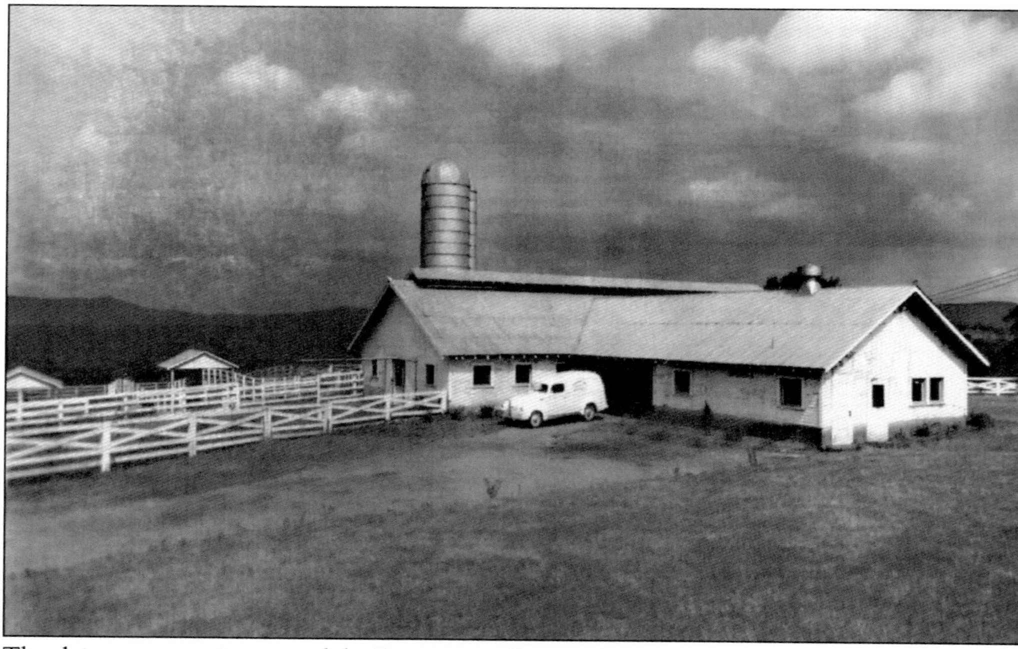

The dairy was a major part of the Bemiston village. It had dairy cows and employees who ran the dairy and delivered its products to the village residents regularly at a nominal cost. It was located approximately one-half mile from the village. There are three dwellings for the manager and employees of the dairy. (Courtesy of Todd Wilson.)

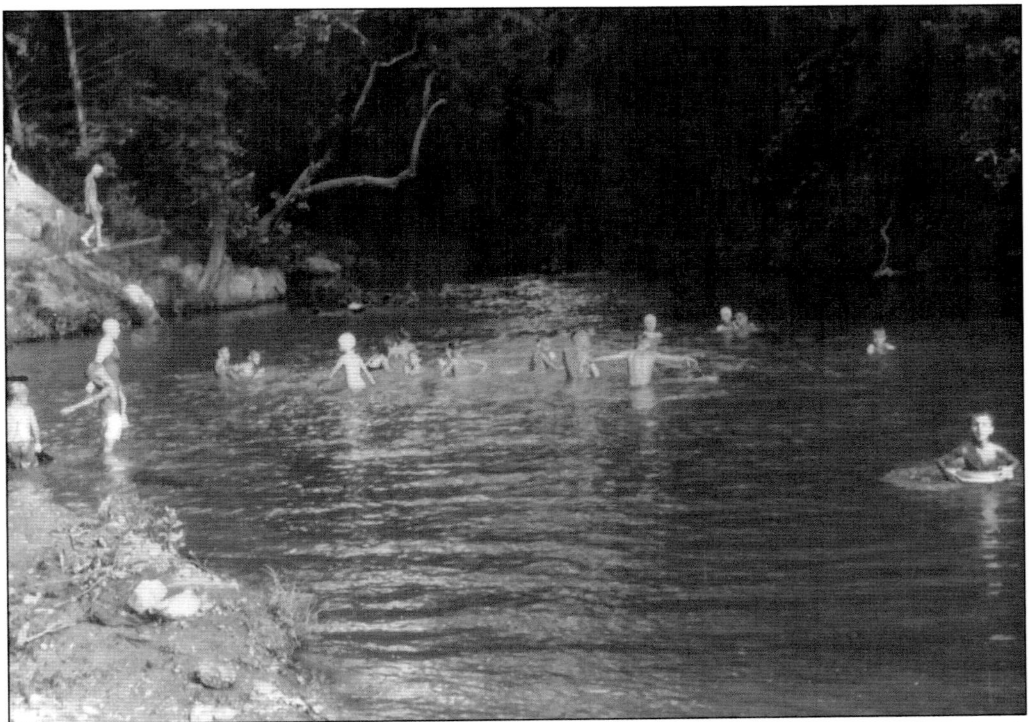

The "ole" swimming hole was the answer to the swimming pool but much better. Talladega Creek bordered the east side of the village, and a beach was cleaned out and the creek made safe for the public. There was a swing and a diving board, and anytime the schools were out, an adult was always there for safety purposes. (Courtesy of Gail Shaw.)

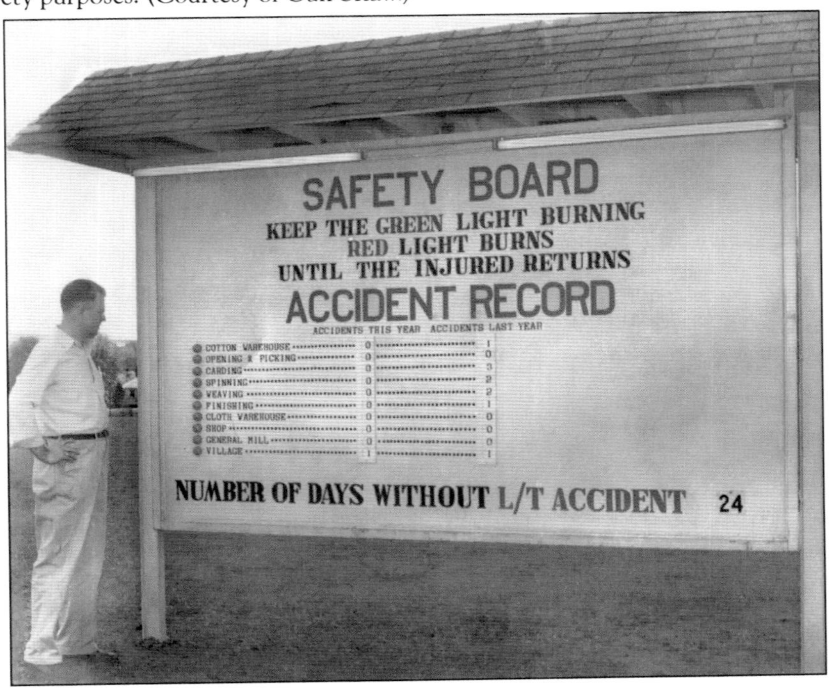

This image shows the safety board that kept a record of any accidents occurring in the plant by department. Malcolm Jones is checking it out. A red light burned until an accident victim returned to work. It was located just inside the gate to the plant so everyone would be aware. (Courtesy of J. W. Baker.)

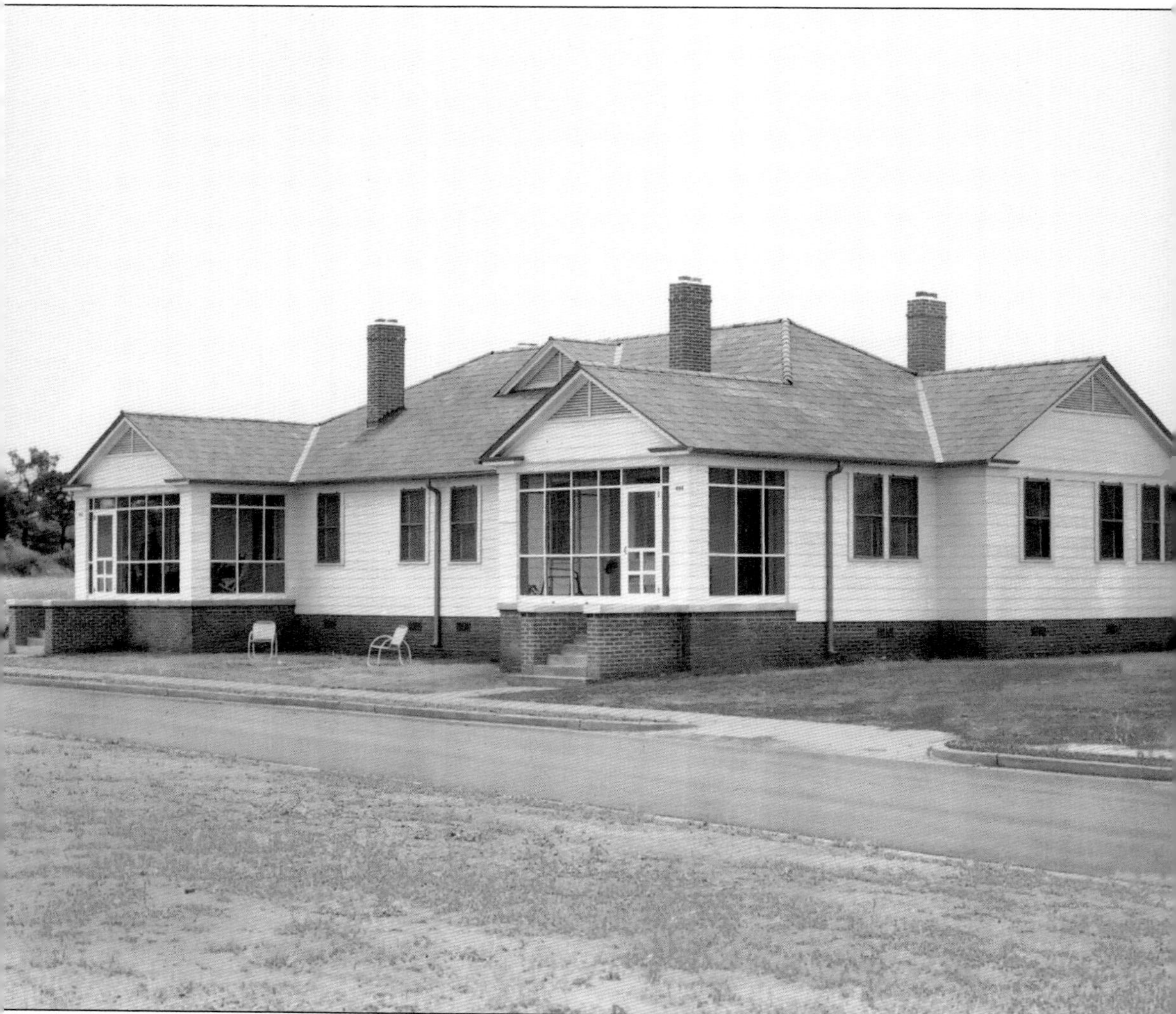

Most of the houses the Bemis Brothers Bag Company built were duplexes. This house was known as a "double four," meaning that it was basically two apartments of four main rooms each. The company rented these to the employees for a nominal rent, which was taken out of their pay each week. There was also a double garage for each house, even though most employees at the time did not have cars. (Courtesy of J. W. Baker.)

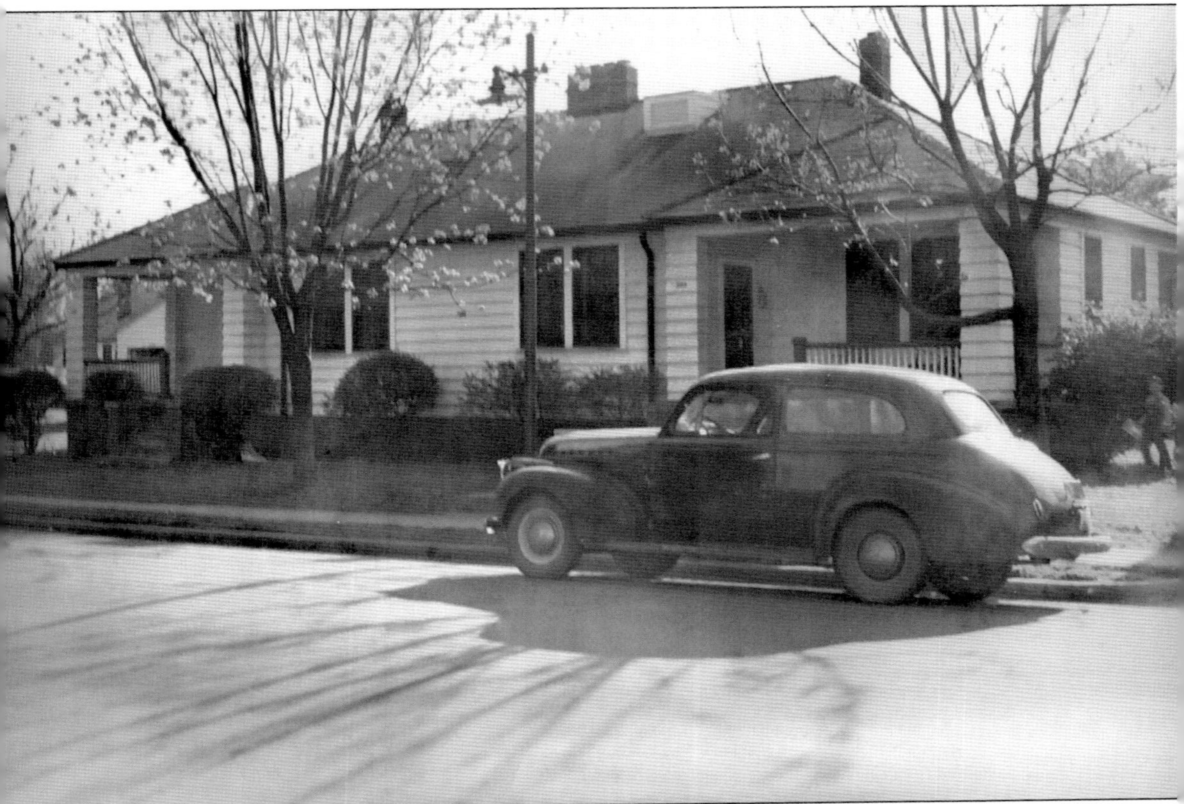

This house was known as a "double three." Employees were assigned houses based on family size and availability. All had two private entrances and a concrete front porch, back porch, and double garage, one for each resident. (Courtesy of J. W. Baker.)

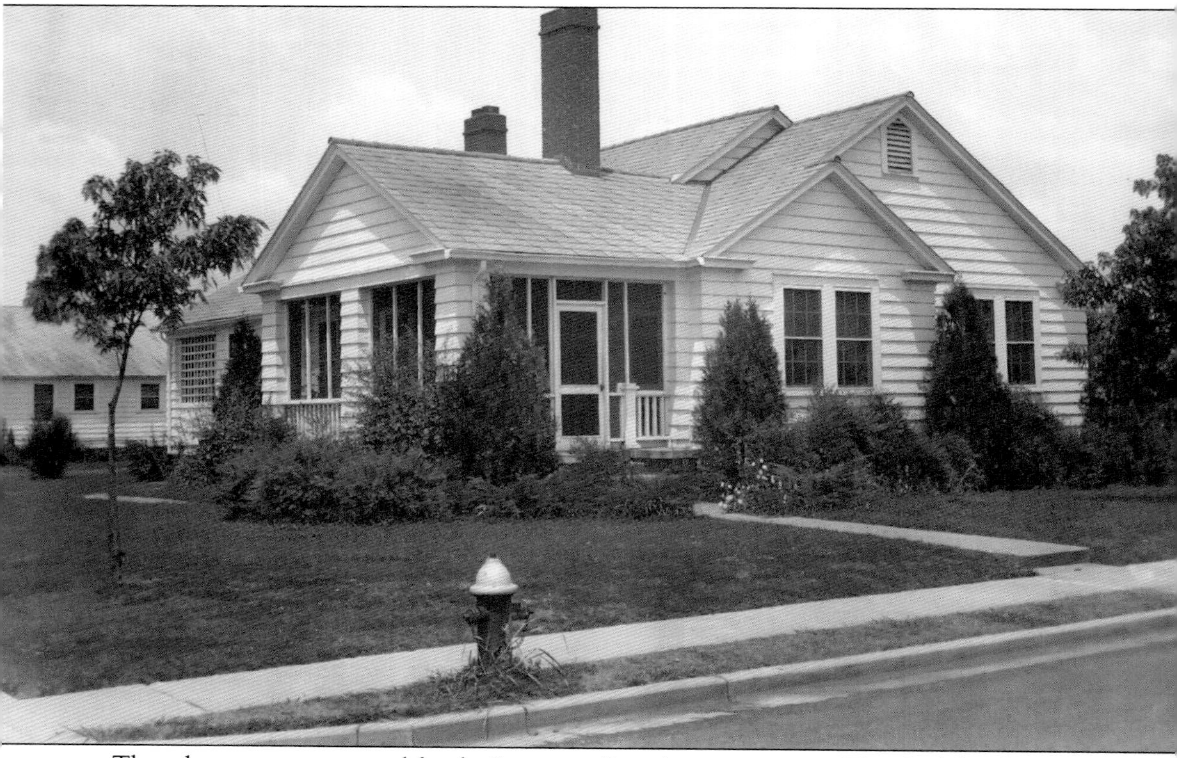

These houses were reserved for the "overseers," or plant supervisors. They had four bedrooms, a living room, a dining room, a den, and a kitchen, along with two baths. The front porch was also screened, and the house included an attic fan. There was also a double garage and a basement. (Courtesy of J. W. Baker.)

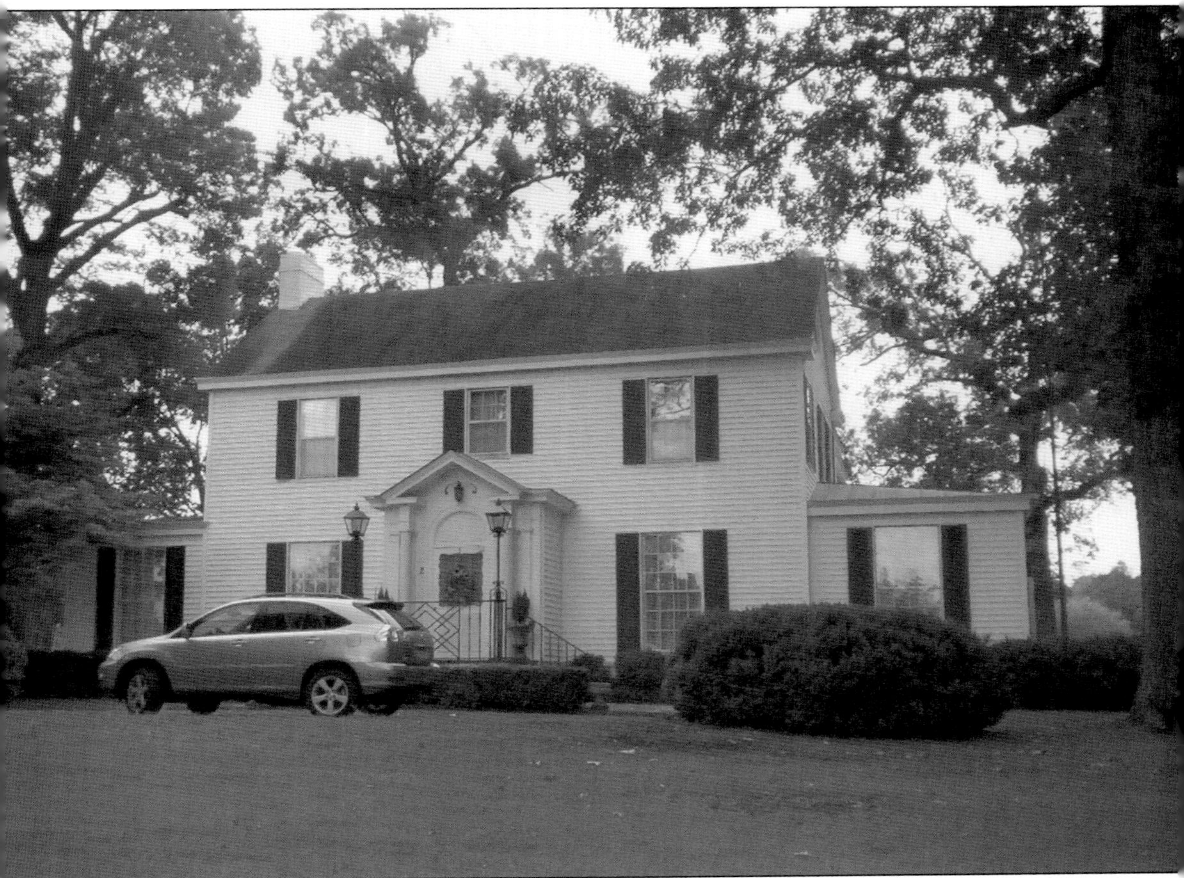

Neal and Linda Rodgers reside in this house. Originally, it was built for the general manager of Bemiston, and it was used for a company house until the homes were sold in the 1980s. It was purchased by the Rodgers family. Linda grew up in Bemiston. (Courtesy of Todd Wilson.)

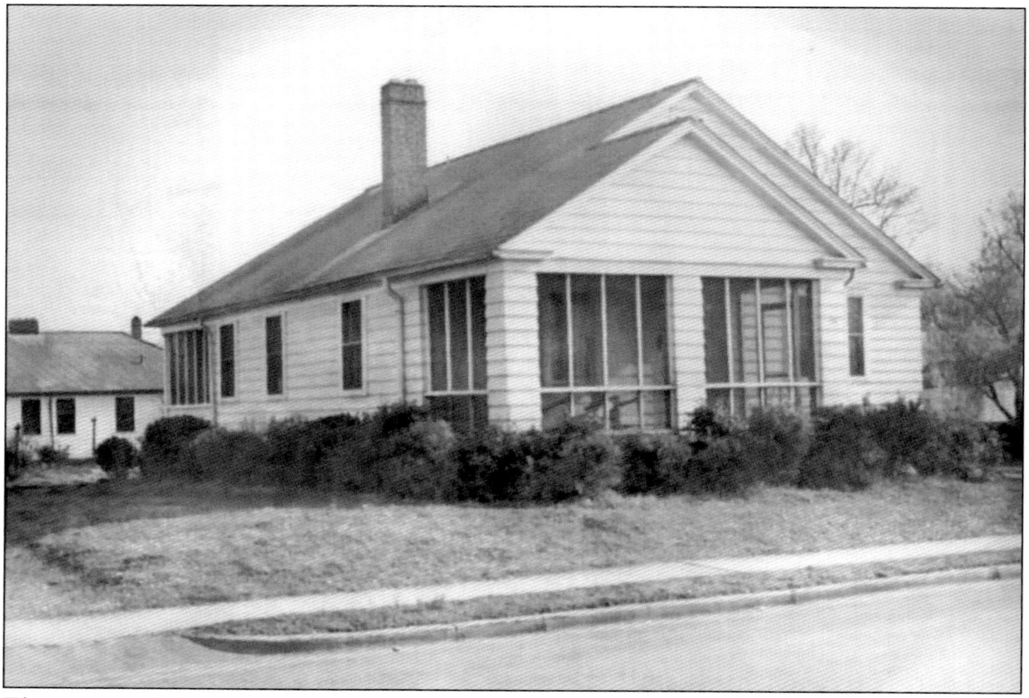

This is one of the larger, single-family houses known as a "single five." It consisted of three bedrooms, a living room, and a kitchen. It also had one bathroom, front and back porches, and a garage. (Courtesy of J. W. Baker.)

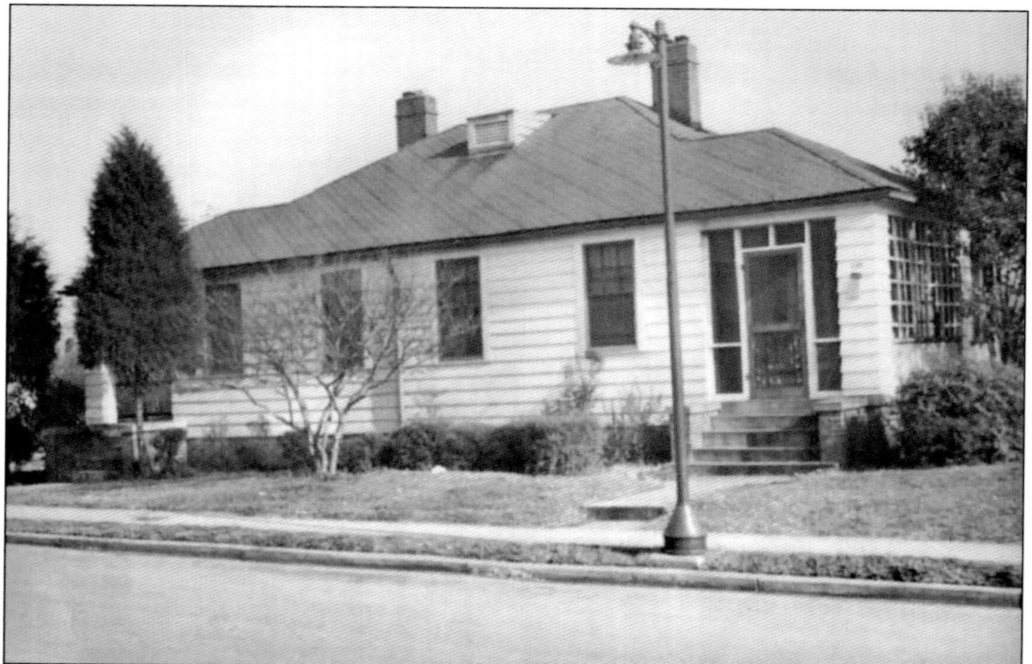

This was another style of duplex known as a "double two." These houses had a bedroom and a kitchen, and were mostly assigned to single employees or newlyweds. (Courtesy of J. W. Baker.)

Six

Time Marches On

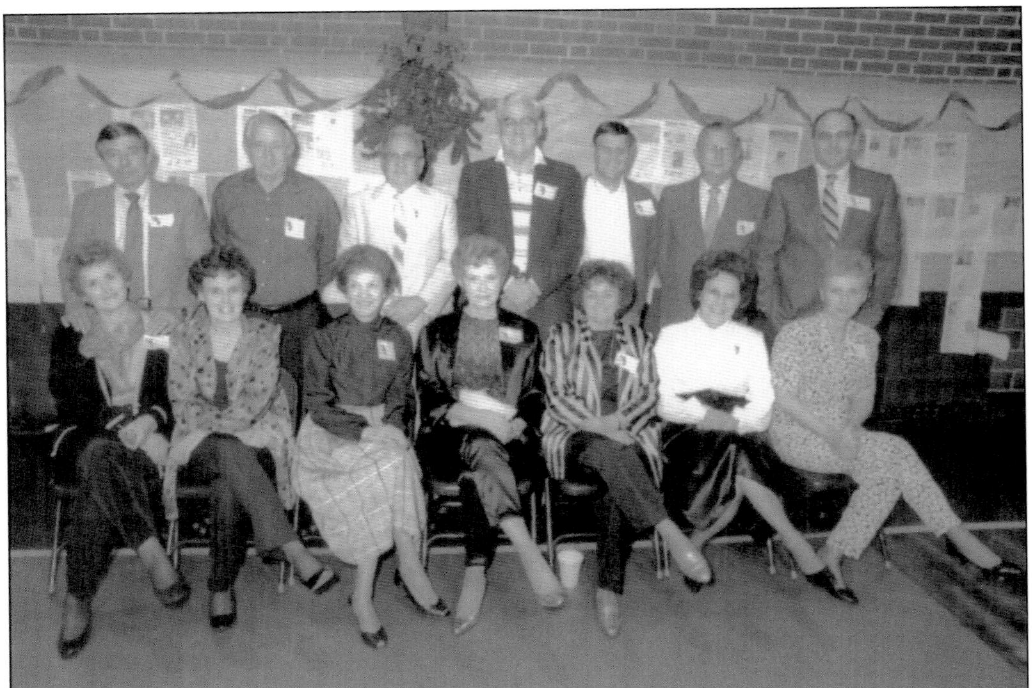

The people who grew up together stayed in touch. After their children grew up, one group got together to plan a Bemiston reunion. Shown is a photograph of the first group to plan a reunion, and ever since, this has been a regular affair. The first reunion was in December 1987. This group was the planning committee for eight years. From left to right are (first row) Betty Baker, Bobbye Trammell, Sue Peters, Sally Mitchell, Yvonne Grice, Bobbye Ellison, and Linda Rodgers; (second row) J. W. Baker, Glenn Trammell, James Mitchell, Sam Grice, Allen "Red" Brown, Harold Ellison, and Neal Rodgers. (Courtesy of Bobbye Trammell.)

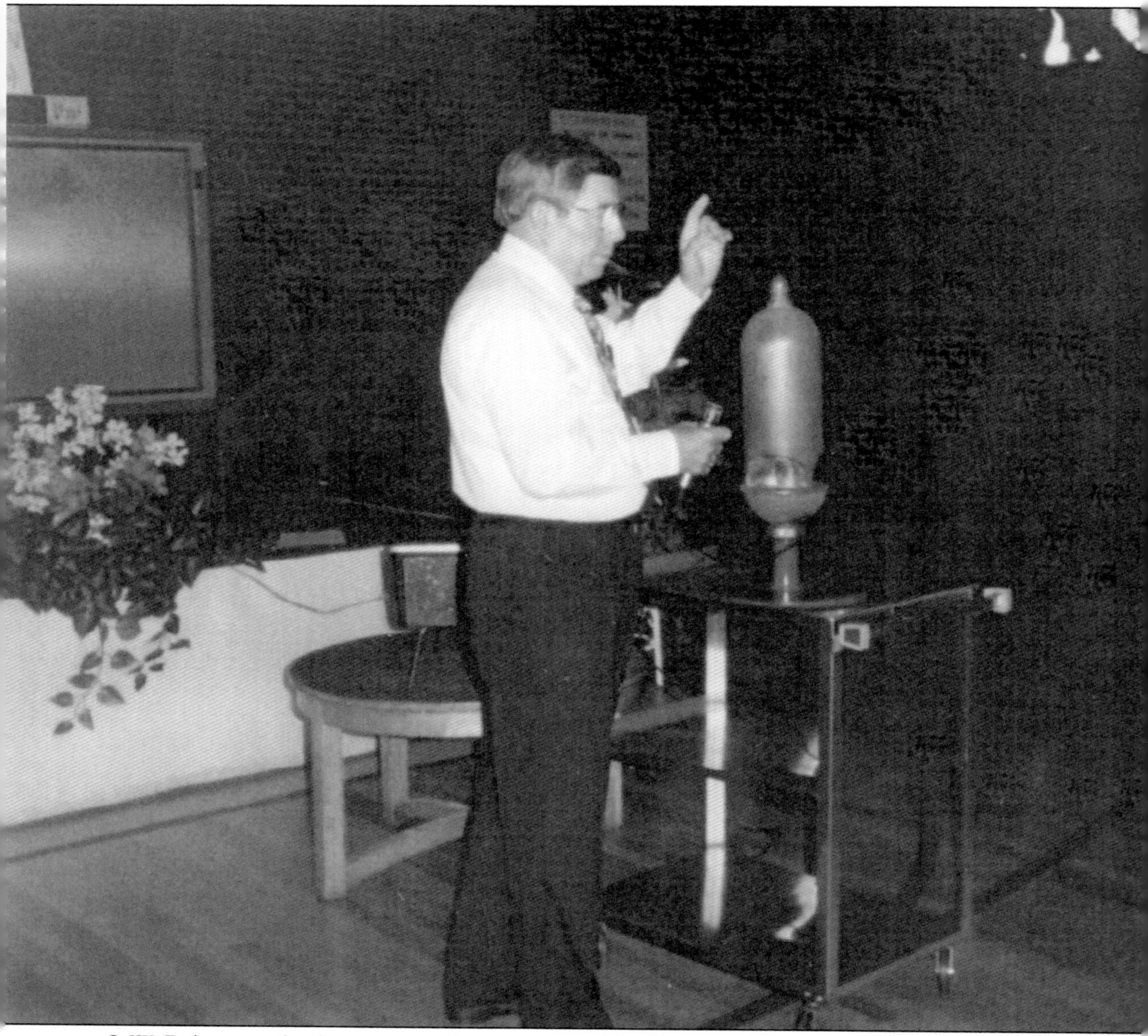

J. W. Baker was the first master of ceremonies of the first Bemiston reunion in 1987. He is shown here with the steam whistle that signaled work time at the mill for many years. Baker has saved many mementos of life in Bemiston and is regarded as the local Bemiston historian. (Courtesy of Bobbye Trammell.)

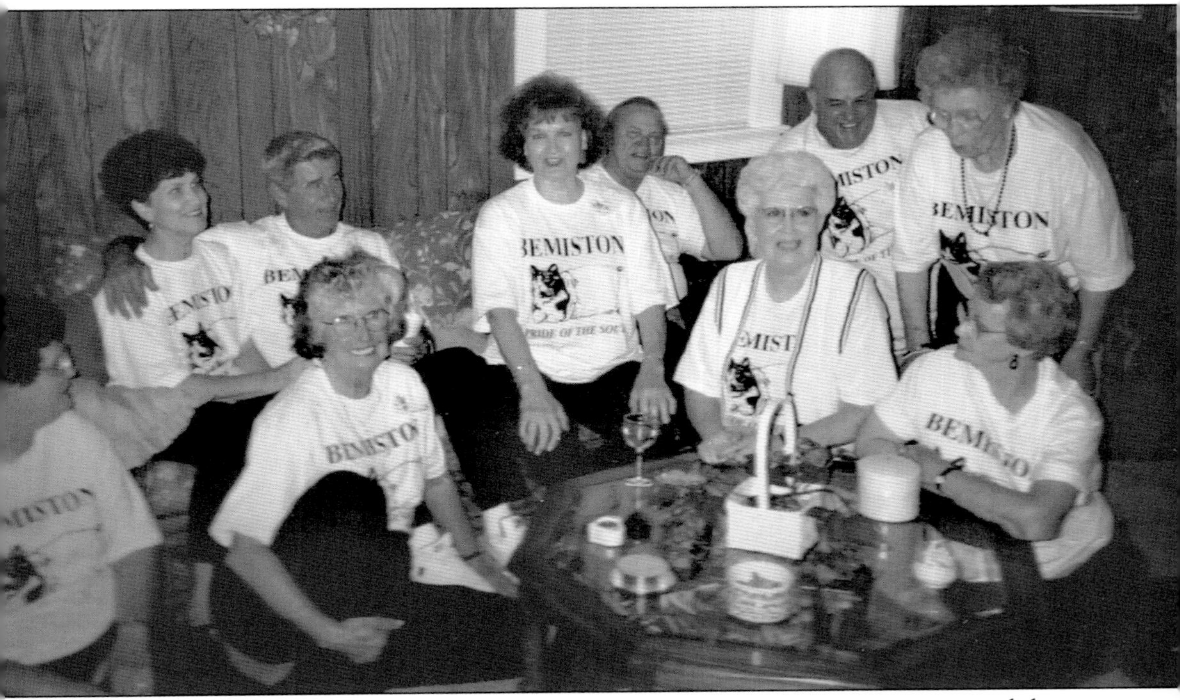

In 1995, the group shown here began to take over as the reunion planning committee, and they have done an outstanding job. They are shown here as they get ready to tackle the job. From left to right are Frances Hughston, Mary Lois Ingram, Joe Wayne Ingram, Dot Jackson, Marlene Moore, John Moore, Geneva Phillips, Mickey Vickers, Lillian Patterson, and Roxie Rogers. (Courtesy of Geneva Phillips.)

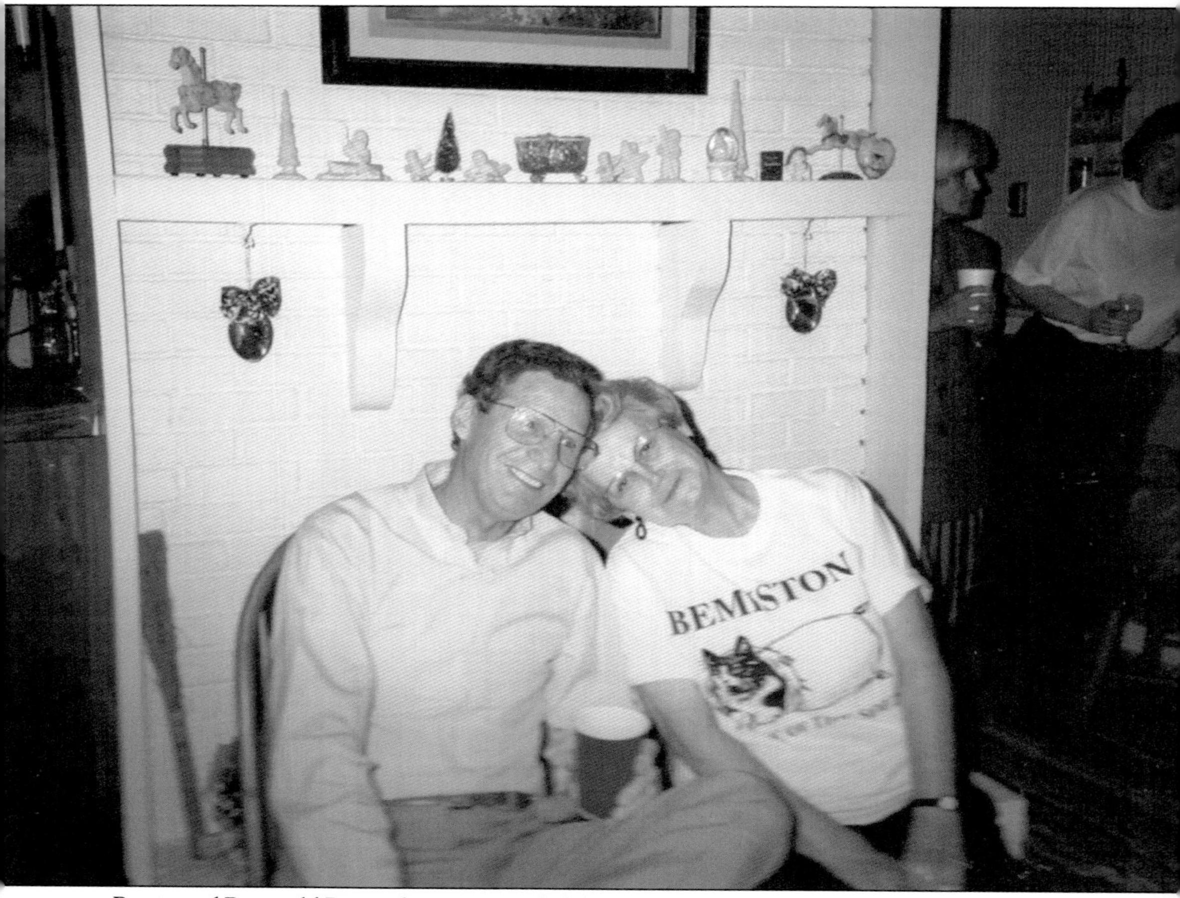

Roxie and Reginald Rogers have just settled down after a long day at the gymnasium getting ready for the next reunion. (Courtesy of Geneva Phillips.)

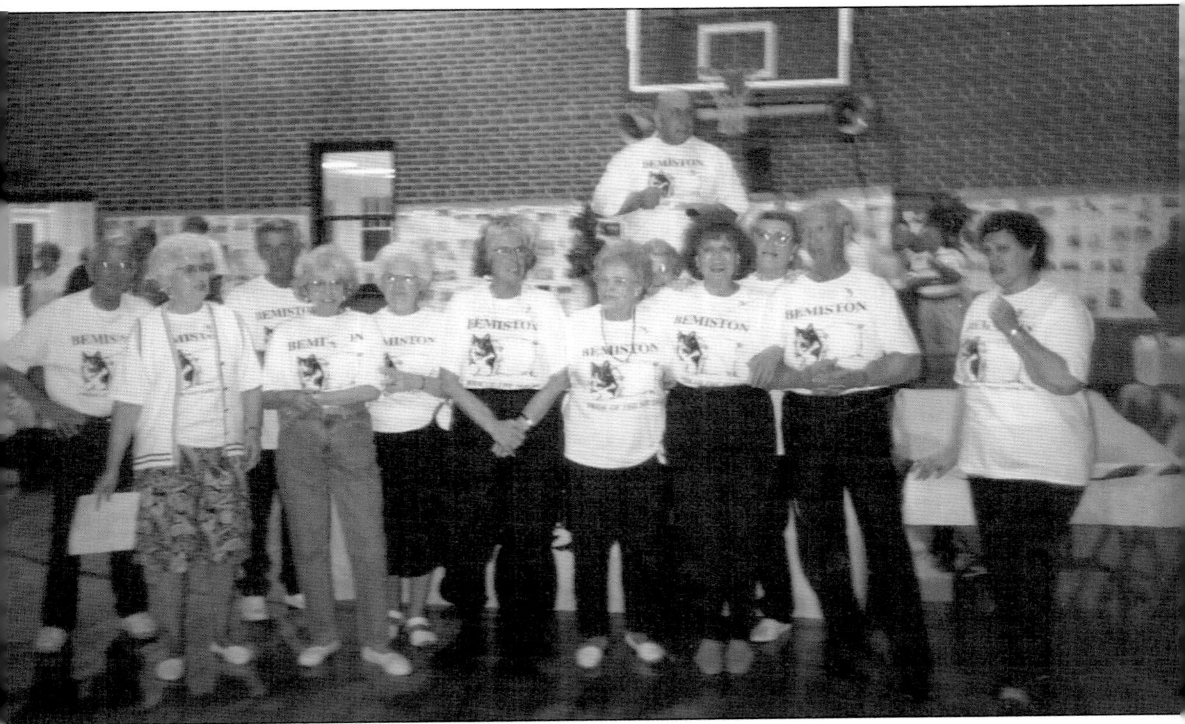

This was the reunion group after all the decorating fun was finished. All of the newspaper clippings were hung to remind the guests of past years. Among those pictured are, in no particular order, Billy Davis, Geneva Mosley, Joe Wayne Ingram, Ann Davis, Mickey Vickers, Sarah Ann Shaw, Elon Pope, Lillian Patterson, Dot Duncan, Marlene Patterson, and Frances Hughston. (Courtesy of Geneva Phillips.)

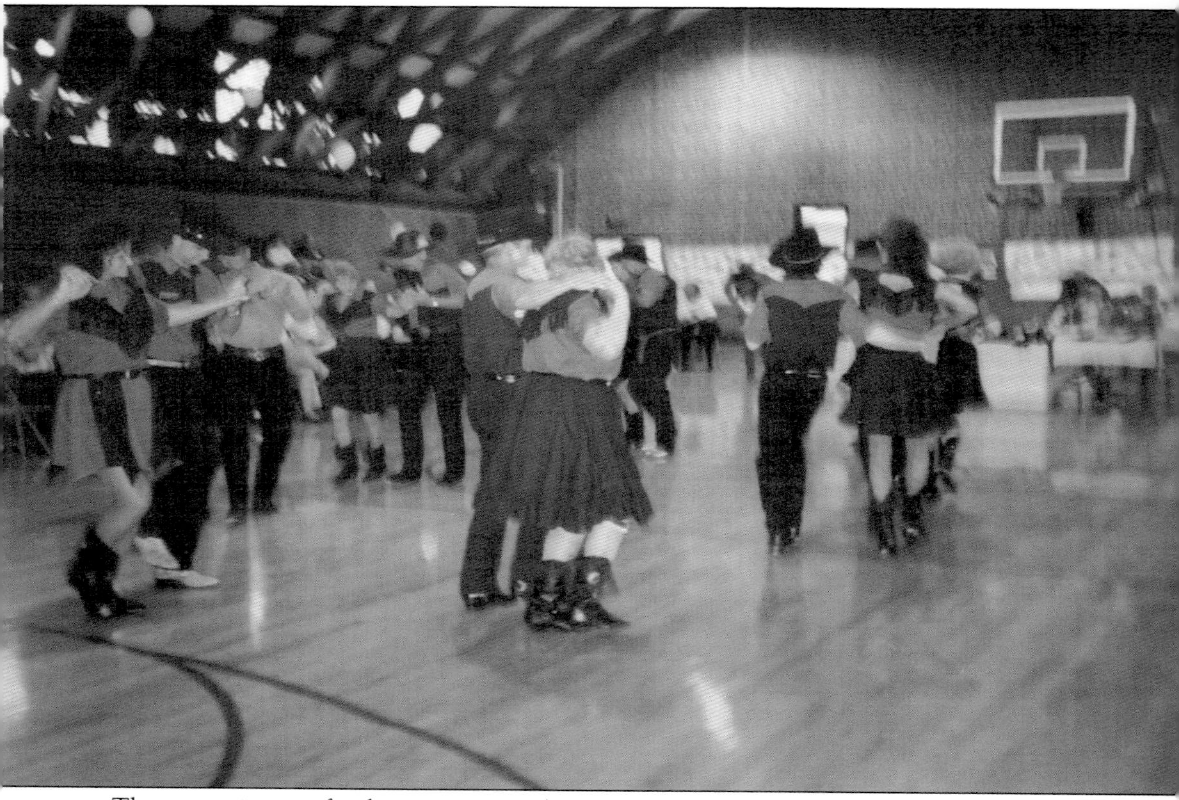

The entertainment for the reunion was the Country Entertainers square dancers. Since this was the entertainment of choice by the community, it seemed to be appropriate for the occasion. (Courtesy of Geneva Phillips.)

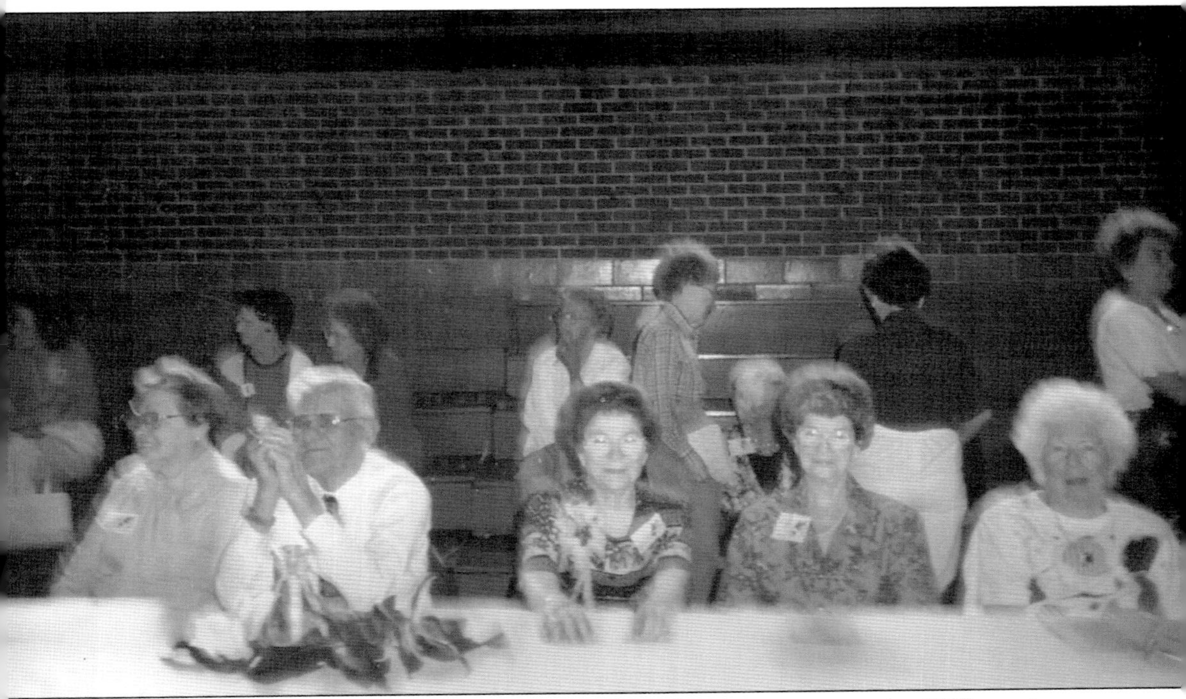

Shown here are some of the first employees to work at the plant enjoying the 1995 reunion. Seated from left to right are Ola Churchill, Louie Churchill, Katie Ruth Morgan, Effie Rodgers, and Alma Bowen. (Courtesy of Geneva Phillips.)